Fresh Tracks

Writing the Western Landscape

Pamela Banting, editor

POLESTAR
BOOK PUBLISHERS

Polestar Book Publishers acknowledges the ongoing support of The Canada Council, the British Columbia Arts Council and the Department of Canadian Heritage.

Cover artwork by Judith Currelly.
Cover design by Val Speidel.
Printed and bound in Canada.

CANADIAN CATALOGUING IN PUBLICATION DATA
Fresh tracks
ISBN 1-896095-42-9
I. Landscape — Canada, Western — Literary collections.
2. Canadian literature (English) — 20th century. 3. Canadian literature (English) — Canada, Western. I. Banting, Pamela, 1955-
PS8237.L35F73 1998   C810.8'.032712   C98-910142-8
PR9194.52.L35F73 1998

Library of Congress Card Catalog Number: 98-84377

Polestar Book Publishers
P.O. Box 5238, Station B
Victoria, British Columbia
Canada   V8R 6N4
http://mypage.direct.ca/p/polestar/

In the United States:
Polestar Book Publishers
P.O. Box 468
Custer, WA
USA   98240-0468

5 4 3 2 1

*This book is for Sinclair Banting and Vera Banting
and for the community of Birch River, Manitoba.*

The truest art I would strive for in any work would be to give
the page the same qualities as earth: weather would land on it
harshly; light would elucidate the most difficult truths; wind
would sweep away obtuse padding.

— Gretel Ehrlich, *The Solace of Open Spaces*

Buffalo memory persists in the grasses, and they have not yet
fully assimilated the cow and the fence.

— Don Gayton, *The Wheatgrass Mechanism:
Science and Imagination in the Western
Canadian Landscape*

A text is information stored through time. The
stratigraphy of rocks, layers of pollen in a swamp, the
outward expanding circles in the trunk of a tree, can be
seen as texts. The calligraphy of rivers winding back and
forth over the land leaving layer upon layer of traces of
previous riverbeds is text.

— Gary Snyder, "Tawny Grammar"

☞ Acknowledgments

First of all, I would like to thank Sharon Butala and Terry Jordan for organizing the Writing the Land Conference which set this process in motion. Astrid Blodgett assisted me with designing the call for submissions, photocopying, faxing and translating and transferring computer files to diskette. The Canadian Plains Research Center at the University of Regina provided a grant to assuage the costs of mailing, photocopying, postage, paper, printer cartridges, long distance calls and other costs associated with this project.

I would also like thank all of the contributors — those whose work I was able to use in this volume and those whose work I regretfully had to return due to considerations of space. Michelle Benjamin of Polestar Book Publishers traced my request for some of her authors' mailing addresses back to the project itself and then pursued the book with the kind of editorial foresight and vision that every writer longs for in a publisher. Lynn Henry, managing editor for the press, won my trust and made me tremble to think how few spelling bees I might have won had she been in my class at school. More important, I appreciate her editorial wisdom and restraint and her respect for the work of the writers herein. I thank Emiko Morita for her superb professionalism and promotional wizardry.

The process of creating and editing this anthology turned out to be one of tracking myself home. The intense and immensely pleasurable work of designing an anthology, corresponding with potential contributors and collaborating with them on the editing of their work inevitably results not only in a book but in the creation of a community as well. I invite readers to join this community.

FRESH TRACKS

Writing the Western Landscape

INTRODUCTION
Pamela Banting ☞ 9

Tracks

RUDY WIEBE
The Wind and the Caribou ☞ 23
SID MARTY
The Rucksack ☞ 28
MURRAY BANTING
Tracking ☞ 30
CHARLES A. FINN
Carcass of a Deer ☞ 33
JOHN WEIER
Excerpt from *Marshwalker* ☞ 36
DAVID CARPENTER
The End of the Hunt ☞ 43
DON GAYTON
Canyon ☞ 58

Maps and Borders

THERESA SHEA
The Unwelcome Railroad (or Gertrude's Revenge) ☞ 63
MYRNA GARANIS
Saskatchewan Accent ☞ 65
Last Train to Millennium ☞ 65
RICK WENMAN
Charlie Butterfly ☞ 67
WADE BELL
Drumming ☞ 74
MYRNA KOSTASH
Medicine Line Crossings ☞ 79

Weather Signs

BARBARA SCHOTT
>   The Farmhouse Poems ☞ 91
>   Blue Snow ☞ 93

JOHN PASS
>   Invocation to the Character of Water ☞ 96
>   Kleanza Creek ☞ 98

CHARLENE DIEHL-JONES
>   lamentations: prairie winter ☞ 100

GREGORY SCOFIELD
>   Excerpt from "Twelve Moons and The Dream" ☞ 103

Names

SHARON BUTALA
>   Grass ☞ 111

PAMELA BANTING
>   Declining Orchids ☞ 116
>   Highway 22 North ☞ 117
>   Novice ☞ 118

ELIZABETH PHILIPS
>   Becoming Earth ☞ 120

FRED WAH
>   Clematis Creek Humming ☞ 129
>   Nose Hill ☞ 129

LEA LITTLEWOLFE
>   "nobody knows how to live off the land any more" ☞ 131
>   indigenous ☞ 132

Histories

FRED STENSON
>   Bow River Expedition ☞ 135

GUY VANDERHAEGHE
>   Blue Horse In A Blizzard ☞ 141

MARGARET SWEATMAN
>   1869 ☞ 144

ELIZABETH HAYNES
    The Great Unlonely Silences & 153
GEORGE BOWERING
    Parashoot!: Diary of a Novel & 159

Cowboyography

ARTHUR SLADE
    Jesus Busts a Bronc & 173
JIM GREEN
    Another Tall Bear Tale & 175
    Scotch and Soda & 176
    Milk and Honey & 177
SLIM DAVIS
    Clearwater Country & 178
    Monty & 179
    Trail from Red Deer to Pine Lake & 180
DORIS BIRCHAM
    The Prolapse & 181
    Equinox Storm & 183
ANNE SLADE
    ghost story & 186
    Company's Comin' & 187
ROSE BIBBY
    Tales from the Hayshaker's Wife & 189
HILARY PEACH
    Outlaw Girls & 196

The Geography of Home

HAZEL JARDINE
    Jumping Jehoshaphat & 209
ROBERT HILLES
    A Career in Farming & 216
SUSAN HALEY
    The Outhouse & 221
LORNA CROZIER
    Joe Lawson's Wife & 228

Country Dweller ☞ 230

Dust ☞ 231

DI BRANDT

This land that I love, this wide wide prairie ☞ 232

SHARRON PROULX-TURNER

sing your song / your children are strong / we are métis ☞ 239

A Sense of Place

BEN GADD

O Canada National Wilderness ☞ 249

MAUREEN SCOTT HARRIS

Being Homesick, Writing Home ☞ 253

JOAN CRATE

The Invisible Landscape ☞ 265

BIRK SPROXTON

A Stickle of Smoke ☞ 270

KAREN CONNELLY

Thoughts on Land and Language ☞ 279

Flesh and Bone

SKY DANCER Louise Bernice Halfe

Telling Tales/Telling Stories ☞ 289

BLANCHE HOWARD

Evening in Paris ☞ 292

THERESA KISHKAN

Undressing the Mountains ☞ 300

THOMAS WHARTON

The Country of Illusion ☞ 304

SUSAN ANDREWS GRACE

Heart Break ☞ 311

PETER CHRISTENSEN with ROBERT J. ROSEN

Canyon Shadows: "Stones" ☞ 319

NOTES ON THE CONTRIBUTORS ☞ 337

FURTHER EXPLORING ☞ 345

Introduction

Glaciers write with rock / on rock.
— Don McKay, "The Windchill Factor,"
Sanding Down This Rocking Chair on a Windy Night

In July 1994, I attended the Writing the Land Conference organized by Sharon Butala and Terry Jordan and held in the town of Eastend in the Cypress Hills of Saskatchewan. For the four years prior to that conference I had been living in an intensely industrialized, commercialized, institutionalized and bureaucratized area where, because of all that "development," the landscape had become — to my sense of space — miniaturized. There were roads everywhere and as a consequence no wilderness or wilder places to go. I sought out so-called conservation areas in order to explore my new and unfamiliar terrain, to learn about its plants, birds and animals, only to discover that within a mere twenty minutes I had hiked the entire length of the path and come out the other side to a dessert emporium and gift boutique!

To someone who, in the three years previous, had been initiated into hiking in the Rocky Mountains and who had grown up in the spacious "middle of nowhere," these experiences were like electric shocks to the body, mind and spirit. Like Gretel Ehrlich who writes in *The Solace of Open Spaces* about her adopted state of Wyoming (the least populated state in the United States), I was accustomed to a landscape which is "engorged with detail, every movement on it chillingly sharp." Space and long distances had always been a central fact of life for me and I felt that my capitalized, dandified and then countrified new home could not contain me. Without having grown up in such a place, I was at a loss as to how to be encompassed, overshadowed and sustained by a landscape so cut up and diminished from what must once have been its glory. Marilynne Robinson, author of *Housekeeping*, writes that "the true, abiding myth of the West is that there is an intense, continuous and typically wordless conversation between attentive people and the landscape they inhabit, and that this can be the major business of a very rich life." I simply did not know how to initiate a conversation with a paved, prettified and potpourried place — a place where landscape was more often referred to in terms appropriate to interior decoration than to the bush.

In *Landscapes of the Interior: Re-Explorations of Nature and the Human Spirit*, Don Gayton introduces the term "primal landscapes" to denote those landscapes in which we spend our most formative childhood years. He offers an explanation for the kinds of ease and anomie which landscapes can induce. Gayton writes:

"Discovering places similar to the primal landscape will naturally evoke strong positive feelings. My wife grew up in a seaside community near Seattle and, even though she has no real desire to live near the ocean now, she finds the smell of tideflats and the sound of waves breaking at night to be urgent, compelling messages. It is as if certain sights, sounds and smells bypass the senses and speak directly to her being. Perhaps we do carry around some fossil genetic coding for an enhanced memory of the natal or childhood place. Dissimilar landscapes, ones that contrast strongly with the primal landscape, can generate unease, even active disgust."

The rhetoric of interior design was not inappropriate to my new surroundings; they were undoubtedly attractive. But over a period of four years the absence of immensity, the sense of spatial displacement and the lack of geographical relief made me feel ungrounded and inconsolable.

The Writing the Land Conference, staged almost entirely out of doors near the river in Eastend, marked a profound homecoming for me, an affirmation that others shared my passion for land and wildness and my powerfully rooted sense of place. Lyric poets, cowboy-, rancher- and farmer-poets, fiction and nonfiction writers, ecologists, range managers, historians, journalists, Jungian therapists and six English professors congregated on the banks of the Whitemud River to discuss, compare and celebrate their different approaches to writing the western landscape.

After the conference, I went home and read everything I could find by the writers who had participated. I began to dream of creating an anthology of new Western-Canadian writing which explored the ways in which we both imprint and are imprinted by geography, especially the geography of our primal landscapes. Creating such an anthology would be a way to reconstruct my own sense of place, which had been rubbed raw by my feelings of alienation. It would also be a way of paying tribute to the conference organizers and participants and to the community of Eastend which had hosted the conference with the grace and elegance possible only in small towns. Finally, I thought, it would be a way of connecting with the larger community of those who respect and love the land.

Reading the Land

This book has its roots in yet another place: my own community of Birch River in central-eastern Manitoba at the foot of the Porcupine Mountains. At 836 metres above sea level, the Porcupines mark the highest altitude in Manitoba, although they are not true mountains at all but the shores of the ancient Lake Agassiz. This is a parkland district where in the 1920s and

1930s when my dad was a boy it was common to see moose around each bend in the road, sometimes as many as twelve feeding together.

I remember learning to read up there in moose country. I, who had been eager to start school, was becoming jaded at what we did there, thinking it a trivial waste of time. For weeks and weeks, it seemed, we had been studying the alphabet. Finally one morning Mrs. Dagg showed us how to do things with the letters, how to make them into words; she taught us how to read. We read pages one, two and three of our reader: "Oh. Look. Look and see." I took my reader home over the noon hour and read it cover to cover. All right, I thought, this is useful knowledge, and I decided to give school a second chance.

My mother had chosen *not* to teach me to read before I went to school. She thought that children should have as much pre-literate childhood as possible and she was right in this, as in almost everything else. I had the luxury of a full six years of my life to explore, largely without supervision, the three acres of land (and beyond) on which we were the first white people to live. Our land was adjacent to the Birch River (the town was named after the river, the river after the trees), a creek in which brook and rainbow trout, minnows, crabs and waterbugs could be glimpsed and some-times caught. Animal paths and Indian trails outlined the river in the same way that we would be instructed in school to outline our colouring. As a preschooler, I set myself the task of retracing and restoring one of the fainter paths through the bush to the river. My only stipulation was that no implement, such as a rake, could be used; I allowed myself to remake the path simply by walking back and forth all day long until it became legible again under my feet.

In *Wolf Willow: A History, a Story and a Memory of the Last Prairie Frontier*, Wallace Stegner, who grew up near Eastend, writes that "Wearing any such path in the earth's rind is an intimate act." Although he is writing about a prairie landscape utterly different from the parkland where I grew up, his attitude toward path-making is strikingly familiar and eloquent:

> And that was why I so loved the trails and paths we made. They were ceremonial, an insistence not only that we had a right to be in sight on the prairie but that we owned and controlled a piece of it. In a country practically without land-marks, as that part of Saskatchewan was, it might have been assumed that any road would comfort the soul. But I don't recall feeling anything special about the graded road that led us more than half of the way from town to homestead, or for the wiggling tracks that turned off to the homesteads of oth-ers. It was our own trail, lightly worn, its ruts a slightly fresher green where old cured grass had been rubbed away, that

lifted my heart. It took off across the prairie like an extension of myself …

Most satisfying than the wagon trail, even, because more intimately and privately made, were the paths that our daily living wore in the prairie. I loved the horses for poking along the pasture fence looking for a way out, because that habit very soon wore a plain path all around inside the barbed wire. Whenever I had to go and catch them, I went out of my way to walk along it, partly because the path was easier on my bare feet but mostly because I wanted to contribute my feet to the wearing process.

Stegner, Bruce Chatwin, Gary Snyder and others suggest it would be worth considering the making of paths as another form of writing and of epistemology, of coming to know and understand the world.

In the process of my path-making, I came to know every individual bluebell, columbine, maple tree, clump of willows, highbush cranberry, chokecherry and pincherry tree along that path on intimate terms. It was no wonder that once our teacher let us do something with the alphabet I learned to read in an instant. Long before I was introduced to the alphabet, multiplication tables or lines of verse I had already taught myself to read the language of tracks, wildflowers and birdcalls, the messages of stones, the semiotics of roots and branches. Lush green ferns were literally my childhood companions. I have few memories of people from the period before I went to school, but I can still remember the three or four enormous balsam poplars south of our house that I thought of as my grandparents. Before he started school my brother had learned from experience all about foxes, squirrels, beavers, muskrats, weasels and many species of birds and had operated his own trapline. Our mother would refer to my brother and me as "little heathen," and we grinned and took it as the highest of compliments.

When I left the bush at age eighteen and went to university, I was astonished to hear my English professors talk about "nature" and poets' special relationships to it. As if one could have a "relationship" with "nature." As if poets and only poets could be "in tune with nature." What about everyone else? What about me and my family? It amazed me to think that at the university people could separate themselves from nature enough to talk about "it" — as if nature was a concept rather than a place, an idea rather than the skin and muscle and bone of your own body. Even my professors' specialized use of the word "nature" was foreign to me. It sounded effete and artificial, as if it had already been skewed or tamed. Gradually, I came to realize the obvious — that the "nature" implicit in those discussions was a foreign geography, that the natural world in question was the one which informed the work of British poets. My professors had been using the word "nature" as if it had universal reference. After my second year of university I went to England to see for myself and was disturbed and vaguely oppressed to discover that even the roadside ditches had a landscaped and gardened look.

Where I had grown up, we referred to the trees and other plants in and immediately beyond our yard — from our front doorstep and continuing all the way up into the Porcupine Mountains and into eastern Saskatchewan — not as "nature" but as "the bush." "Bush" was a term which connoted some sense of respect for the vitality and persistence of the undergrowth which was continually pressing in on our yard from all sides, trying to reclaim territory it had lost to the house and the expanse of crabgrass we called (with no little irony) "the lawn." To some extent, "bush" even incorporated the animals and birds who lived there. We, however, could not have had a "relationship" with the bush because the bush was almost inseparable from ourselves. Place was self. Of course, we had a strong sense of ourselves as unique individuals and as members of our families — maybe more so than in urban centres because we knew each other so well. Yet the closest my contemporaries and our parents came to a sense of self was our sense of place. The two overlapped so much that the boundary between them was blurred and few of us would have thought to try to discern its outlines more clearly.

I had expected university to open up a world of wonders, but this revelation about "nature" exceeded my expectations. I realized I was still a heathen, or rather a barbarian in the original sense of the Greek word as evoked by Jack Turner in his essay "Economic Nature": one who has trouble with the language of civilization. I had been born into a place where white settlement had existed for no more than thirty or thirty-five years — a belated frontier, to use Stegner's term. This meant that I had grown up in two historical eras simultaneously: On the one hand I grew up between the late fifties and early seventies; on the other hand, I was raised in a place and time which had parallels to the post-fur-trade era. It is both a long-term problem and a supreme advantage to have grown up in two historical eras simultaneously.

Nevertheless, for me the university appeared to be a place where my "barbaric" reading skills could be, at least covertly, applied. Over the course of four university degrees I became fluent not only in the primarily oral language of my home place but also in the print-based culture of the city. After teaching high school in Manitoba's Interlake for a couple of years, I returned to university to do graduate work. Today I teach courses in Literary Theory, Canadian Literature, Literature of the Canadian and American Wests, Literature and the Environment, Nature Writing and Ecocriticism and Wild Semiosis: Reading Texts and Landscapes. Through these courses and this book I hope to help create new small and interdisciplinary communities and to trouble and query *my* students' understanding of nature, sense of place, language and translation.

Structure and Contents of *Fresh Tracks*

In my call for submissions, I stated that I wanted to create an anthology which would explore the many ways in which we imprint our presence upon the land, including some of the more disastrous environmental inscriptions we have made. (John Daniel has commented that "Destruction of one kind or another has been our signature on the western land." Despite westerners' desire to think of the west as wilder than the east, our landscape is one of the most altered in North America. It is estimated, for example, that Manitoba's tallgrass prairie constitutes 1/20th of 1 percent of its original extent.) I also indicated that I wanted to incorporate a range of genres, styles and approaches to writing the land, and so I solicited creative nonfiction, memoirs, personal essays, poetry, prose poems, postcard stories, pictographs, short stories, meditations, westerns, fiction-theory, statements of poetics and more.

I stated that I wanted to assemble an anthology which would illuminate the ways in which both our psyches and our flesh become writing surfaces for the forces of nature. I wanted to explore how that imprinting is transferred from our sensory experiences, bodily motions, emotions and visceral impressions onto the written page and into the spoken and chanted air. Landscape writes itself over our sight, hearing, touch, smell and even taste. It constructs our sense of space — it even etches itself over our bodies — but we lack a vocabulary, other than the slightly derogatory word "nostalgia," to account for the impact and nuances of these inscriptions. As a result of this poverty of language, attachments to landscape and to place, especially in the postmodern world, are viewed as childish. I have even heard such ties described as "a kind of madness." As Don Gayton observes, "Socially we denigrate strong attachment to natural landscape as an essentially feminine trait, unless it is coupled with an equally strong desire to extract natural resources from it. Landscape bonds are often kept private, like embarrassing birthmarks." There are voices, however, that affirm the corporeal connection with nature. In *The Perfection of the Morning*, Sharon Butala remarks that what she remembers about her childhood landscape is a "combination of smells, the feel of the air, a sense of the presence of Nature as a living entity all around me. All of that had been deeply imprinted in me, but more in the blood and bone and muscles — an instinctive memory — than a precise memory of events or people. I remembered it with my body, or maybe I remembered it with another sense for which we have no name but is no less real for that." Informed terms for a profound connection with landscape and the natural world are "biophilia," meaning an enchantment with and innate affinity for life, or "topophilia," meaning rootedness, "placeness," knowing where home is.

Given the guidelines, it is not surprising that the contributors to *Fresh Tracks* explore similar fundamental political, aesthetic and personal questions about their relationships with the west. Precisely how does the land imprint itself upon us? What kinds of imprintings do we make upon the land? What are the relationships among tipi designs, medicine wheels, scientific classification systems, fences, boundary lines, pictographs, maps, hoof and paw prints and hiking trails? Does a kind of "marriage" take place between a landscape and its various inhabitants? Is "marriage" a viable metaphor? Or is the human domination of the land — in our writing as in our forestry and agriculture and resource extractions — still the most accurate paradigm of our relationship to the land? What differences and similarities are there between aboriginal and non-aboriginal writers' approaches to writing about the west? Is there such a thing as becoming "native" to a place? How do writers today question notions like civilization and progress without repudiating the struggles, sacrifices and gifts of their parents and grandparents — gifts which have made their own writing possible? To what extent is "writing the land" an effective political gesture, a counter-discourse to agri-business, deficit reduction and western economic policy in general? None of these provocative questions is answered definitively in this volume, although I hope that the writing gathered here goes a long way toward assuaging our embarrassment about our bonds to landscape, and validating our interrogation of these issues so that we can more fully interpolate our voices into political discussions and ethical policy-making.

Fresh Tracks deals exclusively with the four provinces of Manitoba, Saskatchewan, Alberta and British Columbia and — to a very limited extent, in Susan Haley's story and Rudy Wiebe's essay — with the North. The book is about writing the land, not writing the nation. Any attempt to include contributions from the entire landmass of Canada would have forced me to choose politics over geography and would inevitably have lead to a kind of tourist version of the disparate landscapes and bioregions of Canada or to a massive and expensive tome. Only the canonized, the well-known and the famous names make it into anthologies which attempt so much. I am proud to say that *Fresh Tracks* includes Governor-General's award winners and nominees (Wiebe, Marty, Wah, Butala, Hilles, Vanderhaege, Bowering, Connelly, Brandt, Crozier), writers with established careers (Carpenter, Kostash, Stenson, Sproxton, Philips, Crate, Haley) and writers nearer the beginning of very promising careers (Wharton, Schott, Scofield, Halfe, Gayton, Wenman, and others).

It is not my intent to divide Canada along east/west lines. I chose, for this editorial project, to begin from the area I know best and to design a book that would allow me to learn even more. That being said, this book is emphatically not about writing a "region," as the CBC and a few other Canadian institutions prefer to call the territory outside of Toronto. The west is not a hinterland, branch plant or regional extension of some fiction called Central Canada, nor is it even a single bioregion.

There are many different ways in which to organize an anthology, and the arrangement I chose for *Fresh Tracks* was determined by the kinds of inscriptions or "tracks" the individual pieces explored. I want readers to be able to both savour the individual writer's personal essay, meditation, poem or story and to discover the different writing systems or systems of signs the authors within each section delineate. Alternate arrangements — according to theme, bioregion, province, authors' last names — would have highlighted the human writing and downplayed the inscriptions of animals and birds and the forces of rock and ice and wind. An arrangement by literary genre was rejected for similar reasons and because it would have imposed an artificial quota for each genre. I was more interested in finding out what genres are being produced in the field of nature writing than in achieving a balanced ratio among them.

The book is divided into sections generally corresponding to different modes of writing (tracks, maps and borders, weather signs, names, histories, cowboyography) and writing surfaces (the geography of home, a sense of place, flesh and bone). The first section, "Tracks," deals with how non-human animals read and write the land with their footprints, calls, odour markings and scat, and how we and they read one another's systems of signs. Rudy Wiebe writes of hunting caribou with the Dogrib Dene in the north. Sid Marty muses on the scratches, tears, bloodstains and marks on the old rucksack that has accompanied him on so many backcountry trails it has almost become part of his body. When to my surprise I had not yet received any contributions about animal tracks, I asked my brother, Murray Banting, to write something about tracking. Charles Finn meditates on the carcass of a deer, killed on one of the highways which are a major cause of animal fatalities, not only from collisions but because they represent a significant loss of habitat. John Weier sent me part of a manuscript which is a kind of ecstatic catalogue of the birds and mammals he sees during a series of regular visits to Delta Marsh in Manitoba. David Carpenter, noted fiction writer, hunter and fisherman, writes a moving essay about his decision to stop hunting. Range ecologist Don Gayton writes about erasing disfiguring graffiti from a canyon wall.

In "Maps and Borders," Theresa Shea, Myrna Garanis, Rick Wenman, Wade Bell and Myrna Kostash each write about ways in which humans have inscribed upon the landscape our national, provincial and other political and jurisdictional borders, property lines, fences, railway lines and maps. Like Gayton, Shea writes about attempts at "erasing" certain marks:

her postcard story is about a woman who attempts to "erase" the railroad tracks encroaching on her territory. Bell too confesses to a desire to erase, in this case his own words: "I want to erase the words on these pages just as my footprints have been erased from the patches of earth I've walked on." Kostash probes the personal, social and cultural significance of the imaginary invisible line of the 49th parallel — the medicine line dividing Alberta and Montana. Radical thinker, journalist and social historian Kostash even goes so far as to suggest that we share in the dreamtime of one another's ancestors and that those dreams can carry us past the maps and surveys and into a spiritual connection with the land. Each of these writers illustrates how property lines and boundaries are or can be transgressed.

Weather is nature's macro-inscription, and "Weather Signs" deals not just with weather per se but also with its impact on the landscape and on our perceptions of our lives under western skies. The rhetorical term "pathetic fallacy," meaning the attribution of human emotions or characteristics to inanimate objects or to nature, is inverted by Schott, Pass, Diehl-Jones and Scofield. The poems in this section do not rely on the attribution of human characteristics to nature; instead, they show us the ways in which nature elicits human emotions, insights and poetry in us. In Schott's words, "I know the lay of this land / I know its winds and its ways I know / this land and speak its language." Métis poet Gregory Scofield contributes a series of poems which present a contemporary version of the seasons observed by his Cree ancestors. Like the other poems in this section, his poems about the weather are also love poems.

The names we give to places represent a powerful technique for both writing over and erasing the land. Sharon Butala writes of a contest between scientists and indigenous folk over the names of grasses. Which names are the ones "proper" to a place — scientific nomenclature or vernacular regional names? What is, or ought to be, the relationship between these different naming systems? What are the implications of European settlers erasing and replacing the names given by the native peoples to particular places? My own three poems, from a manuscript entitled "Bareback," deal with the scientific versus the erotic naming of wildflowers, how to write about a landscape lightly without insisting too much upon the act of doing so, and about fantasies of life as an animal. Elizabeth Philips tracks the sources of her poems back to specific instances of dirt under her fingernails and a fascination with gardening. Her poetics is a "cultivated" one. She analyzes the connections between "my obsession with helping things grow, and my fitful attempts to marry the earth with words." In their respective poems, Lea Littlewolfe and Fred Wah run their tongues over the names of places and things.

"Histories" proceeds from historical fiction (Stenson) to historiographical metafiction (Vanderhaege, Sweatman, Haynes) to the diary of the writing of a novel (Bowering). "Bow River Expedition" is an excerpt from the manuscript of Fred Stenson's novel "The Trade," an historical fiction that deconstructs the romanticization of the era of the fur trade and unearths the destructive consequences of that bargain in flesh, both animal and human, which went by the name of the trade. "Blue Horse in a Blizzard" is the horse-stealing incident in Guy Vanderhaege's Governor-General's award-winning novel *The Englishman's Boy*, which deals with the Hollywood movie industry of the 1920s and with the Cypress Hills Massacre. "1869" is an excerpt from the novel-in-progress of Winnipeg writer, dramatist and performance artist Margaret Sweatman. Hers is a fabulist novel set on the southern edge of the contemporary city of Winnipeg in the area that was the scene of Louis Riel's 1869-70 resistance to Canadian annexation of the territory which became Manitoba. Elizabeth Haynes, a writer and speech pathologist from Calgary, composes a delightful "ghost" story in which she radically revises the notion of the Canadian wilderness as "The Lonely Land." As its title suggests, George Bowering's excerpt from "Parashoot!" is part of the diary of the writing of his novel *Shoot!*, about the McLean Gang (Métis brothers Allan, Charlie and Archie and their friend Alex Hare) who lived and rustled cattle in the Thompson ranch country of British Columbia in the late nineteenth century. *Shoot!* is at once a western and a postmodern critique of the genre.

Cowboy poetry is distinguished by its focus on the relationships among land, weather, animals and humans, by its oral qualities and by its liberal doses of humour. I chose the term "cowboyography" because it points to the "graph" or writing which is the focus of this anthology. Although the term "cowboyography" seems gender-specific, I have attended several cowboy poetry gatherings and heard the women poets remark that they consider the term "cowboy poetry" to be inclusive of their work. I have asked them about this and they tell me that for them the "cowboy" in "cowboy poetry" is gender neutral, since most of the women who write and perform it also perform most of the same ranch chores as their male partners. Jim Green, who lives in Fort Smith, Northwest Territories but grew up in the Pincher Creek area of Alberta, is working on a batch of poems and postcard stories which write the land through careful descriptions of the physical labour involved in pioneer life. He often incorporates into his poems archival "documents" such as a scratched out inscription on the wall of a forsaken homestead. In other poems, he records anecdotes and jokes passed down through the oral tradition. Slim Davis, Doris Bircham and Anne Slade write about their guiding and ranching experiences, re-spectively. Rose and Garth Bibby are also popular figures on the cowboy poetry scene in the Canadian and American wests. Rose has written a series of "he said / she said" poems about gender roles in farm and ranch life. Like Slade and many other cowboy poets, the Bibbys employ a great deal of humour. Since cowboy poetry is also an oral and performance genre — cowboy poets don't "do readings" or "recite," they "say" their poetry — interested readers may wish to look for the books and audio cassettes by Doris, Anne and Rose and Garth. (Ordering information is included in the "Notes on Contributors" at the back of the book.) Hilary Peach presents a feminist take on the cowboy ballad in her poem about Honey, who was no less legendary and no less wanted ("Honey was an outlaw / she was a wanted poster / she was a photograph") than her male counterparts Billy the Kid and Jesse James.

The section devoted to "The Geography of Home" begins a movement away from outward signs like tracks, maps and weather patterns. It turns inward, toward the personal effects of landscape — how it constructs our sense of place and how, in the final section of the book, it writes itself over flesh and bone. Hazel Jardine and Di Brandt measure how Bible passages and metaphors apply to the realities of life in Western Canada. Sharron Proulx-Turner calibrates another text, the English-language dictionary, against a Métis version of the lived world. Robert Hilles interrogates the record of photographs against memories of his father. In an excerpt from a novel about the Dene of the Western Arctic, among whom she lived between 1977 and 1991, Susan Haley exposes the gap between white, urban, text-based, bureaucratic culture and Dene, village, oral, land-based culture. Lorna Crozier rewrites and recreates in poetry the figure of the despairing and yet endlessly desiring Mrs. Bentley in the classic prairie novel *As For Me and My House* by Sinclair Ross.

Most of the pieces in "A Sense of Place" are about one's childhood senses being imprinted by a particular place. The exception is Ben Gadd's essay. Although Gadd too writes about a remembered place — the North American wilderness of the past — his essay is also about a hypothetical place: O Canada National Park. Its utopian and yet eminently practical vision is sensually appealing. Scott Harris, Crate and Sproxton all write about the crucial relationship between writing and a sense of place. Karen Connelly, who has been travelling and living in different countries since her late teens, contributes a series of erotic poems and a statement about the connection between sense of place and the senses in place.

"Flesh and Bone" opens with Sky Dancer Louise Bernice Halfe's two short commentaries tracing her physical relationship to the land. Blanche Howard's elegant and restrained personal essay is about the sexual knowledge of children and adult predation. It dispels the notion of the idyllic, smalltown childhood and, like poet Myrna Garanis, also presents a vivid and moving lovesong to such places, many of which have already died or are dying. Theresa Kishkan writes about the shameful act of clearcutting the mountain forests and about how that shame is not just political but personal, how it shames our very bodies. Readers who enjoyed Thomas

Wharton's novel *Icefields*, which opens with a fall into a crevasse, will be intrigued to read about Wharton's own fall into a canyon in the Rocky Mountains and to see how a lived incident becomes fiction. Susan Andrews Grace's provocative essay "Heart Break" explores how the imprint of landscape can transcend several generations of a family. The essay raises two possibilities: that the landscape lost through emigration is inscribed as a palimpsest onto subsequent generations, or that there may exist a kind of fossil imprinting or genetic memory of place. To close the book, Peter Christensen writes about his collaboration with Rocky Mountain composer Robert Rosen on an outdoor soundscape performance.

One of my very few regrets about the book as it stands is that I was unable to attract more submissions from biologists, geologists, environmental activists and other scientists working in ecology. I am grateful to those who did respond to my queries but the book could be even stronger with the inclusion of more writers like Sid Marty and Ben Gadd. I wish Kevin Van Tighem, Andy Russell, Charlie Russell, Stan Rowe, Larry Pratt, Candace Savage, Andrew Nikiforuk, Lisa Christensen and others were represented here. It is also too bad that Robert Kroetsch was unable to contribute to the book because of his concentration on his own novel-in-progress, and so I refer readers to that just-published novel, *The Man from the Creeks*. To my regret, Reg Crowshoe's work on tipi designs proved to be unavailable. Despite these regrets, I am extremely pleased by the range of writers and the quality of writing included in *Fresh Tracks*, and I encourage readers to buy and read the contributors' own books.

A more poignant regret is that my dad, Sinclair Banting, died on the morning of April 20, 1998 while this book was in press and that he never had a chance to read it. I had sent him a copy of the dedication, but he himself was a great storyteller and he loved biographies, geography, maps, navigation, the west, the history of our district, community, the habits of the animals and birds, berrypicking, the weather, people, trains (he and his brothers once stole a barrel of rancid butter from their father's store and greased the railroad track with it so that when the train came into town and applied its brakes it slid all the way through town and out again) and laughter. This book follows in his footprints.

— *Pamela Banting*

TRACKS

RUDY WIEBE

The Wind and the Caribou

The Dene Elders say, Who can know the way of the wind or of the caribou? On the open tundra beyond the treeline — fully a quarter of Canada — the movements of the clouds in the sky and the animals on the earth remain as mysterious as they have always been.

If any human beings understand this mystery, they are the Dogrib Dene who live north of Great Slave Lake. Always nomadic hunters, for thousands of years they have known that in the month we call September the immense caribou herds will return again from where they have spent their summer, travelling north to Bathurst Inlet on the Arctic Ocean. So September is the time to hunt them, to prepare dried meat and fat and hides for the long winter.

But this September there were no caribou where they usually are, flowing back into the boreal forests around Snare and Roundrock Lakes, 230 kilometres (as the Twin Otter flies) north of Yellowknife.

So where were they? Six Dogrib men with all our equipment flew northeast to look for them near Jolly Lake. Shortly thereafter, eighteen more of us were in a second plane, following them by radio. Within an hour and a half we circled down out of the clouds, round and round over a terrain more water than land. The other plane was below us, skimming over a large, nameless lake.

Our plane roared its pontoons back into the sandy shore, and when I climbed up the bank, the people out before me were already staring into the distance over the rock-strewn tundra. There against a ragged ridge were caribou.

There were forty, fifty of them. Moving slowly, steadily south, their greyish brown bodies blending into the rocks, although the massive white collars of the bulls hung indelible as snow. And their antlers: through binoculars they seemed too immense to be believed. Great branched lyres, as high again as their thick bodies, the wind whistling in our ears as if they were making music for our arrival.

And as we all stood motionless, watching, they disappeared. It was a disappearance so gradual, so without hurry, that it seemed as if their vanishment were simply the inevitable nature of their movement — and then they were gone.

They are the greatest land travellers on earth, always travelling. In 1820, the English sailor and artist Robert Hood saw them and wrote in his diary: "We have at last penetrated into the native haunts of the

caribou, whose antlers are moving forests on the ridges of the hills."
Within two hours I had seen four caribou shot. One, a bull, took four
direct hits from 30.06 bullets before he went down. He was shot by Ian
Robins, an Australian-Canadian teaching at the Chief Jimmy Bruneau
School at Edzo, NWT, and he cut it up in the careful Dogrib way, as he
had learned on previous hunts. After a time John B. Zoe, who was
finished with his cow, came to help him and together they bundled the
meat into a tight, solid pack. John is head of the Dogrib Treaty 11 Land
Settlement negotiations; as he washed his bloody arms he laughed at
his soft "office hands," though they seemed plenty tough to me. Ian
had no tumpline, so John fashioned one for me with cord and his towel
for a headband.

On a straight lift, I could just raise that pack to my waist, but it felt
good on the small of my back with my legs standing fixed. The problem was moving, and the tumpline. It holds the load in place very well
as you walk bent forward, neck and back straight, but this towel was a
bare padding, the four strands of rope bunched together, tough, tough.
My neck creaked, squashed together by dead weight; in ten steps I felt
I had been compacted two centimetres. But, I argued to myself, this is
a good way to begin; every load I carry after this will seem so much
easier, especially with a proper, broad headstrap.

We went through spongy muskeg, tussocks, over boulder fields, up
the rocky ridges among the erratics sitting on the skyline everywhere
like shattered houses. Balance became the other big problem. There
are superb caribou trails cut into the ground everywhere, always leading over the smoothest paths, but never in the right direction. As John
pointed out when I rested, the pack high on an erratic, the best way to
walk to a tundra camp is not necessarily the most direct route. But from
the ridge I could see our white tents against the indigo lake.

When John took up the pack and I carried his rifle, I couldn't catch
him. He moved at almost a trot, bent low, eyes on the ground, feet
seemingly always certain on the treacherous, ever-changing ground.
And how do caribou walk here anyway, how do they run in massed
herds on such ground as I saw them run? How is it possible that they
don't break their hooves, their legs, on such brutal stones? They have
four legs to place and never watch a single one of them. Perhaps they
have eyes in the hard scoops of their hooves.

John hoisted the pack onto my back again and walked away with
his rifle. I had thought the weather cold, but soon I realized it was
warm — no, positively hot. Previously unacknowledged parts of my
creaking body declared themselves, argued with my split aching head.
I compacted another two centimetres.

At the fire between the tents, Terry Douglas had bannock waiting;

she would have food ready all weekend. "You'll feel it in your neck tomorrow," she said cheerfully. Actually, I already did.

The caribou had let us find them, and then about midnight the wind sought us out. We were all comfortably bedded down in the two big tents, twenty-four of us: two Elders, two boys, seven Dogrib leaders from the community and the Chief Jimmy Bruneau School, and also twelve white teachers, there to learn more about Dogrib culture. When the wind hit, it was with boxer combinations: boom! boom! boomboom! We were in an excellent canvas tent, sewed in Fort McPherson, NWT.

During the night, the stovepipes crashed over the stove; someone had gone outside and was pounding the pegs down, but soon came in and said that only the corners were holding. Sometimes I awoke; a giant outside was kicking my backpack through the canvas wall, kicking me in the head. By morning we had to shout to make ourselves heard over the wind. Two men were holding down the windward corner with their sleeping bags; when someone zipped up the flap, we saw the streaking snow outside just before the wind got a muscle inside and threatened to heave the tent out over the lake-running whitecaps.

In the larger tent, everyone had bundled up their packs and piled them around the centre support and with their body weight were trying to hold the tent on the ground. No fire was possible in the stove. Camp boss George Mackenzie told us: "It can't hold, so we move." A site had already been chosen: a hollow with a small grove of tiny tundra trees. In whipping snow we let the tents collapse over our equipment, fought to roll them up, and began to dismantle the camp.

We were working into the teeth of snow and wind but were calm, orderly — there was not a single order given that I heard. Everyone simply worked, carrying poles, stovepipes, packs, food boxes, everything, as much as they could, trip after trip. Meanwhile, some cleared and levelled the site for the tent and the Elders built a fire, set kettles and hung racks of caribou ribs on sharpened sticks over it. The low density of tiny trees was amazing shelter; when we had drunk tea and eaten as many ribs with cold bannock as we wanted, the snow and wind had dropped and we put up the biggest tent. All twenty-four people moved in, the barrel stove blazing its thick wood heat. The moss floor, spread with spruce boughs no larger than a hand, looked wonderful.

The lake was large but nameless; apparently not even the Elders knew of a name. This was a particular problem for literature teacher Blake Wile. He pored over detailed maps but could not recognize the lake's shape. Finally someone suggested the name "Blake Lake," which he liked until it was decided by general consensus that in order for the name to be valid, he must somehow die there, preferably in great pain. It seemed a high price for a name.

When we came out of the tent, John, whose naked eyes were better than mine with binoculars, saw a single bull grazing lichen against a far skyline. The afternoon wind was steady and fierce; it was time to hunt again.

The hunters I was with did not shoot that caribou: he moved too fast for us. But I followed John as he circled down to a peninsula and startled five other bulls from their ruminations; as they ran past us in their usual orderly line, he dropped the last one. The other four circled uneasily, out of range, then moved up the corridor between the hills where our companions waited. They shot them all.

I went to watch Robert Mackenzie cut up those animals. He was a master with a long, thin knife. Not a single gesture was wasted, the thick saddles of backfat seeming to slip free stroke by stroke from those muscled rumps. One could write half a book about the intricacy of muscle sheathing bone in a caribou's leg.

The next day Robert skinned a two-year-old bull who still had velvet covering his antlers. After cutting off the head, he slit the hide and peeled it off from neck to rump like a body stocking. In sixteen minutes the animal was totally disassembled and wrapped again into its own hide, tumpline attached and ready for carrying. Which everyone did. The four women teachers did not use rifles but helped skin the animals, and every day they carried meat packs for kilometres to camp. Cutting up and carrying: a living ritual as old as humanity on the tundra. And though we might wear Goretex instead of caribou skins, the actions of our bodies remained exactly the same.

That evening, the Elders told stories. And we listened, circled on our bedrolls inside the tent, not a whiff of wind moving the walls. Dogrib Elder Joe Susie Mackenzie told of ancient footprints around this lake, of the hard life he lived on this land, always moving to feed his family. In summer he went by canoe, sled dogs running along the shore, fifty-seven portages in a month of travel from Rae to Courageous Lake with children and elders. He told of hunting accidents and near death; of how men of the first Franklin expedition died here because they did not show the proper respect for animals. And John interpreted his singing Dogrib words, compounding the human mystery of language and memory with that of translation.

Elder George Blondin from Great Bear Lake told stories of the legendary leader Yamoria — stories told to him by his grandmother — and also of traditions of medicine power. He said people lived to be so old in the days "when the world was new" because they had power for everything: for weather and animals and water and sun and sickness and even their own ageing. For years he has tried to define medicine power, and in the stories he told us it is both a spirit and a gift. All the great power died, he said, when the medicine men fought between themselves at Fort Norman in 1926; today no one has any. And though he tells many stories about it and has written and published several books, sadly he says that he himself has none either. So he said. But I have listened to him often and watched others listening, and I doubt that he has no power. A person with real medicine power will, of course, never talk about it.

There was snow, but no wind, Sunday morning. Elder Joe Mackenzie led the morning worship, facing into the sun. Then we went out to bring in the last of the meat. There were twenty-four animals for twenty-four people — a fitting number. The meat was repacked, to distribute among hunters and people back in the community. George Mackenzie had been on the radio regularly, and afternoon planes were coming in with fifteen students to continue the hunt and to learn with the Elders for the coming week.

But before the planes arrived for us, the caribou came again. They appeared at the same spot where they had vanished when we first stepped on shore; it seemed as if they were the same number, the same animals, coming back. But now they were much closer to us than before because the wind had forced us to move camp. We all stood motionless around our fire, watching them move closer.

And then they began to run. They ran across in front of us as they always do, the mass of them breaking into tremendous speed, first running right behind a ridge and then emerging again, running back left across the tundra and up among the erratics until their antlered bodies walked south there, high against the wild, cloud-driven sky.

SID MARTY

The Rucksack

My first rucksack hangs on the wall in my study. It doesn't look like much anymore.

It was built for abuse and got more than its share. It's been dragged up cliff faces with a climbing rope passed through its steel haul ring. It's fallen down a few couloirs, been tossed out of helicopters, gotten washed down the Panther River in Banff Park one time and found a day later — everything inside soaked and covered in sand. It's been run over by a truck, pissed on by a packhorse and burnt by battery acid the time I rolled a Volkswagen Beetle and came within one centimetre of killing myself.

The holes burnt in that pack remind me of something I can't afford to forget.

It served as a pillow under my head more times then I'll ever remember: on the other hand (or end), I've stuck my legs, climbing boots and all, inside it and pulled the bivouac packing up as high as I could to sit out a storm. Saw the clouds clear off and watched the moon come up on the glacier down below, keeping my feet warm inside that old pack and reflecting on the virtues of the watch and compass.

Bloodstains on the canvas remind me of the day a friend peeled off a scaly headwall on Mount Huber near Lake Louise and went tumbling down a glacier at bone-cracking speed. It served as a cushion while I splinted and bandaged his leg. It served as a pad under his bruised behind as I carried him down the mountain on my back in a makeshift rope-seat. The pack reminds me of the days when I was strong enough and bold enough to do things like that.

I've shaken fat ground squirrels full of salami sandwiches out of the old pack, scared nesting mice out of its grimy depths, rescued it from a salt-hungry porcupine and left it as a peace offering to an aggressive black bear, which fortunately declined the offer.

I wish I had them lined up in front of me now, the bottles of wine, brandy and rum — the cans of beer that I've carried in that old sack from one snow cave or tent or alpine hut to another. I wish I had the silver bounties of rainbow and cutthroat trout hauled in that thing from cloud-hung lakes.

Everything from bighorn sheep pellets to elk liver has ridden in there at one time.

A pack like that just grows to fit your body. No fancy braces or webbing. Just an extra sweater or vest jammed down inside to protect your back. What mattered was that every time you strapped it on, you were going outside to do something you wanted to do. You were reminding yourself of something every wanderer knows, that everything you need to survive can be carried on your own back.

Once it had a trademark: a mountaineer with a pipe in his mouth, climbing with true Gallic arrogance and savoir-faire. It's made of heavy duck canvas with a thick leather bottom that won't wear out in this lifetime, and leather straps of a quality that are hard to find now. I bought it from Brian Greenwood, a renegade member of the truculent Calgary Mountain Club, who had a climbing store in his basement.

I bought the pack when I was seventeen and a dishwasher at Lake O'Hara Lodge in Yoho National Park. I chose that model because Heinz Kahl, a big, dark-haired mountain guide with a friendly grin who guided out of the lodge, had one like it. He was one of the gods then bestriding the mountains like a colossus, but he always had time to teach greenhorns a few tricks of the trade. Poor Heinz died while still a young man.

The mountains didn't kill Heinz in the prime of his life. Leukemia, that giant slayer, did that, and whenever I look at the pack, I remember him and I see his face glowing with strength and happiness. I see the faces of so many who were young, full of confidence and quick with life.

I can't use it any longer; it's too full of holes and memories.

But I can't stand the new ones of neon-coloured nylon that smack of the look-at-me age we live in now. I'll probably wind up hiring somebody to replace the canvas and restore the poor old rag to life. It seems like the least I can do, somehow, to keep faith with that boy back there, on the shore at Lake O'Hara, looking up at the first of his mountains, with the smell of larches in his nostrils and saying to himself, "I'm going to climb that peak at the end of the valley," thinking, in his innocence, rightly as it turned out, that if you could do that, you would learn something about life and about yourself that could be found no other way.

MURRAY BANTING

Tracking

Sun-up two hours ago. The air is frozen and dense, and the sound of each step and movement I make is amplified in this barren cold, where sound travels fast and far. A woodpecker taps and probes for grubs on a dried-out black poplar a half mile away. Raven cackles from high in flight can be heard clearly at one mile. My snowshoes pack a familiar trail in the light covering of last night's snow as I follow the fresh track of a coyote through the frozen marsh.

Coyote going here and there, checking out that clump of weeds, looking for a vole or a long-dead duck left behind last fall when crippled and unable to fly south with its mates. Coyote then sniffing cautiously around the muskrat's house built from mud and dead vegetation scoured from the bottom and edges of the marsh and smelling of all things wet, damp, musky and alive. Below, the muskrat rests secure from the menace above, the coyote kept safely away beyond the frozen dome of marsh refuse. On to the next clump of willows, where other tracks preceded those of the coyote — mishmashed and seemingly random wanderings of a pair of sharptailed grouse or "prairie chicken," as they are often incorrectly referred to. I wonder what the coyote calls them, and if it is the correct name. A good meal one of these would have made for a hungry coyote, but he can't catch one simply by being where they were. Tracks are history and, as one old-timer used to say, "make very thin soup."

Ah, but the coyote knew where his best chances were last night when he left his signature on this frozen land, and I follow his tracks in anticipation. Coyote leaves the marsh and cuts into a thicket of hazelnut and red willow. Finds rabbit trails, packed and perfect for a coyote to travel and nab the unsuspecting snowshoe hare whose silent feet seldom leave the trail. Tracks weave and crisscross for miles along the marsh and from thicket to thicket. The minus twenty-five degrees Celsius air fills my lungs with cool fluid from which I extract much more than oxygen. The snow is crisp and with each step I announce to all that a man, a very noisy creature, has entered their world and is also leaving tracks for the next passerby to ponder. Ravens duel in the distance, the sound of the dense air rippling over black-feathered wings as they toss and turn in flight making as much noise as I do breaking the crust of snow. Today I am not stalking my quarry, so there is no need to be exceptionally quiet, even if I could be. Today I am checking a coyote snare that I set four days ago on a rabbit trail.

Tracking a wolf is different from tracking most other animals on a trapline. For some reason — and it doesn't seem to be conscious — you find yourself looking in the direction in which the tracks are going and, equally, in the direction from which they came.

To the hunter or trapper, the tracks that all wild things leave behind have a special power and they affect us similarly. Is it just the track that makes us react so profoundly — the simple mark in the snow or the indent in mud left fresh after a receding water level? No, it is much more than that. There is the feeling of discovery and of respect for the beast that was here to leave such a dignified and bold statement of its presence. "Behold me," proclaim these tracks, "I am one of the four-legged."

Once, when I was about eight, I went with my dad to a trapper's cabin to deliver some hardware supplies. It was a dark, early winter night in the middle of moose season, and it was snowing heavily. The old fellow was in a cheery mood and invited my dad to have a drink with him. As we sat at his table, he and my dad talked about this and that. The cabin smelled of woodsmoke and the pungent aroma of beaver and muskrat hides drying. The woodstove belched out excessive heat, and though the cabin was uncomfortably hot, the trapper wore his dirty, faded, fluorescent orange toque. I sat glued to my chair, thoroughly eyeing the steel traps hanging from the walls, the guns propped up in the corner and the duck decoys and ammunition boxes in the porch. The only thing I recall from the conversation was that the trapper would blurt out every so often, in a "happy-new-year!" type of voice and with ever-increasing volume, the phrase "fresh tracks in the morning." After each of these exclamations he would hold high his coffee mug (filled with Five Star whiskey, straight up) as if saluting some sort of royalty, then take a good slug and let out a big breath.

Later, as my dad backed the truck away from the cabin, the old fellow came out on the porch and looked skyward, giant snowflakes melting on his leathery face. He was framed in the truck headlights as if on stage at the local talent night. He squinted towards us and let out one last salute: *Fresh tracks in the morning, boys!"*

͡

Coyote tracks veer off the rabbit trail ten paces before they reach my snare. I exhale into the cold dense air and glance quickly over my shoulder — an old habit. The steel snare hangs lifeless and undisturbed, not caring about the correct identification of sharptailed grouse or prairie chicken. I wanted to outsmart the coyote and am disappointed, but the tracks offer solace that only I can appreciate. They say: There will be another chance. Where is he now? I ask. I imagine his stealthy paws etching out another tale to be read and deciphered later.

Throughout the day, as I make my way along my trapline, I am greeted by many unseen inhabitants of the land. Some are quarry and others are not, but all weave a tale of immense proportions upon the landscape. I read it like others read the morning paper. Tracks ahead! What or whose are they? Where are they going? Can I get there first? And will they come again?

CHARLES A. FINN

Carcass of a Deer

I was swept by a wave of feeling, then a pang so sharp that,
for a moment, I felt sick, as if all the waste and loss of life,
the harm one brings to oneself and others, had drawn to a
point in this lonely passage between light and darkness.
— Peter Matthiessen, in *The Tree Where Man was Born*,
relating the death of a lioness on the Serengeti Plain.

I am driving north on Highway 3A out of Kaslo, B.C. on my way to
Argenta. It is the morning of what will be Christmas Eve and I have
stopped the car to examine the carcass of a deer, apparently hit last
night and thrown over the side. I'd seen it on my drive in earlier this
morning and thought it'd be a good chance to view death, even a day
or two old, up close. As I pull over and prepare to get out, I'm protect-
ing myself in small ways for what I will see and feel, already catching a
glimpse of a smashed-in eye turned tragically towards me, while ravens,
waiting in their perpetual black but showing no signs of mourning,
huddle nearby.

Because the deer is head first over the bank, the first thing I notice
are the sharp ungulate hooves, heart-shaped even in death, leading
down to the soft brown of the legs, then to the black and brown under-
belly exposed sadly against dirty white snow. It is a doe, a blacktail,
and as I guessed, its death is already a night and maybe even a day old.
To my surprise there is little blood, but the ravens have been poking at
an eye, and where the deer was dragged a pink trail wanders behind it.
Presumably, because there is no sign of debris on the road, the vehicle
that hit it must have sustained little or no damage, but the deer, instantly, was catapulted from life. In a useless gesture I squat beside the
body and pat its cold side. A small cloud of dust, like a soul reluctant to
leave, rises and falls.

This is not the first time I have seen a roadkill, nor do I make a habit
of investigating morbid scenes. But I'm an advocate of following one's
intuitions and this is why, driving home, I knew I would stop. Paused
now in the thin wind coming off the lake I wonder what on earth I'm
doing, and the deer, stiff as the grey clouds skidding into the mountains, makes no effort to answer. Behind me I hear cars going by on the
highway and I know later friends will ask me what I was doing. Already I'm trying to think of a feasible lie.

The first time I saw a dead animal was when I was five years old. It was the black and white kitten I'd picked out two months earlier at the animal hospital. Naming him Boris, I played with him day in and day out, at night letting him sleep curled up next to my belly. Then one evening I imagined him being run over by a car and, in a state of self-imposed tears, cried myself to sleep. The next day when my mother brought me the news, I was unanswerably quiet and did not shed a tear.

I also remember last summer driving twelve hours to Vancouver, arriving just in time to witness a black tomcat getting hit crossing the road. Dodging traffic I scooped the limp weight into my arms and placed the still-warm body on a manicured lawn. I'd always thought death was cold and still, but then again, I'd been brought up on a diet of TV and movies. Even now I can see the great shudder the tom gave trying to get up. It was a ghostly dance, staggering, then collapsing to the ground as if God, the great puppet master, had jerked, then suddenly cut, the invisible strings.

All these memories I have while staring at the deer, and I must force myself to go slowly over every inch of the carcass. Stopping for long periods I let my eyes sink to where my thoughts will not go, and my hands, automatically, move back and forth over the soft, tawny fur. For some reason its neck is of particular interest, and I think of the mornings I've watched similar ones stretching into my meadow. Deer, to me, are the most beautiful creatures gracing the earth. If I were a dancer I'd study their every move. Living where I do, my journal is full of references to their "kind and shy faces," but this one, not surprisingly, has lost all innocence and charm. Blood has spurted from the nose and anus, and the tongue, like that of a child concentrating hard on math, peeks from the side of the mouth. I make myself look into the one good eye; two headlights, then the world goes instantly black.

There's something else that bothers me, but I am hard put to place it. There are the hooves, the twisted neck, the eyelashes and fur ruffled in the strange voiceless wind. Likewise the mountains are mute; also the lake, motionless, stares back at a moody, grey sky. Perhaps because it is quiet, everything around me so utterly still, I feel disconnected from what I am seeing. Vainly I look for signs of death that do not appear. I cannot smell it, see it, sense it with any part of my being. Like an envelope, the deer lies at the side of the road, its life having been opened, read and discarded. Whatever made it run, jump, eat, sleep, blink in the sun — all is gone. There seems no reason to be upset. I know the cycles of nature will take over. But to the sentimentalist there are no circles in such a fate, rather a cutting off of what should have been a continuing line. So much is beyond our ability to understand, to see, that it's useless to speculate on the meaning of any event, especially one as little understood as death or, as is so usually the case, as superficially lived as life. Peering and poking I examine the carcass as if it were an artifact handed me in a museum, and for all the heartache I feel it might as well be a shiny pebble I picked up on the beach. Beauty, I know, attaches itself to the strangest things, and the ears now tuned to silence take on the appearance of angelic brown wings.

Because it is cold I shift my position frequently, thus viewing the body from a number of angles. From below, except for the neck being thrown back in such an awkward position, I can almost believe the deer is sleeping, and from behind it looks like it might be about to give birth. Carefully I steer my thoughts away from such ideas, not wanting to contemplate the aborted fetus of a fawn. Instead I stroke the ears and whisper lullabies, at the end inanely adding, "Time to get up." Miraculously the deer obeys my command and, giving a start, scrambles to its feet. In a vision so real I step back, I watch the deer bounding away through the bushes. I've startled many deer on my walks in the woods, amazed at how nimble spirit remains when wrapped in a heavy earth body. With a flick of the heels my friend ascends deer-like towards heaven. Back on the ground, reality lies frozen with an unmoving eye.

I remember a similar scene when I was fifteen. My best friend called me up excited about the deer he'd just killed and insisted I come see. Behind his house was, and still is, a giant sugar maple, and from one of the arms hangs a braided rope and our favourite tire swing. That day the tire was gone and in its place swayed the upside-down face of a deer. I pretended to be interested and listened unflinchingly to his story, all the while watching poetry running red, seeping into the ground. It seemed incomprehensible to me that he could kill such a beautiful thing, and still I wonder about people's motivation to hunt. Once, driving with the same friend and his father, we hit a deer, and now in my mind, like a sick clap of thunder, I recall the dull, awful sound.

It's cold now and I've been keeping the ravens. To warm my hands, I rub them as I walk back to the car. There's a strange sense of acceptance that has slipped into the air, and the sound of my boots on the crushed gravel fills the tight valley. I watch the ravens from the centre of this calm, seeing how they waddle, twisting their bodies and blinking their eyes. One flutters, then perches in the depression of a shoulder. With a jab it drives its beak into the open pit of an eye. Without waiting, I start the car and it purrs to life like a giant metal cat. I creep onto the road at a funeral speed.

JOHN WEIER

Excerpt from *Marshwalker*

Wings Against a Cross

Wednesday, September 28

Three degrees this morning in Winnipeg. Cloudy, though the clouds are high. A west wind, light. The forecast predicts a high of seventeen, sun, cloud, no rain. I ate my usual breakfast at home this morning — an orange, cereal. Still, I stop at McDonald's to pick up an Egg McMuffin and coffee. I remember how hungry I got at Oak Hammock two weeks ago. I've dropped Susan off at work. By 7:45 a.m., I'm on my way to the marsh.

Even as I left home this morning I thought about guns. I'm upset about guns. The hunters will be out for sure today; this is the middle of the season. I've read stories about the hunt that John James Audubon attended near New Orleans on 16 March 1821. Audubon estimated that 48,000 golden plovers were slaughtered by market gunners in the hunting frenzy of that one day. Those market hunters shot plovers, and Eskimo curlew for their fine taste, knots and dowitchers and even the tiny least sandpiper. Guns! Hunters! I read in a magazine last week that the Canadian Air Force dropped half a million bombs on Oak Hammock Marsh during World War II, target practice. God! What a horror! When I told Susan about this she wondered whether bombs might still be leaking poison into marsh water, whether there were any bombs left unexploded.

I drive north. Past patches of stubble. And one crop standing, a field of wheat on the left side of Highway 8 just outside the Winnipeg perimeter. That's late for wheat, probably because of the rain this year. Maybe this field flooded in spring and had to be reseeded; maybe it's just been too wet for the swather and the combine.

Still no frost this year, but trees are starting to show a lot of red and yellow. Most of the trees sheltering the farmyard on my left have kept their leaves, just a few trunks stretch naked against the horizon. As I approach the marsh entrance, the sky fills with geese. Snow geese, white phase and their black primaries, the blues with white heads; and Canada geese, a white chin strap. Many more geese than last time, all winging south. In the last two weeks, I guess the geese have taken notice of the time. The sky swarms with chevrons and clusters and single straggling lines.

When our son Jonathan was small he was crazy about guns; he must have got it from the television, or maybe it was in his genes. We didn't buy him any guns. We didn't think children should be allowed to play with guns. Guns aren't for playing. So he made them, built them out of LEGO. He had a hundred guns, cartons full of guns, a bedroom full of guns. He knew their names, he knew their purpose. Guns are for killing. What a battle. Old against young, strong against weak. What could we say? "You're not allowed to build guns out of LEGO." He would have made them out of milk jugs, or newspaper. *Ttsshwww, ttsshwww.* He would have used his mouth and his fingers.

My first task today is to collect leaves from the two groups of trees here at the gravel entrance. I'd like to know what kind of trees they are. I've worked with guitars and violins most of my adult life, so I can recognize wood once it's been cut and machined — oak, walnut, spruce, maple — but I know nothing about trees. I park the car, step across the road, search my way through the ditch. Looks pretty muddy. My ears ring with the clamour of geese and blackbirds. A flock of Canadas vees overhead, one snow goose among them. I catch a flash of red in the poplars, red-winged blackbird. Two rock doves strut on the old hip-roof barn. Have the barn swallows gone?

I pick a cluster of leaves from this first stand of trees. A stem with three yellow leaves. I study them, I've brought a book: box elder, Manitoba maple. The other is a bush, still green, some kind of caragana I think. I stalk the second clump of trees. The grass laden with dew, my shoes and pants grow heavy, wet. I pick more leaves — these are oval, egg-shaped, and turning brown. I should have known they weren't poplar. I grew up with two huge poplars at the end of our farm drive. One summer day when I was six or seven, while we were running from the tomato patch in a storm, crash, a bolt of lightning tore the bark off one of them.

Now I hear guns. The hunters.

Back in the car I turn the heater on my feet and watch as twenty Brewer's blackbirds perch in the Manitoba maple. A male with his black and purple sheen, yellow eye. The female, brown, brown eye, and dull. They check and wheeze, jump from branch to branch. A dozen red-wings fly in to join them, sit for awhile, then fly off again. I hear the *tseep* of a sparrow. I see a flash of white on a hunting hawk, a northern harrier. He flaps. Glides. Flaps. Twists and turns. Flaps again, plummets to the stubble. He's up again, flying ten, twenty feet above the ground. He turns his head into the sky, dives. This time he stays down, he's caught something.

The first creek here at the marsh entrance doesn't offer one duck. North and west of that, though, the stubble is spotted with geese, snows and Canadas. I notice the young of the snow geese; not fully grown, they haven't yet taken mature colours. I stop and watch awhile, listen. All this goose gabble, I almost feel they're talking to me, or about me; they have seen me. I wish I could tell you something about the sound of 5,000 geese calling, the way the tumult moves across a field, the way one speaks and a hundred others answer, the way that sound touches me. I'd like to call back. But then the guns again. The hunters are close now. I have seen them crouched in the fields. Their trucks and Broncos are parked in the stubble. My whispered warnings to the geese completely useless. I drive further on.

The car rolls into a stall in front of the interpretive centre. Six ducks rest on this first pond. Five show the sloping beak and forehead of canvasbacks; the other is a dark-eyed American widgeon. The ducks drift on the water: one preens the feathers behind her neck; the other ruffles her wing, shakes her head and beak. They turn this way and that on the water. Four mallards fly up in alarm. I hear the twitter of American tree sparrows, northern juncos, Harris and white-crowned sparrows in the shrubs and thistle.

How will I get used to this, to being here? There is so much to see and know here at the marsh, I'm almost blinded by it. Overload. When your eyes see this much they begin to close. I can't find anything to think about or write about; there's too much to write about. I can't reach to the heart of anything. My thoughts clutter with detail. Ruby-crowned kinglets, robins, yellow-rumped warblers still busy in the willows along the boardwalk. Not much has changed along the boardwalk, the passerines still here, maybe a few less. A common snipe, the blue-winged teal.

Two shirts, two sweaters, a cap, wool socks, I'm glad I dressed warmer today.

An American pipit pumps its black tail on a dried branch ten feet in front of me. I see the white outer tail feathers. Even a western meadowlark still sings in the willow bluff. And those secretive swamp sparrows, they fly up, they rustle through the brush, and then they're down again. Somehow you never get a look at them. Beyond the willows, lesser yellowlegs traverse the grass. I hear a greater legs, there, he flies from the water's edge, stutters along the reeds. Two snipe rise out of the slough grass. I see a coot, a lesser scaup. Has anything changed in two weeks? The air is cool.

I'm like a wild man. I'm so anxious to see, I start to run. There, a pied-billed grebe. I hear the rustle of the cane grass, white plume and scarlet stalk. Out of breath, I walk again. And walk. The same trail as last time, but faster. I hope to get far out into the marsh today. I've reached the lake. The geese to the south of me fly up. They look, and wait. Fly up, and wait again. Here's a dragonfly, one small dragonfly. To the north, that could be the double-crested cormorant that tipped the water for me last time. She's still sitting on the same mound of mud and reeds. The cormorant starts. Is it the wind? The season? Is it me? There's a panic in the air today. I feel it. Is it the same one the ducks and geese feel? Are they as anxious to move as I am? I need to find a place to sit, to shift my thoughts to one small duck. I'll wait for this marsh to come to me. I need to stop running. I can say this for the hunters, they're far more patient than I. I walk faster. I can hear my breath blowing.

This trail is shorter than I thought. Just to my right I see the mound and the bench where I lunched last time. And one great blue heron still left at the marsh. Crook-necked, long wings lined with black, he swings over the mound into the east, passes in front of me. The wings stop, the heron slips by, flaps again, braces himself to land.

Two kilometres from the boardwalk. I have a map. Today I'm walking a big loop, seven more kilometres before I'm back at the car. I hike up along the creek on the eastern boundary of the marsh. The great blue, in the creek, there he is again, long legs straddled, yellow bill fixed straight into the west.

I walk and walk. An injured mallard flops across the trail in front of me. Food for a coyote or a fox I guess, for an eagle. Those human hunters, I wonder what they're looking for. That great blue heron can't get any rest today; he must think I'm chasing him. He's up so close and flies right at me, and I see the chestnut at the front edge of his wings. Before this moment I hadn't ever noticed all his colour.

Sparrows flutter all along this trail, but I have left them to their own designs. Sparrows can be frustrating, especially in fall; they are much easier to identify in spring, by their colour or their song. Are these savannah? Are they Le Conte's, grasshopper? Could they be sharptailed sparrows? Adult or immature? Their sparrow coats are pale and ragged. I hear a rustle in the slough grass. I step closer. A muskrat splashes into the water. What am I doing here? Frightening the ducks, robbing the great blue heron of a quiet morning, giving that group of hunters something big to shoot at.

A ground squirrel, striped and spotted back, rustles in the grass, waits by her hole. When I'm two feet away, suddenly she's gone. Thirteen-lined ground squirrel. Maybe this is the nature of my wilderness, that I am a stranger in the marsh. My second trail sign, I turn west, six kilometres to go. The wind rushes in my ears. I see a flash of white on the north water, something new, a duck I haven't seen since early summer. The white neck and breast, black tail feathers, erect bearing of a northern pintail. What does Barry Lopez say?

The desert is like a boulder; you expect to wait. You expect night to come. Morning. Winter to set in. But you expect sometime it will loosen into pieces to be examined. When it doesn't, you weary.

Here in the marsh, all the usual rules are gone. I can only wait. When I've finally waited long enough, I will wait a little longer.

Now I wish I had my telescope. Of course it's in the car, four, five kilometres away. Off to the south, dark duck-shapes balance in the water. And two bigger daubs of white. Tails high in the air, heads, I suppose, stretched to the water bottom. Must be tundra swans. What was it about swans, how they and ducks benefit each other? The swans stir food from the bottom of a pond while the ducks eat on the surface. The ducks act as sentinels, watch for predators. Tundra swans, I can see the line of their necks, their black beaks. I turn from the swans. A ring-necked duck scuttles, black back, striped bill; I see the trace and curve of his pale sides. A coot gallops across the lake after him.

This bench. I have added and subtracted the kilometres: this is the farthest I'll be from the car today. This is the centre of the marsh. I can hide awhile. I am finally alone. The horizon reaches for miles and miles. In the east the clouds fluff and roll. In the south, if I squint, the glimmer of the city, skyscrapers. To the west, one dark cloud and a line of trees. North, the haze of a farmer's tractor in the distance. The sky is overcast. The grass and earth sponge under my feet. Common groundsel, wild alfalfa, dandelion still blooming, thistle, goose droppings and feathers, a touch of brown earth.

Water pushes all around this trail. Among the rushes and the reeds at the back of the pond in front of me stands a tall wooden structure, a cross. One black cormorant, neck stretched, orange bill pointing up at the sky, spreads and dries its water-soaked wings by resting them on either arm of the cross. Cormorants, I've discovered, need to dry their wings; their feathers aren't waterproofed the way that ducks' are. The pond swarms with waterfowl: mallards, American coot, another pintail, a few scaup, one common goldeneye. Yellowlegs *tu tu* up and down the strand. A northern shoveler bows, down and up, with her wide spoon bill. Down, up, down. Down, up. She gives her head a shake. Down again, orange legs still paddling. Behind her a group of ruddy ducks, three or four, so this is where the ruddy ducks live. Dark cap, pale cheek, tail still cocked, the male has lost his ruddy colour.

Not much happens around my bench in the marsh in one hour. Just the rustling of the grass and the wind. Just a hundred ducks resting and feeding. Just a cormorant stretching its wings against a cross, a ruddy duck with an upright tail, a blue-winged teal flashing by. Just my head, thinking and thinking.

The ruddy duck dives closer. I think for a moment how lucky I am this is September and not June. The mosquitoes, I don't know what I'll do next June. I think of the ducks. Do these ducks think about mosquitoes? Do the ducks think about me? They know I'm here. They watch. They swim away as I walk closer. They must think I'm dangerous. How did they learn that? If I sit quiet on a bench, I wonder if they'll stop to notice me. This ruddy duck doesn't seem too concerned. He dives again and pops up right in front of me. Is he curious about me? I shiver, even with my sweater and my hood, my two thick shirts, wool socks. Fall is here; the cold, the geese moving, that farmer's stubble burning in the northeast, leaves and marsh turning, the sun falling south again.

Even the earth at my feet offers a world of its own. In one square foot below me I see a dandelion, a thistle, quack grass, alfalfa, a spider. All this life growing with so little care from me. A black beetle scrambles for cover. I feel cold and restless waiting here on my bench. I take a deep breath.

In.

Out.

In.

Out.

That's how the marsh breathes around me. In. And out. Is consciousness everything? What could a Buddhist do to be reborn as a duck? Would life be that bad reborn as a duck?

I step from my bench to the water's edge. What does all this marsh grass look like? Cattails, they're easy, a wiener on a roasting stick. Cane grass carries that bushy white broom on top. But slough sedge, I'm still puzzled. Descriptions in my plant book aren't clear enough. A marsh wren chatters beside me. What would the naturalist Ernest Thompson Seton have seen when he lived in Manitoba in 1882? Cattails? Cane grass? Passenger pigeons? Eskimo curlew? Did he write them into his animal stories? How many Manitoba birds have become extinct since then? Whoever said we humans had the right to kill anything?

A flock of smaller passerines chirrups above my head. I see them, hear them, try to tempt them down. *Shpiishh, shpiishh, shpiishh.* Like in the arctic, they say that if you clap two rocks together the caribou will come and find you. Here, these two rocks, I've tried it, no caribou. But I know that chickadees will come to my call.

I sit on my bench and wait. What is it I want to know? The shoveler of an hour ago shakes her head, feeds. That shoveler will winter near Mexico. She has a long way to travel, may already have travelled from Alaska. A red-tailed hawk curls around the sky. A scaup jumps from the water, circles in the air, drops again beside his mate. I look over toward the cross. The cormorants are dried and gone, the ruddy duck is gone. A shadow hangs in front of me, my own, the sun is out. I say goodbye to the shoveler, to the ruddy duck, the bench. I leave little behind me. Just the bruised grass, an apple core, a trail of prune pits. Almost a memory.

I begin the walk back to the car. Suddenly I'm warmer. The moths are too, the sun wakes them. They flutter along the trail. An American bittern flushes in the reeds a hundred feet in front of me. Another trail sign, I'll turn to my left, south. I'm going south. I've walked seven kilometres, two to go. These greater yellowlegs so beautiful here in fall. A brown and speckled black-crowned night heron stands beside a culvert, hears me coming, flies up. Forty-two species today.

I've left the marsh. Now, on both sides of the trail, prairie grass, western dock, big bluestem, rust and green and brown. I stop to inspect a flower, white sweet clover, yellow sweet clover. I shield my eyes against the sun, ache for the days when this land was young, before the white man, before murder of the buffalo and the destruction of most of the native prairie.

Something in the sky behind me. I look up. The pointed wings, black hood of a peregrine far above me. There he is, the fiercest of the hunters, high in the sky above me.

DAVID CARPENTER

The End of the Hunt

I have a problem. As of last September, I have sworn off hunting. Kever and I are driving out to Togo on October 1 to visit with Doug and Barb Elsasser. How do I tell Doug, the greatest hunter I've ever known and my hunting buddy for years, that I have taken the pledge? All morning I've been rehearsing a conversation with him.

Ah, Doug, I begin.

Yeah?

We need to talk.

So? Talk.

That's as far as I've got.

The geese and ducks are driving me wild. Head off in any direction from Saskatoon, wherever you can find water. There they are, flocking and fattening up, getting ready to head south. More ducks than we've had in twenty-five years. I must learn anew how to see migratory fowl — in and for themselves as incomparably beautiful creatures. Not as so many succulent meals stuffed and trussed on a platter. Sounds nice on paper.

These are my thoughts as Kever drives us out to Doug and Barb's cabin. The weather is warm, the sky cloudless. The harvest is almost entirely off the fields, and it promises to be a good one. The year in Saskatchewan is coming to an end.

As we continue east of Kamsack, the Duck Mountains seem to rise up on the far horizon to greet us. They are hills, not mountains, but the blue ridge that forms them is so massive and sudden that they have the effect of mountains after such a wide expanse of prairie. Approaching the Duck Mountains from the west is a bit like approaching the Cypress Hills from the north. The same surprise awaits you.

We turn off Highway 5 and head south on the road to Cote (pronounced Cody), Runnymede, and Togo. This road runs through a valley filled with ranches and farms that have preserved a lot of wild brushland to the west and a huge forest reserve in the park to the east. Real postcard scenery.

Doug and Barb's place is a rambling quarter that overlooks the Lake of the Prairie. This lake is really a very long, dammed-up section of the Assiniboine River Valley. The view from the Elsassers' cabin is expansive, to put it mildly. If you look southwest across their ravine you can see the tip of one of their meandering fields Some days you can spot grazing elk. If you look south and east from their kitchen you see, instead, the Assiniboine Valley. To the north is a mixture of forest and community pasture. Straight east is Duck Mountain Park. This means bear and moose and lots of other wildlife, and an abundance of fish. Bass, muskies, pickerel, pike and perch, and five species of trout.

Um, Doug, we need to have a talk.

About hunting? he will say.

Well, I suppose so, but it's not what you think.

Elsasser will give me a strange look.

Something has happened, I will say.

And then I will say …

Start over.

Doug, we need to have a talk.

He looks up from his cup of coffee.

Talk? About what?

The oldest October ritual in Saskatchewan that I know of is the goose hunt. In Alberta, where the mallards are more plentiful, it would probably be a duck hunt. But here in drought-prone Saskatchewan there isn't always a plentiful supply of ducks; however, with each decade there seem to be more and more geese. Lesser and greater Canadas, snow geese and specklebellies. The majority of these birds nest up north where farmers can't drain their marshes for a bigger field of grain, and the geese gather in early September, the grown goslings and their parents forming huge extended family groups for the big migration south.

The most northerly nesters take their time. The forage is pretty good from well north of the Arctic Circle to the grainfields of southern Saskatchewan. We don't begin to see the huge flocks until towards the end of September. Conservationists who fight for the survival of endangered species have no worry over the wary geese. Since the early fifties their numbers in Saskatchewan have actually increased. Our prairie chicken is extinct, its habitat poisoned and ploughed away. Locals have since taken to calling the sharptailed grouse a prairie chicken, but even this magnificent lookalike is on the wane.

Not so the wild geese. They honk their way north in March to bring in spring, and they honk their way back south in October to draw down the blinds of winter. For those two periods, their shrill voices are as familiar to our ears as the song of nightingales to the English or the mockingbirds to the people of the Deep South. It makes sense. A region's birds come to stand in some mysterious way for that home place. Their calls seem to give voice to the very spirit of the place. And just as a nightingale might, in some way, come to embody the yearning spirit of rural English romanticism, so the cries of the wild geese give voice to an entire way of life up north.

They enter your territory, not gently like a songbird, but like a force of nature, a storm or a weather front. Their high fierce barking is the voice of harsh necessity, a response to the violent contrasts of the seasons that run our lives. The sound emerges from a great feathered body with nearly a pound of goose fat to keep the bird insulated from the blizzards; it flows up the length of a long powerful neck with vocal cords as resonant as the workings of a Swiss horn. Out the beak it goes, hoarse, falsetto, urgent. Valkyries. An attack from the very gods.

My father raised my brother and me to hunt with him, just as his father raised him and his brothers, just as my mother's father raised his family to hunt. Every October in southern Saskatchewan. Both of these grandfathers came out from Ontario as young men at the turn of the century, and in both cases, when they learned of the great abundance of geese on the prairie, they took to the hunt as though it called to them from a long time ago when life (yes, even for the genteel Anglos) was tribal, and hunting was not a sport but a great need.

Think of it. We've been out of the woods for a thousand years or so, living in relatively stable communities enclosed by political boundaries. But we lived in the woods for three and a half million years. An entirely tribal, pagan world is what we came from, and in hunting we can still communicate with that world, if only in rituals and faint re-enactments. I hasten to say, this communication doesn't happen to every hunter, but it happens to me and it happens to Doug Elsasser.

Never before in history has the annual hunt been so much under attack. Chemical companies are flourishing. International arms trade has never been hotter. Almost any industry involved in the depletion of the ozone layer (cars, air traffic, fossil fuels) seems to be thriving. But Canadians are massing against hunters as though they know something about evil that I simply cannot grasp.

We hear a great deal about hunters who are incapable of responding to the wilderness as a powerful numinous presence. They drive all-terrain vehicles or hunt from power toboggans — anything to avoid walking and listening and paying attention. They bring ghetto blasters to their campsites and listen to sports news, deejays and their favourite ads. Regardless of the season these hunters will shoot pregnant cow moose or nesting ducks. They will shoot from pickups and abandon their quarry to rot. Or they leave wounded birds and animals to die a slow death in the bush. They kill a bear only for its gall bladder or a huge breeding elk just for his antlers. They scatter their garbage on the roads and campgrounds. In spite of years of practice, they handle their booze very badly.

These jerks are real enough. But they get all the publicity because they attract all the attention. Perhaps we've all met a few of them.

Perhaps they are your next-door neighbours. But rest assured, there are better hunters than these among us.

You almost never hear about the many women who join in the hunt year after year. This includes my university office mate, Maria Campbell. She and her daughters have hunted moose and deer through all the lean years of life in the north. Her ancestors are among the great hunters of this part of the world, so no one in Maria's family is aghast at a woman's love of the hunt.

You almost never hear about the depth of appreciation in the hearts of ordinary urbanites for the hunt. I have hunted with friends who go out one or two weekends a year, who call themselves sportsmen, who wear plaid shirts from designer catalogues, who live in the heart of an urban sprawl; and among them all, something awakens out there in the goose pit or the woods that is so entirely primitive that on a good morning it brings up those vestigial hairs on the back of the neck.

Time and again I am asked the following question: What is the appeal of hunting for these city slickers?

Let me begin with the obvious. City life everywhere tends to create a need for its opposite. Too much noise creates a need for quiet. When the brain has to process too much information (video games, stock quotes, computers, TV shows), it yearns simply to think. Too much fast food or processed meat creates a need for something healthy. An almost entirely domestic world creates a yearning for the wild earth. The body wants to live again.

This will sound preposterously romantic, but there was a time when we used our noses and ears for day-to-day survival. Perhaps someone inside us, wiser than we have become in the city, wants to tear off that walkman and listen to a stream gurgle or a chickadee call. Someone inside us wants to rediscover excuses to pay attention.

On a hunting trip you tend to pay attention. You notice which way the wind is coming from. When you stalk animals, you need to approach them with the wind in your face. You come to learn that certain birds take off and land into the wind. You examine footprints carefully. You study fallen trees, large rocks and other landmarks and remember them or you tend to get lost. You smell things, at first because you can't help it. But then you come to rely on your sense of smell to perform dozens of little tasks. You walk quietly because you have to, and when you do this, you begin to hear the tiniest sounds and you learn to identify them. A whole world begins to return to you, a world that becomes more and more sacred the more it is ravaged by mindless human expansion.

Another question I get asked is this: To attain this dramatic state of awareness do you have to go out and kill something?

I always say, Of course not. Many hunters, myself included, eventually forsake the gun and find other excuses for getting back into the bush. These older hunters are glad to leave the killing to the young. It is a specific feeling they are hunting for. Hunters are addicted to it: that surge of well-being that comes over a man or woman when the senses are on full alert, the body in motion, the mind focussed. As your senses return to you, walking in the cold fall air, something hits you like a drug, a second wind of epic proportions, the ultimate jogger's high. Your body becomes infused with a strange and powerful flow of energy, many times more powerful than you thought you might possess. The need to stay warm promotes the need to keep moving, and ordinarily walking long distances would make you tired, but because all your senses are focussed on the pursuit of your prey (to hunt it or simply to see it), your body becomes strangely energized.

I'm now into my fifties, and I find that a four-mile walk in the city is taxing. But every time I go hunting I discover that, day after day, I can cover twenty or more miles and return from the experience fit as can be. In my case, under the right circumstances, this surge of energy comes on the very first day out.

Another frequent question: How could you bear to pull the trigger on those beautiful creatures when you claim to love the wilderness? How are you any different from anyone else who destroys our environment?

This question is the most frequent and bespeaks the most innocence. The question presupposes that there are two kinds of people: those who destroy the environment and those who leave it alone. The people who ask this question will often place hunters on one side of the moral fence (with developers, weapons manufacturers, producers of farm chemicals and other such villains), and themselves on the other side of this moral fence (with vegetarians, ecologists and urban protesters of all kinds). Perhaps someone told them or their parents that one is either part of the problem or part of the solution. Remember that argument?

Many of these same people will wear leather goods. They will shop for hunks of dead meat at a mall (which they will refer to by comfortable names like "veal" or "groceries"). They will never learn or want to learn what it is like for steers or pigs to line up at the abattoir watching the animal in front of them being electrocuted. Fear of violent death elicits a peculiar smell, and pigs are especially sensitive to that smell in the abattoir. They frequently die in a state of terror.

Hunters live with a paradox that very few non-hunters understand: They prowl through wilderness in order to kill the creatures that they love. This paradox helps to explain why hunters are such strong conservationists. If you recycle religiously, contribute time or money to environmental causes and are a vegetarian, environmentally speaking, you have the moral high ground and my respect. But bear in mind that a true hunter is like any other passionate lover of the wilderness. Call him (or her) your enemy if you will, but most hunters would never dream of destroying natural habitat.

When you fish and hunt with any regularity, you also become involved in a host of other equally healthy activities. You learn how to marinate grouse meat, how to prepare butterflied trout, how to dress and roast a mallard. But before you can do any of these wonderful things, you need to learn how to gut or pluck or field dress or clean your quarry. You learn what kind of animals and birds provide good meat. You learn which meat is better pickled, which is better smoked. You gain an intimacy with the food that may well feed you all winter long. Never again will you take good food for granted as you have in the past. Never again will you make the mistake of assuming that food comes painlessly in packages. In every North American city I've ever seen, there are always commercial forces at work that serve to distance you from the food you eat. Food becomes exotic. Food becomes someone else's business. Food becomes anything but bloody. If there's any virtue in this process of obscuring our vision of the things we eat, I have yet to discover it.

Lately, over the past six or seven years, I've been missing a lot of shots. My mind is engaged with the hunt, but my body finds itself moving in a contrary fashion. The goose flies this way, so the body should move in such a way as to line up the bird and fire. But my body wants to go that way. It wants to do something else. During recent trips I catch myself waiting, waiting, when I should be shooting. The mind knows this, but the body seems to know something else.

Carp, shoot! comes the cry of my exasperated friends.

What is my body doing, exactly?

For one thing, it's watching the bird. How close will it come this time? How old is this one? Is it a lesser Canada or a specklebelly? When will it discover me under this blind? Let's wait and see.

I don't want to shoot things anymore; it's come to that.

Some years ago, when the geese were almost as prolific as they are now, Doug Elsasser, Jack Gilhooly and I went on a goose hunt to Sceptre. This village is a four-hour drive southwest of Saskatoon. We did some reconnaissance to confirm the location and the flight patterns of a good-sized flock we had found.

I can remember this hunt as though it happened last fall. We are parked in a straggle of trees under the shadow of the Great Sand Hills. About three thousand geese are feeding in the stubble of a recently harvested field of barley. We take turns spying on them through a pair of field glasses. Back and forth the geese go in groups of up to a hundred birds: from our field to a big slough nearby, and from the slough back to the field. A fat noisy gaggle if ever I've seen one. By the time it grows dark, at least a thousand of them are still feeding there. Some snow geese and lesser Canadas, but mostly specklebellies.

At last we get out of the car and trudge across the field, spades in hand. When we reach a dip about two hundred metres from the edge of the remaining flock, they all take off in a histrionic explosion of goose outrage.

"They'll be back," says Doug.

It's too dark to see exactly where the birds have been concentrating. By this I mean the very centre of feeding activity. So Doug hauls a flashlight out of his knapsack and begins to pace along the stubble in search of the greatest concentrations of gooseshit. At Elsasser's bidding, we begin to dig our three holes, side by side. We have to guess that the wind will again come from the northwest, so we dig the holes in such a way that we will all be facing side by side in a row as the geese come in, rather than one behind the other. The geese will likely return from their water for a morning feed by circling our pits and landing into the wind. In other words, they will come from the southeast.

The holes take a long time to dig. There is little talk and much puffing. Gilhooly is getting antsy.

"Remember," he says, "bar closes in two hours."

Doug looks over at Gilhooly like a plumber examining a particularly vexing problem with a sewer drain. Doug likes it if you take an interest.

Gilhooly yawns, Doug frowns, and the three of us return to the silent business of digging holes.

After a long sweaty time of it, the holes are finished and Doug dispatches Gilhooly and I to round up a big pile of straw. We scatter the straw all around our three holes and toss the rest inside. Then we cover our holes with boards.

The night is a bit too warm for October. We would prefer to have a stormy wind and low overcast skies. In fact, the forecast is for rain and cooler weather. But tonight the breeze remains resolutely mild and the stars come out one by one. Out on the big slough nearby, the geese gab and cackle by the thousands. They are having a high old time.

Someone's alarm is ringing and I haven't the faintest idea whose it is or why some demented sonofabitch would set off an alarm clock in the middle of the jeezly night. It isn't my alarm clock. I've got enough on my mind without this damned machine. I've been arguing with this pigbrained slug of an editor about my title. It's a good title. He insists that I change it to the one his girlfriend likes. My title is pure poetry: The Floating Kisses of Eden. The one his girlfriend likes is such a cornball title no publisher in his right mind would accept it: Going Stacey's Way.

Going Stacey's Way? You've gotta be kidding! For one thing, there's no one named Stacey in the entire book. Look! Check it out! Not one trace of a Stacey!

"Well, maybe if you get out of bed, Carp, you'll find her in the coffee shop."

Doug Elsasser is standing over me. He is holding a big duffle bag directly over me. He is about to drop the bag on top of my head. He drops it on top of my head.

"Come, Sah'b, we are not wanting to be late for the Maharishi. I am have saddled your elephant."

This voice belongs to Gilhooly. This morning he is a mahout.

It turns out that we are up too early for the coffee shop to be open, but Elsasser has already covered this contingency. There's a pot of coffee brewing in our little room. And a plate full of doughnuts. He is dressed, arranging his shells on the bed. He takes one kind and slips them into his cartridge belt and then dumps the rest into his jacket pocket. He turns to me.

"Eat."

At such times when the urgency of the hunt is on him, Elsasser becomes something beyond taciturn. He becomes a combination of Sergeant Preston and Chief Little Bear. Nods, hand signals, one-syllable words. Hurry. Geese fly at dawn.

Gilhooly is his opposite. This morning he sings a selection of Johnny Cash in his newly fashioned mahout's accent. "I am falling in to a bahning ring of fire, I am going down down down as the flames are going higher."

"Can it, Gilhooly."

"And it is bahning bahning bahning, dese ring of fire — "

"Enough!"

The doughnuts and the coffee go down fast and delicious, as though they were destined to be the last comfort from civilization. I have a feeling it's going to be cold. The wind is up. It vibrates the basement shutters. On go the longjohns and wool socks, on go the wool shirt and the sweater, on go the canvas pants and canvas hunting jacket.

"Could be wet, Carp."

Off comes the canvas hunting jacket. On goes the rain gear, top and bottom. Back on goes the jacket. On goes the canvas cap. On go the boots. We trudge like football players down the hall and out into the street. The street is covered with snow.

"Snow!"

"Snow?"

"My gracious heavens, not since the Khyber pass have I beheld such — "

"Gilhooly, enough awready!"

It is only a five-mile drive to our pits, but will the water be open? In other words, will our geese still be there when we arrive? If so, will they feel disposed to land among our decoys for a last feed before heading to Texas?

We park in the trees, and the whole scene is almost unrecognizable. The branches of the trees and bushes are feathered with snow, the ground covered with several inches of powder. The visibility is not good, but better than I had expected because everything seems to glow in the dark. We load up with decoys, shells, food, thermoses of tea, and move out in single file toward our pits. Fortunately, Doug has marked them by shoving sticks into the ground by each hole. The wind sweeps across the field like Doom himself.

When the wind falls, I catch the rising babble of goose talk. Once in a while there is the dissident quack of a lone duck.

"Let's move it!" says Elsasser in an urgent whisper.

We arrive at the pits with the aid of Doug's flashlight. I choose the left pit and Gilhooly takes the right one. Elsasser shakes out the decoys. He will take the middle pit and call the whole hunt. We place most of our decoys in front of our holes, heads into the wind. Elsasser discovers that we have laid some of them down in too regular a pattern, so he disperses a dozen or so with the heads facing in random directions. We are down into our pits before we know it. Over our heads goes a bundle of straw about as wide as a sombrero. All I can see is the pure white field before us and the fringe of trees that separates us from the big slough full of birds.

And then the sound of Doug's goose call. A bassoon warming up? A clarinet blown by your mischievous little brother? Anyway, a very ragged sound.

"The slough is twelve o'clock," whispers Elsasser after a few honks. "The truck is six o'clock."

"Ah don lak it owt thar, boys. It's too quiet."

Gilhooly has become Slim Pickins as an old Marine.

Something seems to rise above the trees to the right.

"One o'clock," I whisper.

"Get down," says Elsasser.

I crouch down into my pit so that my shotgun barrel is poking up into the straw that covers the entrance. Then comes the noise of approaching birds, a high frantic barking.

"Carp, three goosks coming in from behind. You'll have to turn around."

I come up slowly from my crouch, ease off the straw, and spot them.

Three geese, flying low across the decoys. They drop down from tree height, and because of the semi-dark and the renewed snowfall, they can scarcely make out what I am. My head pokes out of a straw-covered hole. I could be just another goose having breakfast in the snow. They drop even lower and set their wings. This manoeuvre looks a bit like an airplane coming down to a landing strip in a high wind. A wing dips, the bird tilts sideways, it rights itself. All five geese do this in unison: dipping, tilting, flapping back to the horizontal. You can get mesmerized by the acrobatics of it. Then the wings set in a downward curve. This is the moment when those vestigial hairs stand up on the back of my neck.

"Now," says Elsasser.

The time is 8:15 a.m. The snow has stopped falling and the sun is up, though still not visible. We have shot our limit of fifteen birds, plus a couple of mallard drakes. Weighted down with them we move off the field. A very good morning.

"I've got this friend who always winters in Mexico," says Elsasser. "A biologist from Mississippi. He keeps asking me why I don't come down there and escape the cold. I can talk till I'm blue in the face, and he just doesn't understand."

Elsasser is beaming. He always looks this way after a successful hunt. The smile emerges because he can no longer hide his satisfaction.

After breakfast at the café we head back out to the sandhills. The sun is shining and the snow melting. The tops of the sand dunes are already free of snow and the air is cool and sweet with the smell of sage and stubble. Doug parks his truck and begins to set up the process of plucking, which will take us a good two or three hours. I'm not looking forward to this.

First, Elsasser goes into his truck and puts on a big pot of boiling water and parafin. This pot is for the birds. You dip them into the parafin, let it dry on the feathers, and then pull off the wax, feathers and all. But even after the parafin has done its work, there are still many feathers to pull. The idea is to make it all enjoyable.

The next step is to find a nice dry spot up on the sandhills. The view must be exactly right. Doug and Gilhooly choose a high dune with a south-facing view of row upon row of sandhills. We can see so far south that we imagine we can make out the northeastern edge of Montana.

We each grab a bag of geese and climb up to the top of the dune. Elsasser lines us up so that we are side by side, as we were in the pits. Between himself and his two plucking buddies, Elsasser places two opened, chilled bottles of haut sauterne. He pushes each bottle into the sand and then packs snow around it. Then he lays down cushions for us to sit on.

"Got your harp?" he says to Gilhooly.

"Yep."

And so the morning plucking begins. We tear off the feathers, toss them up to the wind, then gut the birds. As we pluck the birds we swig from the nearest bottle. Since Doug is in the middle, he has the privilege of drinking from either bottle. Wine in the morning. How did I become such an epicurian?

After we've plucked and cleaned a half dozen birds or more, Gilhooly pulls out his harp and begins to play. This is a blues harp, of course, a mouth organ for those of you who haven't yet become blues buffs. Gilhooly begins with a slow stately hymn, "Just a Closer Walk with Thee." He sucks his notes out of the little holes and bends them, sends them mournfully in the direction of New Orleans.

My bottle of wine has acquired a downy neck. This is only a bit disgusting. The wine gets better and better as the day wears on. The breeze is at our backs. It lifts the goose down from our laps and drifts feather after feather towards Montana.

"America," Elsasser calls, Paul Revere to the hunters. "The goosks are coming. The goosks are coming."

"Doug, we need to have a talk."

We are sitting out on Doug and Barb's veranda. Kever and Doug's wife Barb are stretched out on their deck chairs, eyes closed to the warm sun. Already since breakfast we've heard some elk bugling just below the rim of the valley. A perfect morning.

"Is this guy-to-guy talk?" Doug says in a lazy voice.

"'Fraid so."

"Well, if you two want to have a guy-to-guy talk," says Barb, "we are not movin'."

She says this through closed eyes, stroking their dog Brewer. Brewer opens one sleepy eye, yawns and closes his eye again.

"Let's go, Carp," says Doug. "I have to put out some leech traps. You can come along for the ride."

"And don't let him lift anything," says Kever.

She is protective of my health. Doctor's orders. Lie still and no vigorous movement. As my blood supply builds up, I go everywhere slowly, like a very old man.

Doug and I climb into Old Blue, a truck he's had since he was in his late teens. His leech-gathering equipment has been loaded into the back. He sells these leeches to bait and tackle stores that in turn sell most of them to anglers in pickerel tournaments. It's a good sideline for Elsasser, because these days the stores pay well.

We head on down through the gate and out across the road to a valley filled with small marshes. Perfect for leech gathering. Doug slows down at the wheel and begins to survey the nearest little slough.

"Okay, Carp. What's on your mind?"

"Our annual hunt."

"Good. I had a few ideas. Amazing hatch this year. Imagine that. Thousands of goosks right around here."

"Yeah."

I take a big breath and turn to face Elsasser. He continues to stare out at the slough where he will lay down his first set of leech traps.

"Something happened up north," I begin.

"So I heard."

"Yeah, but I mean in addition to the bleeding and stuff."

Elsasser turns to face me. He wears a skeptical look, almost hostile, as though I'm about to announce that I'm going to run for the leadership of the Conservative Party of Canada.

"Have you ever been scared?" I ask him.

Elsasser is close to scoffing. "Well, I suppose I've been in situations where I couldn't let on how I was feeling."

"I'll take that as a yes?"

"Get to the point."

"One more question, Elsasser."

He sighs.

"When you look out at all this, the big hills, the Assiniboine Valley, all the deer, all these marshes and meadows, do you ever get to thinking what might have created it all?"

The skeptical lines of his face shift from a "don't tell me you're runnin' for the Conservatives" look to a "don't tell me you've been born again" look.

He says, grudgingly, "Yeah?"

"What do you call it?"

"Well, Carp, I guess I'd call it the Creator."

"Great!"

Elsasser swears under his breath.

"When I was coming down in the car, things got sort of weird. The bleeding got kind of bad."

"So?"

"Well, I got quite worried at one point, because I was gulping blood. I mean, too much blood."

"Yeah?"

"So. I said, like, a prayer. To the Creator."

"Yeah?"

And I said that if He could get me out of this one alive, I'd promise never again to — "

"Oh, fuck."

" — shoot another creature."

Elsasser scowls at the gas pedal. He says, "Can I interrupt this to talk a little sense into you?"

"Go ahead."

"How did you word it? What word did you use?"

"You mean in my — "

"Yeah. Did you say fishing too?"

"Elsasser, I was worried. I wasn't crazy."

"So it's just hunting?"

"Shooting. I said I'd never shoot anything again."

"Well, does that include a bow and arrow? A rabbit stick?"

"Yeah. I think so."

"But it doesn't include fishing?"

"You don't shoot fish."

Without a word, Elsasser climbs out of the truck and begins to lay his leech traps. I watch him as he goes. When he returns to the truck, he starts it up and doesn't speak for several minutes, not until we reach the top of the next grade.

"Well, Carp, I guess when you make a promise like that, you have to keep it."

"Yeah."

"I mean, not that you had to worry all that much."

"What do you mean?"

"Well, the last few times out you couldn't hit the broad side of a barn door. I mean, hell, what is it exactly you've given up on?"

"There's no need to be sarcastic."

That day last October was one of the loveliest times I've ever spent not hunting in my entire life. Kever loved it in the same sweetly idle way. Doug and Barb planned a supper picnic for when the heat of the day had passed. They loaded up the car with various necessaries, including a roasted goose carefully packed away in the back trunk. Doug had shot it only a week earlier. As we drove into the heart of the Duck Mountains, the aroma of goose in the roaster moved all through the car and drove us mad with hunger.

We arrived at the shores of a small deep lake surrounded by big hills and heavy forest. It had heavy marshes all around the side and a small dock for boats. We brought out the supper and the folding chairs just as the sun was beginning to set. Barb poured the wine, and with our eyes on the water, we all tucked into our Thanksgiving meal. Doug had stuffed the bird with a hot curry that made me think, oddly, of Gilhooly.

I spotted a rise near the dock, and then another rise.

The supper was almost too perfect to spoil with conversation, but I said, "I swear I saw a trout rise."

"Where?"

Just as I started to point, another trout rose, this time only several metres from shore, a good one this time.

"What's in this lake?" I said.

"Thought you'd never ask," said Doug, grinning. "Some rainbows and brookies."

"You're kidding."

We ate our curried goose and looked on in astonishment as the trout continued to dimple the surface. An October rise. It was almost a contradiction in terms. It felt like it might be the last warm day of the year and the very last rise as well.

"Too bad we didn't bring our fishing gear," I said.

There was a knowing silence, conspiratorial.

"Actually," said Kever.

"You're kidding."

Doug opened up the trunk again and took out an arm-load of fishing tackle. There was still time, maybe forty-five minutes before complete darkness.

"If you promise not to exert yourself," said Kever.

"I promise."

It had been almost three weeks since I came home from hospital, and I hadn't had enough energy even to walk around the block. But now, with the day and the warm weather fading so beautifully, I felt a tiny surge of youth.

In another existence, perhaps I would have said no to fishing and just sat in my chair and savoured the sunset and the goose curry belches and had an aesthetically satisfying moment and maybe thought briefly but deeply about mortality and life's seasonal rhythms. But of course, having learned early on that the path to hell was paved by unfished lakes, I forsook my lawn chair.

I joined Kever and Barb and Doug, casting from the shore of the tiny lake. In twenty minutes we had four trout. The largest was a sixteen-inch male brookie, dazzling in dark olive and bright orange.

The day, the meal, the fishing, the people, even my confessional conversation with Elsasser and his leech traps — it had all felt like a continuous offering of thanksgiving. I had even extracted a promise from Elsasser that I would be allowed on his future hunts as a bird dog, game cleaner, cook and plucker. I've been called worse.

Conclude with the obvious. The best thing about October is Thanksgiving. For many, it's the end of the harvest. It's the end of all that wonderful fall weather, the end of a whole year in Saskatchewan. The pause before winter that says thank you to life for life.

DON GAYTON

Canyon

I had a ritual for my visits to that deep and narrow canyon. At the end of the walk up from the ranch, I would stop short of the mouth to wait and collect a few sticks for the fire. After a few moments I would enter, crossing from plangent afternoon sun to a kind of separate and constant dusk. The canyon's layered rock walls would glow with a faint bluish tinge.

Buck Creek starts somewhere above treeline and flows through the canyon all the way down to sagebrush. Originally the creek ran parallel to the main river, but sometime in the distant Pleistocene it turned abruptly, confronting a massive sandstone ridge that separated the two. The result of that unrecorded confrontation was a narrow, vertical canyon cut through bedded sandstone, and a contented Buck, now joined with its central drainage. Whatever violence had accompanied the creation of this tiny canyon was resolved in total peace. Even during spring flood the Buck flowed like silk down its smooth and rounded bed.

Just inside the canyon entrance, the sandstone walls widened out to form a circular plunge pool, about twenty feet across. There were four pools in all, one above the other, the first one being the largest. The water in the pools was tea-coloured, even though the Buck ran clear both above and below the canyon.

As a dusty young hired man on an Okanagan ranch, this canyon and its water provided retreat and solace at the end of the long workday. After my token wait at the entrance, I would move to the first pool. My work clothes, sticky with hay dust and sweat, would go into a neat pile on the first ledge, next to the sagebrush sticks I had collected. Only then did I slide quietly into the water, to float on my back and look upward. The west wall of this pool was a series of ledges leading up to a sheer sandstone face; the east wall formed a broad, curved overhang, reminiscent of a church nave. Halfway up the west wall a scrappy ponderosa pine had established on a ledge. It presided over the canyon, a modest icon.

After a few minutes in the first pool I would climb the narrow sandstone spillway to the second pool, float for a time, then go to the third and finally the fourth. Sometimes I felt suspended, as if I were floating through the rooms of a fantastic sculpture gallery, each one a different statement of colour, texture and form.

After my swim, I would return to the ledge of the first pool to build a tiny fire from the gnarled and twisted sagebrush sticks and drink from a canteen. Pungent sage smoke would curl straight upward on its way out of the windless canyon.

The rancher I worked for was an old man in those days and is long since dead. At the time I saw him only as a kind of grim coordinator of cattle, grass and barbwire, but later on I realized he must have known of the very personal, mystical nature of the canyon. That would explain his casual, well-timed remark about "those pools on the Buck, up above Bigsage Pasture," for the benefit of one he must have known would seek them out and then his prompt denial of anyone else's presence there. Certainly it was not long before the water of that canyon flowed only for me.

For years I thought about revisiting the place. In my experience of natural landscapes, the canyon stood out in my memory as one of the more openly spiritual places, rising above the level of simple nostalgia. Buck Creek was prominent on my itinerary for re-exploration.

Memory, however, can be vindictive, contemplating change with bitterness and anger. It was the potato chip, balanced on the first ledge like some obscenely alien butterfly, that first caught my eye. The chip, a nearby paper plate and several large, garish graffiti now lay strewn across a personal tapestry of my own memory, one that had lain inviolate for twenty-five years. The graffiti were spraypainted in orange Dayglo on the sandstone overhang of the first pool. "FERG89" and "TORCHY," they screamed. There were a few other initials as well; "B.D." was one. The authors would be high school graduates desperate to enhance personal identities by hijacking the spirit of the place.

My long-awaited reunion with the canyon destroyed, I stopped only long enough to survey the litter and the damage. A cold wind passed through my guts and I felt as if I had come home to a break-in. I left cleanly, not wanting to waste time in useless rage.

I was well into the long, furious walk back down through the pasture when anger finally gave way to duty and to the service of memory.

First I built a fire on the rock ledge, reversing the old ritual, and immolated the potato chip, the plate and some bits of candy wrapper. Then I stripped, waded into the first pool, took a handful of gritty sand from the bottom, and began to scrub the graffiti off the sandstone wall. It was slow work. A handful of sand would last only a few strokes before slipping through my fingers. I had brought nothing with me, so I put my socks over my hands to better hold the sand.

Parts of the sandstone were deeply stained by the paint. I scraped those areas with the sharp edge of a stone and then feathered the slight depressions back by scrubbing with more sand. It seemed appropriate to remove the graffiti from this place with primitive technology.

Resting once or twice, I lay back into the water and into the significant memory I was trying to repair. It was here, in the first pool of Buck Creek canyon, that my future wife and I saw each other naked for the first time. Brown water flowed over white bodies, sand gradually sifted over and covered our feet, and the luminous sandstone somehow softened the enormity of those first moments. Spirit, flesh, naked and humble: the meeting was a human use of natural landscape that was as valid as a mountain, as legitimate as a tree.

The very fragility of the sandstone was an asset to my work. I was able to scrape deeply enough into the body of the wall that I could get beyond the paint's deepest penetration. I could train my memory to accept change, since change is a dynamic of nature, but I would never let it accept degradation.

Before visiting the canyon, I had stopped in to see the rancher's son. He was a little older than I; in the early days we had talked about becoming partners on the ranch. He warned me about the state of the canyon and said that some aboriginal rock art further down the valley had recently been defaced by people who had chipped their own initials right into the figures. A comparison of aboriginal rock art with graffiti crossed my mind momentarily, but I dropped it. Rock art and nature were not derivative; they came from within themselves and had no need to parasitize the purity and sincerity of another's intent.

When the wall was finally finished, I returned to the ledge and dressed. This time, my clothes had none of that fine old stink of hay, sweat and horses. They could still, I mused, if I had stayed on. I could even have guarded this place on grad nights.

As I left, I took a last look up the canyon. The ponderosa pine up on the west wall had prospered, and the place was clean again. Fresh sandstone was evident on the overhang, but no paint could be seen, and I had scrubbed broadly enough that even the shapes of the letters could no longer be made out. I hoped that a few years of weathering would bring the entire wall back to its original grainy blue-white, and memory would then be served.

MAPS and BORDERS

THERESA SHEA

The Unwelcome Railroad

(or Gertrude's Revenge)

For forty years, Gertrude had craved silence as a drought craves rain. Her daughters had married local farmers years ago and her husband had recently returned to the earth. Alone at sixty, she had prayed that solitude would be her reward for servitude. But when the workcrew made its way over the hill at the edge of her property, Gertrude knew her heirloom of silence was a memory. The dull thud of wooden ties invaded the wheat fields like a natural disaster beyond her control. The metallic ring of mallets on spikes rang through her head every second on the second in time with the pulse visible on the thinning skin of her temples. Sooner imagine a man on the moon, she had never believed her homestead could be so trespassed upon.

It was weeks before the mallets swinging over muscled shoulders were in the distance. Then, in the eye of the hurricane, she allowed herself to believe once again in silence.

A fortnight later she awakened to a thunderous noise, and the accompanying vibrations spread a road map of goose bumps over her flesh. Outside her window a fireworks of sparks rose high above the tree-tops, and Gertrude imagined a dragon was erupting its way over her hillside. The vibrations grew until the freight train's light nuzzled the hill's crest and, laying heavy on its whistle, vanished sedately into the harvest moon.

From that night forward the train disrupted her dreams, and each waking moment only brought her closer to its return. Every morning she laboured to erase the railway from her life, scrubbing the skin of soot from her kitchen. She soaped everything from top to bottom, and when she ran out of soap she made some more, stacking it in large bricks in her barn. So much soap.

Early one evening she climbed the hill and surveyed the slope ascending from the north. The rails spread as long as winter to the horizon. A sense of powerlessness covered her like a blanket as she stared and wondered what she could possibly do to stop this intrusion. Suddenly it seemed so obvious.

She returned later with her arms laden with soap. Rolling up her sleeves she headed for the base of the hill and began rubbing the soap directly onto the rail in hard strokes, methodically chipping the bars until a thick coat covered both rails up to the hill's crest. She was exhausted and her hands were red, stiff and cramped by the time she returned home to pick vegetables from her garden for her dinner.

That evening the noise was deafening. The locomotive strained more than usual to mount the hill, only to fall back again and again, like a faulty zipper. Gertrude lay in bed and listened to the forlorn wail that signalled the engine's repeated defeat, and a smile spread over her face when the train reversed itself back into town.

For the next week, Gertrude continued to soap the rails, and every night the train slunk back into town. If the rain hadn't come, the railway might have believed in a curse and switched its route.

But on the eighth night, the rain fell. Incandescent bubbles burst forth from the friction of wheels on rails. In the locomotive's light they beckoned like pearls; the engineer jumped from his panting beast and put his tongue to the froth.

On Thursday, Gertrude's morning tea was interrupted by a knock on the door. A railroad official presented her with a fine for obstructing traffic and threatened to confiscate her soap. He returned late in the night to insure the freight train's safe passage through her property.

Once again came the sparks, the noise, the vibrations and the soot. The engineer leaned on the whistle, gloating in his victory. And Gertrude lay quietly in bed, a mysterious smile lingering at the corners of her mouth. Already she had begun to imagine an alternate plan.

MYRNA GARANIS

Saskatchewan Accent

been on courses tried therapy
 even chawed on stones
  still can't ditch
   that home-canned sound
    that prairie tone

most likely the water
 affects intonation or
  maybe the doin' without
   n' all those years
    yellin' into the wind
     must 'uv made a contribution

potatoes could be at the root
 heaped plates of boiled n' mashed
  milk'n butter rivers, half canna pepper
   yeah that 'ud do it

talked to a man in P.E.I.
 he'd been there 30 years
  learned to speak Atlantic
   yet in and out, around his phrases
    telltale prairie telegraphs
     skittering vowels along the tongue
     close calls with rusted wire

Last Train to Millennium

I thought you knew

Millennium's a town in Saskatchewan
baseball team won a pile of trophies
they're in the Millennium Museum, second floor
along with catchers' mitts, umps' uniforms

in space donated, what used to be the Red and White
now a hardly/any porno/store

no one climbs the stairs, players dead or relocated
to Millennium Lodge, leading town employer
Pool elevator latest shutdown, trucking grain is cheaper
and freight train's a foreign word
the only track remaining a narrow gauge
built by an outside crew the time they shot that baseball movie

you can still catch a bus, special luxury coach
for gamblers, one week south across the border
alternate weeks Regina, three-night package tour
plus a hundred dollar casino credit, whole thing run
by the province's original owners

most Millennium traffic heading out
except the Japanese balloonists
seeking launch locations and space to burn
their record-breaking flight assured
discounting wind and freezing rain

Frank Aiken
shortstop through the whole Depression
known in the Lodge as the Come-Back Kid
can't make out the soaring basket
spies a patch of native grass
miracle it was spared
when they moved the CP station
rebuilt it board by board in another town
new owners serve authentic railway food

nearly naptime, Frank intent on Main Street

the swift fox pair two sandy brush salutes

they vanish into thin air or perhaps their den

four cubs waiting, Millennium waiting too

RICK WENMAN

Charlie Butterfly

Funny thing. Last night I'm lying in bed thinking about fencing, about the wind whistling through the wire, and me, pulling down on the fence stretcher, tighter and tighter, until the wind and the wire become a voice, and the voice begins to weep. Pulling the handle down again, all the way down until it clicks, and the weeping becomes a song, a song from a Diva, and the Diva singing it for me.

Then today, halfway through my first cup of coffee, I look out the window and see my neighbour, Bob Shank, with his truck stopped out in my hayfield. Behind the truck are tire tracks of flattened crop. I grab my binoculars. Now he's taking down the barbed wire fence between the hayfield and the cow pasture.

Then I'm in my truck in the cow pasture, parallelling the downed fence, bottoming out on a pocket gopher mound and spilling my coffee. Badger holes too. They make a minefield for any equipment.

Bob looks like a scarecrow, hair sticking out of his cap like straw. He works with rigid fervour, the summer sun scorching his arms below a filthy T-shirt. It's only around eightish, but he already has urine-coloured circles under his armpits. He's pulling out staples with a pair of fencing pliers, examining each carefully before dropping them into a rusty coffee can. I pull up, roll down the window, take a deep breath. "Howdy Bob. You sure look busy."

Bob grunts as he pulls another staple. "Yeah, well, you know when I sold this land I never sold the fence. I just never needed it till now so I let you use it till I did. You most likely forgot." His face looks fierce, like a hawk, and his voice sounds like a rusty well pump.

I look down the crooked fence line. The posts are rotten and too far apart. The wire's loose, the cows are always leaning through to the hay crop. That's the problem with cheap wire, you can't get it tight enough to sing. Snaps every time.

"The fence is mine and I'm taking it." Bob turns back to the fence and rips another staple loose. "The staples too. They're mine."

"You're welcome to the fence, Bob." I watch his back for a minute before driving to the road, then around to the hay barn. I pick up five bales then bounce across the cow pasture. The cattle haven't noticed the downed fence yet. Hopefully the hay bales will keep them busy until I can get a new one up. The cattle mob the truck as I fling flakes of hay with my pitchfork. Then I stand in the truck box and look back to the fence line. The scarecrow is still walking, post to post, holding the fencing pliers in front like a witching rod, bending forward and pulling the staples, then holding them up to the sun before dropping them into the coffee can.

Rumour has it, old man Shank left a lot of bad debts when he died. The farm went from four sections to one within a year of Bob taking over. That's when I bought the hayfield and the cow pasture at a fair price. Then Bob got the idea that yuppies will pay more for meat if they think it's special. He jumped into the natural beef thing. You know, no chemicals or antibiotics, just natural silage. He rented some space in a big mall in Calgary, and his wife Mary worked in the store. Bob came up with the advertising slogan. "Green Beef." Cover the environmental angle. Well, no one wanted to eat green beef, natural or not.

Then, last year, Bob started talking about selling out. He showed me plans for a new golf course and condo deal that was going to make him a millionaire. However, after the developers took a closer look at Bob's financial situation, they decided to wait him out. Pick up the land at auction instead. I remember watching the stream of trucks rumbling past our gate on the way to Shank's on the day of the auction. Syl and I sat on the porch and listened to the windblown chatter of the loudspeaker as Bob's cattle, tractor, loader and manure spreader were put on the block and like dry topsoil, drifted and settled with his neighbours. The poor bastard went from retiring in Palm Springs to flat bust within six months. The bank left him the house and two acres of land.

I reach the blacktop and turn south, away from Calgary, the city crouching on the north horizon like a cluster of thistle. I do most of my business in Okotoks. Sometimes I pay a bit more. I only go to Calgary when Sylvia and I go to the opera.

People look at me, sitting in the second row in my good suit and new haircut, and maybe think I'm some kind of executive, until they see my gnarled hands. But once the houselights go down, I become part of the uneven mass of heads, like a broken field, and across the landscape like a fine wire tightening blows the voice of the Diva. I hold my eyes open until they swim, my ears open up to her voice and it runs around the walls, up to the first balcony. Then up to the second balcony, across the roof and back down to where she's standing, a glowing white pillar on the stage. In the second act, when she's singing "*Un bel di*," I stifle a sob and Sylvia digs her elbow into my ribs. She thinks I'm asleep.

After a few miles, I turn off the blacktop, onto the gravel and take the back way in to town, through the small industrial area, and pull in at the green UFA sign. I've got about twenty posts at home. I'll need another thirty, some two-inch staples, a small can of white paint, and a few rolls of good wire.

Betsy has worked behind the counter for decades, her brown shoe-polish hair welded to her head. Long purple fingernails, thick and curling in at the ends of her fingers, like overgrown hoofs.

"Cash or charge?" She looks at me. A flap of wrinkled skin flickers over her left eyelid.

"Uh, make that charge, if you don't mind."

"Oh, no," Betsy says. "Charge is fine."

When I get back to the fence, Bob has finished pulling staples and is rolling up the rusty wire. I see several broken ends of wire sticking out of the coil. "Stuff's pretty brittle eh?"

Bob snaps his sunburned face up and bares his teeth. Looks like a weasel now. "Nothing wrong with this. Wire's good as new." He continues rolling.

I pull the gearshift into reverse. Always do it by feel. The PRNDL on top of the steering column quit working as soon as the warranty was up. Not like my old International. Now that was a truck. First time Sylvia let me kiss her was in that truck. Since then I've had a Ford Ranger, a Dodge Power Wagon, even a little Datsun I gave to my daughter when my belly started pressing the steering wheel. Peg's at university, in pre-med. I might as well have taken ancient history for all the good my agriculture degree does me now.

I back down the naked fence line. When I reach the cross corner I stop the truck again. My new fence will go up strong and straight, with the anchor post painted white. I hoist myself up into the back and start rummaging through the filthy wooden toolbox. I know I have a roll of string somewhere. There it is, right on the bottom. I pull out the roll and with it trail out the chainsaw, some shredded baling twine, a roll of black tape with mouse shit all over the sticky side, and my booster cables. Where the hell is my pocket knife? Here it is, in my pocket.

I use my rifle to make sure the fence is straight. Set the rifle on the anchor post, then look through the scope and keep the other posts in line with the cross hairs. Even though I know the rifle isn't loaded, I pull the bolt out, for safety's sake. Bob's still up ahead, rolling wire.

I'll use the post pounder. It's a brute, my dad bought it in the fifties. Hooks up to the power take-off unit on the old Massey. I pull the battery out of Sylvia's car and put it in the tractor. The Massey was red.

Now it's hard to tell what's red and what's rust. It's one of those ones that has the gasoline start-up motor, then you switch to diesel. When I switch over, the tractor starts belching and popping irregular black clouds that hang over the yard. I grab a coffee and watch the clouds of smoke until they turn grey.

Bob's rolling the last coil of wire when I ride the tractor into position, about a foot over from where the old fence was. He drapes the wire over his shoulder and walks down to where I'm working. Bob won't want these old posts. I doubt if he can retrieve them without breaking them off, and even if he does, they'll never take a staple.

His normally fluid gait has a jerkiness, and several wire cuts on his hands ooze red blood over black crusty scabs. He stands right in front of the pounder. Now, Bob knows that pounder as well as I do; he's borrowed it enough over the years. He knows to always stand behind the tractor because the pounder has a habit of firing the occasional post straight out. Bob stands, wire slung over his shoulder, staring intently at the post being punched into the dry soil.

"Er, Bob, you better not stand right there, if you catch my drift."

Bob looks at me like I'm screwing his wife or something. He wags his head and his voice rattles out. "Leave me room to take my posts. Nothing wrong with them."

I shake my head and look over the horizon to the next section road where a red pickup is making a contrail of dust. "Sure thing Bob. You know, that rusty wire can give you lockjaw. You better see your doctor for a tetanus shot. Can't be too careful."

Bob sets the roll of wire carefully in the box of his truck, then pulls out a long iron bar. "Lockjaw," he says as he plunges the bar into the ground next to the first of the rotten posts and wiggles it back and forth. "Lockjaw. That's fine. Lockjaw. That's good." He yanks on the top of the post and it snaps off underground. "Perfect," he declares as he places the post in the box of his truck. "Nothing wrong with that."

It's about time for dinner. I figure Bob can use some food, get out of the sun for a while.

"Nope," Bob says as he attacks the next post. "Got lockjaw, can't eat."

I've got to stop eating so much. All I feel like doing now is snoozing for a couple of hours. But it's after one, and it looks like Bob is over half-way up the fence line.

The new posts go in straight. With the scope and string they look like a column of soldiers. Keep the line perfect all the way. Gaining ground on Bob, I see him look back every once in a while and it's driving him to a faster pace. The wind is blowing from the west, carrying the occasional grunt over the steady thunk of the post pounder.

I look up and I see my Sylvia standing in the field with her hands on her hips, her fresh lipstick in a straight line while the wind's fingers muss her hair and flutter through her new, cream-coloured blouse. I must have done something. Oh, oh. Now I remember. Her icy eyes tell the story of trying to start her car. Nothing. Lifting the hood. I can picture her pacing down the road, her jaw set, her narrow shoulders hunched. When she's angry her actions become very deliberate. Her voice too.

"Okay Charlie. Where's my battery?"

I look at the tractor, still puffing smoke over the thunk of the pounder. "I sort of needed it for the tractor. I forgot you were going ..."

She takes a step closer. "Yeah, well, you can un-forget and put it back where it belongs."

"Aw come on Syl. Why don't you just take the truck?"

"I don't want to take the truck. It's filthy inside and I've got a skirt on. Charlie, I don't have time to argue, I told mother I'd be there by now. You get your fat ass moving and get that battery back in the car."

There was a time when Sylvia would never say "ass" or any other expletives unless under severe fear or duress. Then she'd blush. I guess twenty years of marriage to me has loosened her tongue a bit. We agree to take the battery out of my truck and put it in her car so I don't have to shut the tractor off. We even hold hands on the way back to the yard. Her hands are cool and soft.

We pause for a moment and look to the stick man on the horizon, bending over and working the bar down beside yet another rotten post.

"I could call Mary." Her voice sounds edgy.

"Don't bother. He's not doing any harm. Let him take the damn thing if he wants it."

"It's not the fence I'm worried about."

Syl drops me back near the fence on her way out and I see Bob carrying two posts down to his truck. He has them over his shoulder and one has slipped crosswise. I want to ask him why he doesn't drive his truck up to where he's working, but I just stand and watch.

Bob finally carries down the last of his old posts. After he gets into his truck, I mosey over to the driver's side. The old Ford's windshield looks like a spider's web with all the cracks in it. The metallic brown paint has faded to shit brown and the name, River Road Ranches, is barely distinguishable. A dusty scoped rifle hangs in the back window.

"Did you get all you need, Bob?"

Bob gives me that look again. Then he looks east, over the stubble fields to the horizon where a new tractor is making dust. I can see a thin, purple vein pulsing above his left eye. He points to his clenched jaw, then drives across the field to the road and turns south toward his house and his two acres of land.

The last post thunks into place at four-thirty. I know I can get the wire stretched before dusk. Sylvia's car speeds down the road, and I see her behind the wheel, a dark statue with an arm raised as the double rumble of the cattle gate welcomes her home. The biggest tom turkey trills a greeting. If only he knew that on Saturday, instead of the scrap pail, Sylvia will be carrying the cleaver, and her lovely long fingers will be painted with blood. She'll save the giblets; Syl always uses them and spud water for the gravy. Then I'll eat too much and have to lie down on the couch until the dishwasher's loaded.

The bottom strand is easy to pull tight. Not much to snag on. But the stapling is torture for a guy like me. I have to kneel down to knock the staple in each post, and by the end, my knees are swollen and sore. I have to stand with my hands on my hips and arch my spine to try and relieve the back spasms. I'll need Sylvia's cool hands just to get out of bed tomorrow.

I rip the back of my hand with the middle strand. It snags on the bottom wire when I'm stretching, and I'm pissed off because I have to walk down to the snag. I boot the wire once, but the two barbs are mashed together. I have to pull the snag by hand and then it snaps up and rips right through my glove. I pull my glove off and examine the wound. A good rip, just below the knuckle on my index finger, but doesn't need stitches. I jam my hand back into my glove. I'll clean it up later with some disinfectant. At least it's new wire, no rust. Maybe I'll do it the old way, get the dog to lick it.

I'm a little more careful and use the fencing pliers to release the snags on the top wire. I grab the handle of the fence stretcher and pull it another click tighter. The wind whistles through the wire. I pull down again and listen. The Diva can be heard, weeping softly, and with the last pull, finally, she starts to sing. I close my eyes for a minute and let her song wash over me and down my cheeks. Nothing wrong with that.

I hammer the last staple and release the stretcher. Then wrap the extra wire around the anchor post and twist it tight with the pliers. I slap on lots of white paint. I want the post to glow, just like the Diva.

I stand behind the white anchor post looking east, down my new fence. A yearling heifer is already scratching her butt against one of the posts. To the west, I feel the sun settling behind the mountains, turning my collar to sandpaper. Then Bob's Ford glides down the road and stops in line with the fence. From behind the wheel of the truck, a flash of silvery light reflects the sun back up the fence line to where I stand with the Diva. I know he's lining up the fenceposts and I should step clear, but the Diva is singing her song, more beautifully than I've ever heard her sing before.

The Diva sings her song to me. Only to me.

WADE BELL

Drumming

"I have to make some chaos out of this sense."
— Jim Carroll

Drumming is beating the skin of the earth with human skin. Drumming is heartbeat, shout, language, rhythm. Drumming is a wind, a blizzard, an eruption of human spirit. Drumming is earth. Drumming is earthquake. You do not drum the land. You drum deeper than surfaces. You drum the earth.

Land is a word with diseased associations. The image of a speculator in property values; a landman for the oil company with his fast talk and booze on the farmer's kitchen table; the faceless developer; the Department of Indian Affairs "negotiators/compensators" working in collusion with industry to remove natives from their homeland. Real estate, ownership, forced displacement of people, profit. A good deal or a bad deal. The absolute denial of music, heart, spirit, dimension.

Real estate. Demesne, domain, dominion of the lords of the manor, domination. La tierra real: royal lands, royal property, royal rights. Medieval conceptualizing. Vanity.

Nothing new in this. The drum doesn't say anything new. Repetition stimulates. The beat brings on the dance. The dance renews the spirit and the spirit makes us fly, if we are able.

"Keep the hell off this property or you'll have a load of buckshot up your rear ends!" says a gamekeeper in Scotland, roused from his dinner to carry out his royal and ancient duty in the sullen night. We wanted to walk to the shore of Loch Lomond on the other side of the estate. We were driving from Manchester to Glasgow to Oban for no reason other than that my friend had a car and I'd never seen Scotland. We took the narrow highway that skirts the western side of Loch Lomond, but the road was just far enough from the lake that we couldn't see it in the rain and growing darkness. So we parked the car in trees by the road, scaled a high, stone wall and trespassed, already soaking wet. We got about a hundred yards into a section with tall, black trees that smelled good in the rain. We thought we were skirting the buildings, but we didn't see the gamekeeper's stone house hidden in a copse nor, as we stopped to assess where we were, did we hear the man come up behind us. His shotgun at our backs, he marched us to another stone building where a bulb above the doorway switched on, the door opened and a woman stepped into the pool of weak, yellow light to judge our infraction. It was like a fairy tale. Smiling as reassuringly as I could, I explained that I wanted to see the lake and that I meant no harm. "I'll never be in this part of the world again," I said. She looked at us closely, studying our faces. Then she said, "You can't," and stepped back through the doorway. The light went out. The gamekeeper saw us to a heavy, locked gate, onto the road and to our car. We drove, soaking wet, away from the mystery and the myth of a lake I doubtless will not return to.

"Get off this land before I shoot!" — a rancher on horseback somewhere in that hidden, dreamy micro-world southwest of Longview, Alberta. His rifle raised, he was the erstwhile guardian of the royal might, the government's right to grant leases for the private use of public land. It was part of the most appealing landscape my friend, who was from another country, had ever seen. Dappled with shocks of red and yellow wildflowers, it spread out before us like a novel, inviting us to enter and forget our problems for a few hours, freely and unhurriedly. We desired only to wander in the sensuous sunlight of those foothills, perhaps to make love in the powerful wind and listen to the drumming of ghosts. My friend was frightened and horrified by the severity of the man's threat. Later, she whispered that she was not impressed with "cowboy manners" and recalled the time we strayed onto a finca in Andalusia where, when we were approached by the overseer, we were invited for coffee and a sandwich in the living room of his vast house and then given a tour in his Land Rover to see up close the fighting bulls he bred.

It doesn't matter where in the world you happen to be; if the land isn't yours, it isn't yours.

So. Delete "land." Insert "earth." The substitution has something to do with escaping from the restrictive linear grid that partitions our minds just as section roads divide the prairie. I won't even try to justify it otherwise.

Earth. What we play with. What we smear on our faces to amuse ourselves, to disguise ourselves. And to frighten, to delight, to seduce and give pleasure. Playing with the spirits, collective and personal.

Land: practicality.

Earth: spirit and ritual.

Land: the result of the anarchy of greed.

Earth: the paths of human feet.

Land: resistance, borders, denial of the wandering human foot that needs to be grounded on a trail no matter whose rules of ownership would keep us off it, would suppress thought, history, feeling, imagination, growth.

Children know their right to cut through yards, follow paths, walk barefoot in the mud by the river. Whose mud is it, anyway? Why, exactly, keep off the beautiful grass?

"Land! Land! Free land in Canada! Settle the bloody place. Displace the Indians. Put the land to USE! Put up fences, barriers, roads. Cut off the endless paths across the prairie. No more horses. No more human feet. No more drums. Keep the Indians off!" yelled the royal decree by the people's government to the people who had no idea what was going on, but trusted.

Legal terrorism, political obsession.

"Get off my land!"

Why? Who says? I just want to be by the river, walk in the mud, listen to the drum, play my own in my own style. Or else I'll give up hope and wither. Use your drum to tell me what you need. I'll drum my story in reply. My story is not unusual. Do not be afraid of me. My footsteps are not so loud. Do not be afraid of me. I am not death, I am not mutilation, I am not pain. I do not want your soul. I am guided only by my own and there is no evil in it. Guard yourselves not from me but from yourselves.

Earth: the soil, plants, vegetables (eaten raw with a child's appetite for freshness) of a small backyard garden in the city.

The North Saskatchewan River's bank along Keeler Road in Edmonton, west of the stables. Sixteen-year-old boys parked in cars with girls. Alcohol and drugs.

On the south end of the city, a disused field in which to wander alone in the wild grasses before they built the houses and the shopping centres on it. It was a good place to stare at the sky, wonder at the silver light and the "air so dry that rain disappears before it hits the ground," as Anne Tyler's character says about Edmonton in *The Accidental Tourist*.

Medicine Lake, a pool of snowmelt nestled tightly between mountains in Jasper National Park, a five-year-old's paradise with wild animals, sudden summer storms and the forest's mysterious sounds of death.

The thin woods and lightly covered dunes stretching north of Lac la Biche, oilfield roads impassable in the constant rain yet conquered nonetheless by force of will.

A cluster of wolf willows in the soft, dry folds of the coulees of southern Alberta where one can sleep in summer.

In the centre of a field ploughed for eighty years, an island of trees, grasses and water where no one but a child from the city ventured. When the child discovered a deer there among the morning shadows, the island became a sacred refuge where heaven touched earth.

Sexual, cultural, spiritual awakenings.

The excitement of love, creation and limitless thought. The ecstacy of freedom in the sunlight of the countryside and lust in the city streets at night.

I've always been one of those people who wander off and get lost. Was as a child. Still am. I do that in my imagination too. Maybe it has to do with the mesmerizing landscapes here. All you have to do is stare off in any direction to get lost. Gazing from schoolroom windows in the city, driving the long roads of the countryside, staring out windows of office buildings, contemplating thunderheads, wall clouds, hail, rain and snow storms, summer prairie or winter mountains, I felt, I saw, I played my drum and wrote about wanderers.

Earth. Stripes of mud on my children's smiling faces.

Earth. The plates we ate from.

Earth. The clay goblets from which we drank the purple wine of the Spanish countryside.

Earth. Graves. My great-grandparents' bones beneath shortgrass and tiny cacti a long ride from Wardlow, the closest town; my grandparents in the earth of cities, Edmonton and Calgary; my mother beneath dust at the edge of the Hand Hills.

Earth. Its colours, from white mud to yellow clay to black loam to red soils. Its people, living and dead.

Earth. The unknown. Fear and wonder.

I've never had title to a piece of land so I don't know what the pleasures of land ownership are. Maybe one day I'll own something, somewhere. A little house in Costa Rica, an apartment by the sea in Sitges, just south of Barcelona, or in Rio. These days, though, that would be expensive and Canadians aren't as rich overseas as they used to be. I won't settle down on this land, not here where the summers are disappearing and the winters are too long and the drums hang on museum walls. Not that these landscapes aren't the blankets I was born onto, not that they weren't the ground of the aesthetic that guides my consciousness, not that my sense of the natural anarchy of the spirit did not come to me on the wind off the mountains. No. The shifting kaleidoscope of my being was laid out on this terrain.

The tropics call, but what the south will look like after twenty years of drastic climatic upheaval no one knows.

Land: a corner of a schoolyard, a corner of a park, a place to play baseball.

Earth: the school, the baseball itself, home base.

My father is in Mesa, Arizona, for the winter. For a few months thousands of us spread along the sunbelt from San Diego and Palm Springs to Vegas, Phoenix and Tucson. Not many choose to stay year round. It's too hot and the cost of insurance is high. My father has a lot of friends to play cards with and talk to. He can still play a mean game of golf and loves to do it in February while he imagines the ice on the streets at home.

My father knows Alberta. He was born in a homestead on desiccated buffalo prairie 150 miles straight east of Calgary. In various careers he has travelled more of our roads than anyone I know. The part of his life that is philosophy and poetry, reflection and dreams, is wrapped in a lifetime of visuals of here. In my way, I know the land too. The quiet, the stillness — too still for a manic child — the solitude, the boredom, the somnolence of childhood and the reveries that forge daydreams of escape.

With thirty-five permanent addresses on two continents behind me, here I am in Alberta again, still with a lot of the gypsy spirit in me, still landless, still dreaming of elsewhere and remembering the periodic sensation of being trapped by rooms, by buildings, by land you couldn't see the end of, the boundaries of, the walls to be scaled.

Land: safety, security, a hedge against fate, karma or destiny.

Earth: fear, challenge, discovery.

Land: doctrine.

Earth: enigma.

Land: what we fight wars to acquire.

Earth: what suffers as we destroy in order to acquire.

We are not taught the spirit of the earth. Instead, we are fed the colonist's dream, the surveyor's dream, the developer's dream, and the dream of the owner, stuffed in a drawer with the mortgage. We are taught that it was good to lay out rules on the land, unaware that the land has its own immutable rules.

As the essayist Octavio Paz wrote in "The Dialectic of Solitude," way back in the fifties, "Modern man likes to pretend that his thinking is wide-awake. But this wide-awake thinking has led us into the mazes of a nightmare in which the torture chambers are endlessly repeated in the mirrors of reason. When we emerge, perhaps we will realize that we have been dreaming with our eyes open, and that the dreams of reason are intolerable. And then, perhaps, we will begin to dream once more with our eyes closed."

I want to erase the words on these pages just as my footprints have been erased from the patches of earth I've walked on. Maybe that's what living here, in these surreal landscapes with their unusual light phenomena and odd perspectives, has done to me.

In this place you can see what seems to be a man from a very long distance. Sometimes it is a man; often, although he breathes, eats and defecates, it is only the appearance of one. To know for certain you must get close enough to listen for the drum.

MYRNA KOSTASH

Medicine Line Crossings

> *"... and now Montana opens before you everywhere.*
> *Keep walking."*
> — Paul Jenkins, *Custer's Last Stand*

As a boy, the writer Wallace Stegner contemplated the boundary survey stakes on his family's farm in southeastern Saskatchewan and could "see" no boundary there. He imagines walking along that invisible line, from post to post, and knows that he would find only "more plains, more burnouts, more gopher holes, more cactus, more stinkweed and primroses, more hawk shadows slipping over the scabby flats" on the Montana side. Yet it was no mere figment of the imagination that separated North Americans of the plains into Canadians and Americans. To the Indians of the plains, in anguished flight from the United States army, the line of cairns was the "medicine line."

Sniffing the Wind

My old friend Duane, who grew up in Lethbridge, Alberta, hangs her head out the Toyota's window and listens to the wind. It reminds her of where she grew up. Her mother, who moved down to Lethbridge from Edmonton, hated the wind, but Duane, who grew up with weather fronts careering in from over the Rockies, whipping up dust devils and twisters, learned to trust it. You could see it coming. It didn't blow up, sneaky-like, from shaggy bushland, or suddenly whip itself into a frenzy overtop the reed-clogged lakes. It swept in a broad swoop from the horizon, sending tumbleweed skittering across the schoolyard and her mother's bedsheets in corkscrew twists around the clothesline. They say it eventually makes all the barbs on a barbed wire fence point the same way.

When we drive around Missoula in western Montana, Duane is pierced with memories of Lethbridge — the wide residential streets shaded under the canopy of cottonwoods, the Russian thistles in the autobody shop yard, the black-eyed Susans. Cruising around town looking for an open laundromat, we hear hymn-singing on the radio on Sunday morning, and she remembers the Mormon Tabernacle Choir on Lethbridge radio. It was part of her "churching."

She thinks Montana has more horses though, more cowboys. She picks out their hats navigating the promenading crowd. "Here they have cowboys year round. We had farmers in Lethbridge," she says, as though they were necessary but insufficient, "and cowboys at rodeos." Her cousins had horses. They still do. She rode every chance she got down in the coulees all her childhood long. I tell her we didn't have coulees where I grew up in Edmonton. We had the great wooded trench of the North Saskatchewan River. She goes on, in a reverie. "We all seemed to live a block away from the prairie — tumbleweed rolling in on my street from the field, horses in the 'backyard,' out in the coulees."

I tell her we didn't have cowboys, either; we had farmers from eastern and southern Europe. Duane says she had "Mormons and lots of Hutterites." We go on like this, trading her memories of Japanese in the beetfields for mine of Chinese in the Avenue Cafe. She tells me about Mrs. Helmer, "the Russian," who had a house down in the coulee — lucky Mrs. Helmer down in the flats with the horses. Duane recalls a glamorous family across the street, rolling under their white Stetsons, decked out in their glittering cowboy outfits, never too snooty to say hello in their Miles City drawl. They had once been Montanans.

I come from north of this geography. I come from bush and fenceposts. Cattle do not wander over the face of the earth, but farmers stand at the gates, guarding barleyfields. Cree are on the traplines in the moist woods, clean of the dust raised by Blackfoot powwows beating the desiccated plain to the south. Rivers run north. The first killing frosts of autumn bring the whiffs of frozen tundra so long undisturbed you cannot dig a grave. The Rocky Mountains belong to the legends of those who passed through; we think of forests, and then nothing.

It was the great Scots-Canadian cartographer David Thompson in the 1840s who delineated the Great Plains as the unforested lands from the Gulf of Mexico to latitude fifty-four, just one degree north of Edmonton, bounded on the east by the Mississippi and on the west by the Rocky Mountains. We travellers are the descendants of seven generations of European explorers and adventurers bent on finding something "there" in that uncharted, uterine back-of-beyond. Indians were off-centre, outside the frame, not part of this picture. In something like 200 years, the strangeness of the interior declined with the departing shadows of the woods. Farmers were coming, and they would have familiar names for things.

It is semi-arid land and, some say, we have no business to be farming it. Thompson had warned that the grass was too short for cutting, and in 1857 Captain John Palliser noted in the valleys of the Red Deer and Belly Rivers the "calcareous marls and clays that are baked into a compact mass under the heat of the parching sun," seedbed only to sage and cactus.

Canadians invented summer fallow and strip farming but even so, grass cover is lost forever, soils are depleted, whole contours of the land are eroded. Rains come, and they go. Each year we have needed a little more water than we were getting. Irrigation drains the aquifers. Species are in jeopardy: black-footed ferrets, whooping cranes, kit foxes, trumpeter swans, burrowing owls, the prairie chicken and ferruginous hawks. "We are engaged," the Canadian naturalist Stan Rowe has written, "in a giant experiment of uncertain outcome ... to test under stress the resiliency of the prairie." He chastises us for continuing to act like "foreigners" in our own home place — disappointed Europeans with our forest-dwellers' yearning for wood and water. Let us love what is actually here.

Jon Whyte, the poet from Banff, enumerates the flowers of the foothills and the plains

Goldenrod, silverwood, water calla, dragonhead,
bunchberry, ragwort, paintbrush, and sedge,
Indian pipe, meadow rue, bur-reed, silverthread,
hornwort: growing at the water's edge.
Bog myrtle, sun dew, bracken and pincherries,
pitcher plants, touch-me-not, milfoil and brome,
twinflowers, bishop's cap, running pine, cloudberries:
garland the one who returns slowly home.

— Homage, Henry Kelsey

In 1910 the grass in Montana was smooth and dense, not high but thick, and soft on the sole of the foot. Deep, sheltering wallows, scooped out in the grass, harboured the white ribcage of the vanished buffalo. The long stone spoke of a medicine wheel measuring astronomical time from one solstice to the next — the clock between hunts — poked out from the bluebunch that had been blooming since the last Ice Age. Bluebunch wheatgrass, Indian ricegrass, tufted hairgrass, slender wheatgrass, blue grama. Junegrass, squirrel tail, foxtail barley, prairie cordreed, sand dropseed, rough fescue, little bluestem.

Sediment

George Melnyk is a writer and ideologue of regionalism based in Calgary who likes to reconnoitre the western territories. Example: he takes off on a trip south. On his way out of the city he stops to have a chat with a cowboy riding in the ditch. Slumped at his steering wheel, his left arm resting casually on the open window frame, he is eye level with the horse.

"When does the antelope season start?"

"Today."

"Many around?"

"Nope. Gone south to Montana."

By the time he is east of Medicine Hat he has already seen two herds of pronghorn. What did that cowboy mean, they'd gone to Montana? Maybe he didn't mean Montana, the place with licence plates and state taxes, but Montana, the place beyond, the way south of here, the "there" over the southern horizon.

Down from the glaciers of the Rockies that Melnyk thinks of as "orphans" of the last Ice Age, stranded in the high country above the sedimentary layers of the plains, the rivers dash clear and blue from the ice only to subside in a slow, muddy meander across the prairie on their way to the Arctic Ocean, the Hudson Bay, the Gulf of Mexico. Now Melnyk is in the Montana foothills, admiring the Missouri River that once was freeflowing, 2500 miles through the continent, until the federal government threw the Fort Peck Dam and Reservoir across it in 1937. Underwater lie the pastures of the pronghorn.

Melnyk is wearing sneakers, white man's moccasins. He feels at home. He lifts up his nose to sniff the air. It smells of cottonwood, willow and wild rose. He smells the musk of beaver, the matted black feather of the cormorant, the fish on the breath of the blue heron. Over his left shoulder he catches the passing shadow of the disappeared — the plains grizzly, the prairie wolf, the bighorn sheep. Humans, on the other hand — Crow, Blackfeet and Chippewa-Cree — he sees straight ahead, hurtling past him on the highway in big, raucous cars dragging the haunches of their chassis in the dust.

Pile of Bones

There is an extraordinary clutter in the grasslands. In the shadow of the grotesque shapes of brown ironstone in the valley of the Red Deer River, from the hardened sand, mud and lime-ooze of the Cretaceous, the geologist J.B. Tyrrell, while stopping for lunch on a survey of the country between the Bow and the Saskatchewan Rivers in 1884, became the first white man to collect dinosaur bones in the Badlands. They had lain there a hundred million years in this landscape that had slowly been pried open by corrosive Nature — and now, having seen one pile of bones, it was impossible not to see them suddenly everywhere. In the hundred years since Tyrrell's discovery, some thirty complete dinosaur skeletons have been carted away, not to mention the countless fragments of bone and shell carried downstream into the valley from the dinosaur deathbeds on the lush tablelands.

At Egg Mountain in northwest Montana's Pine Butte Swamp Preserve, Duane and I squint at a swollen bulge of limestone, its features erased in the hot glare of the sun bouncing off the boulder fields. Not all dinosaurs reared up on colossal hindlegs, brandishing claws and a jaw like a chainsaw. Eighty million years ago a duck-billed lizard laid her eggs in the lake sediments of Pine Butte Swamp and now the paleontologists peer through the fossilized shells at her unhatched babies within and write lyrically of this precocious "nesting behaviour" of the species. She is called Miasaura, meaning "good mother lizard," and I imagine her lumbering, gravid with the unborn, impatient to find a safe place in the warm mud for the new life.

The travel guides tell us that if you travel U.S. Highway 89, not far from Pine Butte you will see in a narrow channel to the west the remnants — the animal prints, the travois ruts, the stone circles — of the Old North Trail. The trail began in the awesome migration of the peoples south along the eastern slopes of the Rockies, dragging food and supplies on the travois, staying a uniform distance away from the mountains and forests on their right, the retreating ice sheets on their left, walking past the future sites of Calgary and that of Helena, walking, trudging, hauling. We stand on the highway's shoulder, backs turned to the fast-food drive-in and the shunting railroad cars, faces to the mountains, and stare through our sunglasses into that undulating grass, that scraped-over, blizzard-torn, rain-pocked earth, and try to see the ghosts.

Ribstones

Years earlier George Melnyk had been travelling north on Highway 14, near Wainwright, Alberta, when he spotted a highway sign that pointed "This Way to the Ribstones." He knew what they were — hand-carved stones venerated by generations of aboriginals — but not why.

In his book *Radical Regionalism*, he describes how he drove down a gravel road where a marker pointed the way to a rising slope of land. It seemed at first a hill among hills, but when he got to the top "the rest of the earth fell back from here to provide an unobstructed horizon stretching in every direction to the limits of vision." Melnyk understood the aboriginals' point of view: he was standing in the middle of a circle. Later he will write: "On the prairie one twists around and around till the straight horizon line turns into its opposite, a circle, and the visual turns visionary."

Farmers find aboriginal stone hammers in their fields amid the rubble of the medicine wheels whose stones have been flung from their alignment by cattle and ranch vehicles. They covet them as though to forge a link with those who knew the prairies before they did. The Piegans of southern Alberta tell the story of Creation, of how Napiwa, the Old Man, created the world as a floating island from a single grain of sand. I imagine the medicine wheel as a skipper's wheel on a boat, piloting our lonely planet in perfect circular motion as we float serenely through the detritus of the cosmos.

Hierochloe odorata. Sweetgrass. It grew fragrant on the river bottoms, not a perfume but a scent thickened from wind and dew and released under the hooves of the grass-eating mammals. Then, within a fifteen-year period, 1870-1885, ninety-thousand square miles of grassland died. And now the sensitive ecology of the grasses is threatened by massive ploughing and overgrazing. In the spaces between the feedlots and the highways, sweetgrass is being nurtured back by enterprising gardeners and you can buy it in dried and braided handfuls in tourist shops for five dollars.

The reddish base of the strawlike stems is a sign that the Creator chose this plant for sacred purposes, or so says Long Standing Bear Chief in the copy of the *Waterton-Glacier Views* we pick up in a grocery store in the park. "This mark symbolizes the blood of our ancestors and the Spirits of our grandfathers and grandmothers who have gone to the Spirit World." It makes Bear Chief uneasy to witness the commerce in sweetgrass. We do not understand the gift we are handling; as we hold it up to our noses, inhaling its green spice, it blesses us.

Medicine Line

From the Chinook Museum, between Havre and Harlem, sixteen miles north of the Bear's Paw Battlefield (by Clarence "Beartracks" Murray, 1987, his account):

> Joseph and his band, numbering 168 warriors and about
> 600 men, women and children of all ages, headed for
> Canada where they could live in peace and where they

were welcome. Canada was British, and they (England)
had some experience with the U.S. and very little sympa-
thy was given the U.S. government by the British at that
time. So they offered sanctuary to the Indian people ...
Chief Joseph and his people thought they were in Canada
and so at first they offered no resistance to the oncoming
U.S. Army and when White Bird and his warriors made it
to sanctity and peace in Canada they could really shout —
and for good reason — God Save the King!

The battlefield of 1877 lies aslant that kind of prairie terrain that yields
up the subtleties of its structure only after long and slow hours of travel
through it, headed nowhere in particular, have blunted the traveller's
focus. Broad swells of dun-coloured earth, tinged green with prairie
grass, pile up in imperceptible elevation to the low-slung horizon.
Crouched on the skyline are the humps of the foothills of the Bearpaw
Mountains. For shelter, imagine burrowing in the soft furrows of the
coulees, trying to flatten yourself out on this earth stretched open to the
sun. It is a good place to rest, with game and water and grass in the
creekbed, but if you fight a battle there you are going to die.

The siege lasted five days until October 5, the vastly outnumbered
Nez Percés frantically trying to shield themselves from the U.S. Army's
gun and cannon fire aimed down at their camp on the benches of
Snake Creek. With knives, with pots, with their bare hands, they scooped
out shallow trenches under hail of fire and fired back, but they were
running out of ammunition and had lost their horse herd. The warriors
Looking Glass, Lean Elk and Toohoolhoolzote were dead. The wounded
lay unsheltered in a blanket of snow while the babies and the elders
succumbed to the autumn cold, and everyone still alive was hungry.
On the last day, a shell fired from an army howitzer landed on a cave
shelter, killing and burying a young girl and her grandmother. It was
the last straw, and Chief Joseph determined that no more of his people
should die in this bloodied place. He surrendered his rifle to Colonel
Nelson A. Miles of Fort Keogh, and made a speech:

It is cold and we have no blankets. The little children are
freezing to death. My people, some of them, have run
away to the hills and have no blankets, no food. No one
knows where they are — perhaps freezing to death. I want
to have time to look for my children and see how many of
them I can find. Maybe I shall find them among the dead.
Hear me, my chiefs. I am tired. My heart is sick and sad.
From where the sun now stands I will fight no more forever.[1]

Under cover of darkness, the warrior White Bird and a band of some 300 followers fled to Canada. They hoped for (that "sanctity" of) sanctuary and sustenance north of the border, but its legendary medicine had been enfeebled by the tactics of the American army that deflected the migrating buffalo herds south of the line. By the end of 1879 the buffalo had disappeared forever from the Canadian plains, and the Indians were starving. By 1890 they were dancing the Ghost Dance to bring back the buffalo, tatterdemalions trembling in the chinook.

Medicine Line

The town of Sweetgrass is just about as far north as you can go on Interstate 15 and not be in Canada. Butch grew up there on a ranch spread out on the flanks of the Sweetgrass Hills and always thought that "Great Britain" lay just across the border. He could reach "Great Britain" by sneaking up Pioneer Creek across the borderline to Writing-on-Stone and then look back to where he'd just scrambled from, the tawny folds of prairie and the black barrows of the hills. Even then it all looked deceptively wild. Yet the big ranches had been there for a hundred years and then had come the waves of sodbusters and the dream of gold spilling out behind the plough.

Butch left home to study engineering at Montana State in Bozeman. It was the tail end of the inauspicious 1950s. He tells the story of the Black musician who came to Shelby once and could be accommodated only on the reservation at Browning or in Shelby in a private home, "if someone was willin'." His hosts would know to pack him a lunch, for Shelby's lunch counters had not been integrated. Shelby hangs just thirty-five miles south of Sweetgrass and the border with Alberta. It's an important town on the Burlington Northern Railroad that links the Great Lakes with Seattle. On a downtown sidestreet, planted in asphalt, an abandoned gas station flies an inspirational message on a yellow signboard: Shelby Crossroad to America. A brochure from the Chamber of Commerce lists "101 Things to Do and Know About Shelby and the Surrounding Areas," among them an Automatic Teller Machine at the town pump on Highway 2 West. We have also been recommended the eight-ounce filet at the Sports Club restaurant and the house band at the Mint Bar. This is not an awful lot of action, I am thinking. Shelby is redneck country and unashamed of it. You do not come to Shelby with petitions for gun control laws, and if you are in a union, you do not go on strike for longer than two days. You carry a picket, get your picture taken for the newspaper, go home and then go back to work.

When Butch graduated in 1962 with 600 others, only one of them found a job in Montana. Butch didn't feel like sticking around to see what happened next.

Instead he went to "Great Britain," to Alberta, where there is universal health insurance, gun control and two official languages. It doesn't feel like Montana. That's okay with him.

Landscape on Canvas

"For a view of how Montanans like to see themselves, go look at Charlie Russell paintings," Nutter had advised us. Russell painted 4500 canvasses, so they aren't hard to find. After a while, you recognize one from half a mile away: action-packed and panoramic. Rough-and-ready cowboys on fire-breathing steeds handle guns and animals with finesse, Indian warriors with respect and the ladies with gallantry, all the encounters being played out in vast landscapes that shimmer in purple on a far, crenellated horizon.

But he also painted "Waiting For A Chinook," his elegy for the cowboy dream. Under a grey sky saturated with snow, five wolves, prowling almost nonchalantly, circle a dying steer. They are biding their time while their prey, gaunt and dismal, can barely hold his head up. Snow cakes his haunches. He wobbles. There is no resistance in him or defiance. Just endurance, until the bitter end.

Boneyard

Melnyk goes back to the ribstones. He keeps going back because each visit is a little different from the others. He notices different things. Sometimes he notices the historical stuff — the manmade contrivances already rotting and disappearing within the grass, the old barn, the cairn with the plaque, the gravel road washing away a few inches under each thunderstorm. Other times he notices what the Indians have made — half-buried stones carved in ribbed relief whose very smallness creates the meaning of the place: the monumental amplitude of Nature. The works of humans and the works of Nature meet at their boundaries. We walk on the face of the plains and we build according to the shapes we feel at our back: wind, bone and ribstone.

The Map

I'm travelling south. I'm still in my own country but the dreamtime of others' ancestors is pulling me down the map past the buffalo boneyards and the chinook winds blowing the snow off the tufted grass. Eventually I will cross the medicine line.

[1] According to the literature distributed by the Nez Perce National Historic Park, the speech is no more than apocryphal: "Legends are easy to create but hard to prove." True, but the words still make my hair stand on end.

Sources

Wolf Willow, Wallace Stegner (many editions)
Home Place, Stan Rowe (NeWest Press, 1990)
Homage, Henry Kelsey, Jon Whyte (Turnstone, 1981)
"On Being an Albertan," George Melnyk, *NeWest Review,* February/March 1990
"Ribstones," *Radical Regionalism*, George Melnyk (NeWest Press, 1981)
The Portable North American Indian Reader, ed. Frederick W. Turner III (Penguin, 1978)

WEATHER SIGNS

BARBARA SCHOTT

The Farmhouse Poems

Bees drinking from the wet cloth of the laundry I've hung out to dry.
Farther out, the black fields steaming in the early morning. I can
    remember
carp in those fields, in the drowned barley, the year it rained too much
and the ditches couldn't hold the runoff.

Water was a way to think, growing up, the sparse baths
in the rust-stained tub. Tadpoles fluttering in a Gemstone Mason jar
on the kitchen window sill. Treading water by the hour
in the weed-choked slough we called a lake.

This is not about lack. This is not
about need. Or how you move around the
cage of my body in a dark room giving off the heat
soaked into you all day, the parenthetical
enclosure of your arms, a thumb
endlessly circling the areola's rim, like a moon, a star
the sun creeping closer
every year
it gets hotter and dryer, the parched truths
wrung out of me when the body's logic
is the only logic

What metaphor would I use for myself?
The straight spine of a poplar sapling. Like now
right now, when my leaflessness
startles you.

                          I know this land like the curves
                     of my belly I hold it in my hands I hold it
                          in my head I know the lay of this land
                          I know its winds and its ways I know
                          this land and speak its language

the air is bone dry
the soil is bone dry
my skin is bone dry
the gravel road to town is bone dry
the slough is bone dry
my mouth is bone dry
the carcass of a horsefly
the siding on the barn is bone dry
the grass is bone dry
my bones hold together
like a birds nest

Having made
a hinterland
my body a bone
house
he retreats
through alkali
sloughs, the mineral
richness I breathe
the whiteness, the barley
dust, salt
rim of his
mouth having made
a hinterland
nothing keeps him
home or any place
like it
the field of stones
the plowshare, the
mineral richness
I have known
his droughts
like my own, the sweat
that evaporates
before it stains
I give him
the always thirsty
heart, how now
brown cow
?

Blue Snow

1.

I measure my life in snow
blue in the long low light

reading for what it contains
the hooded rocks, the yellow stain

a creek seeping through, stems of
flag grass tell you how deep the drifts

until you winter in a place
you haven't lived there

2.

wolves watching from the background, waiting
with their eyes, following the senses

confusion, a nape, the long wail
that begins where you breathe

ending in perilous harmony
then the rest of your life takes place

in systolic bursts, endless shades
of white, there are iceflowers

nesting between windowpanes, entire gardens
rupturing, growing by memory

from tropical beginnings
lichen, fern, a vineyard, they say

if you drag a scarf behind you
the wolves will leave you alone

3.

there is snow on the ice on the river
and nothing more naked than these trees

or mammals drinking snow
so little light to inhabit

rooms painted white for the illusion
of space, a room to winter in

ash on the houseplants
woodsmoke curling through the room

settling somewhere near the ceiling
and the sun never comes

4.

          highways scarring
          the land, snow licking
          across the road
          in flames
          the long drive
          across your
          body and the scar
          that invents you
          dividing
          you like a river
          that too must be
          crossed and remembered

          now
          is the time
          for the hand to
          mouth existence
          of a wolf
          blue snow under
          fingernails, the long wail
          that begins in

the mind and
ends in demise
spring
is a fiction

5.

the day was a colour you compare to other days
grey bird sipping red berries

a circle of yardlights, the stout light
making the dark less possible

washing jackpine from your clothes
the bitterness of an open door

then an armload of wood, if this is need
if we survive, too long, too blue

this winter, the cold makes you hungry
it makes you lean and spare

as you enter with flesh-warmed
bones and what you remember of the sun

JOHN PASS

Invocation to the Character of Water

As today, past fate or motive
                              it falls

first light in the air
then accumulating weight, authority

I implore
             for thinking, and the writing hand

snow's impartial emphasis, expansive restraint.
What to do short of shovelling?

Though friends brave the driveway for my party
and arrive!
                 And the laden firs, masters
of what, in one place, is attainable, strain
in their resins and sinews, their elastic greenery

to reply: a limb sporadically unsprung, waving ...

Just so come spring my clumsy paddle stirs, missing the J
stroke. Somehow afloat, dissolute as a Long Sloe Screw
in the sauna (ice-dregs over the coals)
I seek admission at the membrane, agency
in every cell. Let the roofs shed

what they must in my hearing and the molds
be under my nose. Let me through

with the native women in the first canoe
into the Stikine's hole into the glacier.

And let me carry what comes to me
with equanimity, easily

with as smooth a countenance the coffins
sucked by the North Sea from cliff-face graves near Cromer
from *The Garden Of Heavenly Sleep*

as the up-river biffys floods in the fifties delivered
to Winnipeg on the Assiniboine.

Permit me the ancient, relentless return
of what has been taken deep and hidden.

I won't deny it. Nor the brackish bouquet
habitually acquired, particular
to where one wallows. A sip

or two of essentials is sufficient.
Certainly cataracts, be they directly

grief or pleasure. And the jocular creek
to knock the fisherman off his feet.

That swimming moonlight the night she showed me
our bodies' phosphoresence where we woke the water.

For my signature, your many inks.

I want to work and shape my way, but partially
I ascend and adhere to particles. Forgive me.
The disembodied babbling.

The bank collapsing and the silted flume.
The emissions stain on the marble lip.
The clear-cut bruise on the Naiad's hip.
The harbour's sheen that is not just pretty.

And the bathtub ring.
And the angle askew to the eye to things

plunged into you. That seem not to stand
on certainty. That waver.

Kleanza Creek

How will we get up Kleanza Creek
who deserve it least, road-dozy, teeth afloat
on litres of coffee? We gotta stop somewhere

and this is it, exquisite twist
of water from the miniature gorge, a sheen
of pool behind the boulder, a riffle across

this pristine gravel
back-filled and levelled for picnic tables, grass —
the facilities operator even now sweeping
the parking area.

Its beauty is a pang, a duty
we get free. *Fish me*, it burbles.
Take the trail. But ours is a serious

recreation, the camping with kids denouement:
motel-hopping home. Re-load the camera
and back of that, let poetry do it.

Poetry goes where no-one follows anyway...

me and that utterly mythical beast, the reader
dreaming a way up Kleanza Creek
for our arcane two-step ...

last-ditch landscape sleazes wheedling
Show us, you'll be famous, really.
Open the cliff's cleft, the spigot

in the bedrock. Let's taste the salt-
lick in the alpine meadow

from the highway, the *open road*
before that delusion swung off at every exit
shopping

the next (some chalk-blue pot-hole

of the disappearing pickup, the cast-off
gear, some well-bucket for the soul)

scoops me weeks later on a lake on *lack of ...*
a cutthroat sudden on my line, a catch, a whine

in my voice at, *what grinds me
down is the lack of ...*

get the trout in the boat and come
back to it: gracious, humbling

in-your-face reflection ... *attention.*

CHARLENE DIEHL-JONES

lamentations: prairie winter

reluctantly to settle
into the unfamiliar bones of a melody
distant drifts of snow
blue in the afternoon sun

the frozen prairie knows by heart
the ancient rhythms
bitter ache sudden plenitude

the perpetual weight of her skylover
bellying down

no one speaks the grace
of winter
sculpted shadows & tawny grass
barbed wire puncturing holes in the wind

you can't anticipate the long brilliance
of space
empty highway chaperoned by telephone poles
fence posts etching fields
onto a white ground
fleeting ranks of stubble measure
what defies the eye

a snowy owl cants off into the air
its wake a blinding trail
of grief
silver against the sky

at night constellations
scatter across the flat lands
the distance of a coyote

barking in frozen air
semaphore to tell
a searching soul
how far is far
vertigo & the trick of glory
stolen from the milky way

pain requests its interval
ventriloquy for the reluctant
voice   one false note
& the world folds up

the sun is noncommittal
familiar voices waver somewhere
out of breath
sudden as ice on your cheek

winter's surgeries sever
extremities from shivering flesh
you perch on your one remaining leg
numbed & wishful

up off the flats
& into the sudden bush
i can only summon ghostly bluebirds
knitting sapphire into the grey scarf of hazel
vees of geese hauling autumn southward
carcasses of young herons
early flyers unprepared for the taste
of earth
up through memory
to arrive here
astonishing forests of lace
brides & angels
what is precious what is lost

i bring the body's terrible lack
watch fenceposts march off the edge
of the earth

drab winter birds
skitter by accident to a new patch of scrub
pin branches in place

the land absorbs grief
holds it in trust
the missing child already here

late afternoon sky a sudden orange
oath of fire
& bare tree bones
leaping

in january's sharp sorrow
my night prayers are freighted
with sweet bedstraw & portents
loons
on the late lake
laughing

GREGORY SCOFIELD

Excerpt from "Twelve Moons and The Dream"

Niski-pîsim (March ➢ The Goose Moon)

> *Reconcile yourself to wait in this darkness as long as*
> *necessary, but still go on longing after him whom you love.*
> *For if you are to feel him or see him in this life, it must*
> *always be in this cloud, in this darkness.*
> — Anonymous fourteenth-century mystic from
> *The Cloud of Unknowing*

They had come to nest
in the wet marsh, trumpeting
long into the night
their reunion.
You had come silently
like the day's dew, each footstep
a tiny pool
breaking on a leaf's surface.
For this, I loved you.
Loved you, and the geese
in all their unceasing chatter.

All winter
we clung like marmots
burrowing deep in the bed,
kicking snow in moon's face.
I loved you even more.
Loved you
and the whole frozen earth
in her slumber.

Now it's another spring.
She wakes
and all her dreams, readily bound
are sung and cast.
It can only be
she lost her mind, her heart

during the blizzard.
Why else would she pull you
from my sleeping arms?

But sometimes, when I hear them,
I rise from our bed,
slip between the tall grasses
to the muskeg's edge.
Like us, they are throat-singers
pitching
higher and higher, breathing
all their wild heat,
vibrating
the night, the stars
to such frenzy

and still

I go on loving you. Loving you
while the moon,
laughing her reprisal
sinks me deeper, deeper.

Pâskwêhowi-pîsim (June ☞ The Hatching Moon)

Nothing is as it should be.
Moon at my table
is a black wick smoking.
She chokes me on swamp frogs
snickering
to the first sun.
The ducks mind their eggs,
their eyes loose,
loose as snare wire.

Me, I've kissed
the flicker of lizard's tongue.
Now
I want to pluck out his eyes,
pluck out my own

and cast them, all in wailing grief
to the laughing wind.

Nothing is as it should be.
The lake in me is a dry bed
cracking to the bone.
I ache, ache
all that is new
and green and sacred,
all that is reflective of you.

I ache in my smallest bones
but still you won't come
to defend this love.

maci-manitow, I curse you
the moon and lizard.
don't you hear me splitting
bones like wood?
don't you hear the lullaby
so sweetly red, it bleeds
from the pale stone
cutting my lips?

Nothing is as it should be.
There is only this waiting
and so many songs.

maci-manitow: The devil

Paskowi-pîsim (July ⌒ The Moulting Moon)

The days go on jaggedly
beneath the skin,
my sinew-slack drum
more silent than the nights
or moon's echo
pulsing her crippled silver.

Everything comes to stillness
at this hour.

How many dreams, now
without you?
The stars hang on the sky
waiting coyote's lulling song.
Me, I have skin and veins
to offer anyone, hungry.
I have at least these,
torn and diluted as they are.

Everything comes to silence
at this hour.

On whose pillow do you lay
your vagrant head?
Whose hands
pulled you from my dreams?

Tonight
I sleep under a duck's shadow
whose naked wings
sew my mouth like a seam.

Everything comes to death:

the room, my heart.
I plot the migration south,
declaring my last breath
to the hopeful moon.

Ohpahôwi-pîsim (August ⌒ The Flying-up Moon)

Most unexpected,

you roll into me like a stone
sinking deep in the earth,
settling deeper
than all the moons

having crawled across the sky,
crouched low and silent,
soft-boned and remorseful
as the skinny willows
rattling in the wind.

Now
I cannot name your absence
or its taste,
a strange language
neither bitter or sweet.

Only you've returned,
a heavy winged bird
and the bed is a pulse
with the weight of desire,
songs that swim beneath our skin,
lay drunk like fish
in stifling pools.

Though my longing is no secret
you hold it close,
press into me, helpless
against your shame.

Finally you've come!
piko kîkway miyonâkwan.

You sing the summer's end
between my thighs, kiss
the swollen moon
in the curve of my belly,

me, flying-up
like the ducks in the marsh,
you, new-feathered
and weightless,

ushering the dancers to my lips.

piko kîkway miyonâkwan: Everything is beautiful

NAMES

SHARON BUTALA

Grass

"All flesh is grass," the Bible says, meaning that our flesh is as finite as grass; it might also be taken to mean that those of us who eat meat are eating animals raised on grass, which ultimately makes us dependent on grass. Knowing this — that on our death our flesh decays to soil and becomes grass — and living more than twenty years on the southwestern Saskatchewan grasslands, it is hard to remember that I was once like the young city woman who said to me that as a girl she'd thought the prairie was wheat, "That's all, just crops. I never thought of it as being anything else before it was crops." And I never thought that the uniform green carpet I was looking at out there could actually be broken down into around 200 kinds of grasses, forbs and sedges, each with its own characteristics, life span, habits and types, and that one day I would know something about many of them. I too, as ignorant as any child of the northern bush country and then the cement and asphalt terrain of cities, never understood the prairie world for what it really is: a kingdom of grass.

When I first came here, I was surprised by the way the mere sight of the miles and miles of yellow grass changed the way I felt. Others have said the same to me, that a gently undulating field of grass is soothing in a way no other landscape, beautiful as it may be, is. When you approach it, then walk out onto it, your heart steadies in its restless tripping, the muscles that you were not even aware were clenched relax and stop their gentle, relentless aching. You stand and stare out across it and in those long, subtle miles your worries retreat and grow distant too, diminishing toward the horizon. It is said that it was the appearance of savannah grassland that made it possible for our ape ancestors to begin the transformation into the human race. Surely that is the reason grassland holds the key to that closed door in our hearts, because it is home to our species, and the heart knows when it is home.

In North America the icon of the grassland is the cowboy riding meditatively across wide expanses of nothing but grass, through herds of grazing cattle, past antelope and deer, the occasional coyote lurking on the brow of a nearby hill or loping past nonchalantly or sitting on a grassy hilltop yodelling to the sky.

And cowboys — ranchers — know their grasses. It's their job, the way a doctor knows the human body: they know the indigenous from the introduced species; they know their names, sometimes several of them: red fescue, blue grama or buffalo grass, green needle grass, needle-and-thread grass, speargrass, June grass, western wheatgrass, northern wheatgrass, blue-joint, little bluestem ... They know when they mature and how nutritious they are, that is, their percentage of protein in the spring, the summer, the fall, and over winter as hay (example: June grass: twenty percent in spring, dropping to four percent in fall), whether cows like to eat them or not, whether they're harsh on the mouth and gullet and stomach or not. In fact, to a rancher or a cowboy, a cover of good grass is more beautiful than a bed of the most exquisite, exotic roses, and the grasses they love most are those indigenous to their particular prairie. Such plants, in their eyes, are the ones with a rare and shining beauty.

You can't make your home on the prairie without coming to an understanding of and with grass. When the Nature Conservancy of Canada, at our instigation, turned the Butala ranch into the Old Man On His Back Prairie and Heritage Conserve, we wound up in an unexpected controversy with grass botanists and ecologists about names. In no time at all the grass scientists were lined up toe to toe and nose to nose with us — the ubiquitous but non-specific "folk," revealed now as a synonym for idiot — over terminology: the correct use of the commonly used terms "shortgrass," "buffalo grass," and "prairie wool."

No, our grass, which we'd always called shortgrass, is not shortgrass, they said. The most extreme of them declared there is no shortgrass in Canada. Shortgrass is prairie dominated by buffalo grass and blue grama. And no, that pretty little grass you call buffalo grass isn't buffalo grass at all; there is no buffalo grass in Canada, or maybe there is but it grows only at such-and-such a place, certainly not on the Old Man On His Back Conserve. (Not that I've ever been there.) And while we're at it, prairie wool is simply a specific fescue; it has no other definition.

I freely admit I've practically zero scientific education, but that doesn't necessarily mean I'm stupider. I reasoned that shortgrass, buffalo grass, prairie wool are not scientific terms to start with; they're folk terms. That is, they were coined by the "folk," who therefore are the ones who know best what they mean.

Take shortgrass, for instance: the grass mix on the Conserve, no matter how much moisture it gets, never gets much taller than a foot high. And it almost never gets more than about twelve inches of precipitation per year, which classifies the area as semi-arid — not quite desert. Characteristically, it's an attractive, fairly dense, curly grass only a few inches above the ground, and that is why the people called this range "shortgrass." It was the scientists who confused the issue by appropriating the term and imposing their own system, that is their own view of the world, onto it, declaring this shortgrass range to be, in fact, mixed grass because of the composition of range grasses and the intensity of certain grasses, thus giving themselves yet one more reason to look down their noses at the folk who persist in calling it shortgrass because it's shorter than other grasses in regions with more rainfall and better soils.

And as for buffalo grass: a more amiable botanist explained to me that what we folk call "buffalo grass" has a scientific name, *Bouteloua gracilis*, which is really something like a third cousin to what scientists have declared is the "true" buffalo grass — *Buchloë dactyloides* — that grows in Montana, Colorado and Wyoming. But, I sputtered, to the naked eye the only difference is that our grass has fewer shoots and it's maybe a bit shorter, and that surely that could be attributed to the comparative lack of moisture here; further, many of the first settlers here right next to the Montana border were Americans, and they were the ones who called our grass that. According to the *Oxford English Dictionary*, the ultimate authority on the English language, "buffalo grass" was first used in the American magazine *Harper's* in 1883 and is therefore a folk term and not a scientific term, I said. You can stick to the scientific term, but don't try to tell one of the folk what is buffalo grass and what is not.

I tried the term "prairie wool" out on another of these annoying scientists. As I expected, it turned out that we folk don't know what that means either: it's such and such a fescue, the man said, and it's called that because its leaves curl. Yeah, right, I said to myself, but instead of getting mad, I got myself to the library, where — I already knew the term wasn't in the O.E.D. — after much searching through Canadian, American, and then more specialized dictionaries, I discovered it at last in a collection of the terminology of Western Canada. This lexicon was compiled by a former journalist who placed ads in all the newspapers and magazines in Western Canada asking for prairie-specific terminology along with their definitions. He accepted the most commonly used terms and the definitions of them which were agreed upon by the most correspondents.

Now my husband Peter's father was one of that first batch of settlers out here on the plains early in the second decade of this century, and the definition the journalist published was the one Peter had learned as a boy over fifty years ago from his father, who said that "prairie wool" was called that because when the first settlers set down their mowers to cut the grass, certain stands of grass would roll up behind the mower just like freshly sheared wool. Peter says it was a mixture of grasses that did that, but fescues dominated. In all such matters, I take Peter, whose entire life has been spent here on the prairie of Saskatchewan only a few miles from the Montana border, as my authority.

I envy him all he knows that can be learned no other way, although much of his experience I wouldn't care to have first-hand: nearly freezing to death in a blizzard that came on when he was out checking cattle on horseback; riding fifty and more miles a day, day after day, during the time when there were open herd laws here and no fences; or riding four miles every single winter morning, forty below or not, down to the south dam where he kept an axe against a rock to chop a waterhole for the cattle. And yet, even as I write about these shivery, thigh-aching things, a tiny part of me wishes to have been there. Maybe that's why I put them in books; writing them is a way to experience them.

While we're looking at the bad side of life on the grasslands, it is also true that neither can you ride or walk in silence across native prairie without having your calm troubled by all that has gone, for its history is written everywhere on the land: the buffalo horns that can still be found (nearly all the bones and skulls were long ago carted away); the stone circles embedded in the soil, deeper as the years pass, slowly growing thick coats of colourful lichen; the stone flakes from tool-making; and the tools themselves. The bison, a species that was once synonymous with prairie, all gone; a people who for generations made it their home, gone too. It's instructive; it makes you keep in mind how expendable you are too, in the face of rampant wheat-growing, the urban back-to-the-land movement spawning acreages, many of them badly ill-used out of sheer ignorance (check the acreages in the Black Hills around Rapid City, South Dakota; there's a few around Calgary too), and environmental initiatives that would keep the grass but get rid of people. It makes you treasure your grass, and the right to ride or walk through it, even more.

A friend once showed me a picture of his farm in Malawi: three men leaning on their hoes laughing, at their feet the richest, blackest earth I've ever seen, behind them a dense, many-shaded green wall of jungle, and above their heads, hanging unnoticed as if only to be expected, a thick cluster of yellow bananas. It was, in its vivid richness and super-abundance, the perfect contrast to my own grassland home where all is paleness all year round: pale blues and greens in the spring and early summer, pale yellows, creams and duns midsummer to late fall and, if we're lucky and have snow, glistening white with blue shadows, and, if we're not, charcoals, browns and dull greys all the long winter.

Yet I found I didn't envy my Malawi friend. I'm used to the sparseness, the aridity, of my own Great Plains landscape: I wouldn't know what to do or how to live in such abundance. I couldn't even get a mental grip on it; I stared at the picture till, smiling and saying in halting English to me, "I will carry it away," he took it gently from my fingers.

Maybe that farm in Malawi is the Garden of Eden, or else it's a hint of heaven itself. Or maybe when we die, each of us will find the heaven we dream of: my African friend would find his picture, but without poverty, tropical diseases and poisonous snakes. And Peter and I would find our grassy plains to be the gateway to a different Eden. It is here, riding the range in the sun and the wind, small birds lifting out of the grass near your horse's feet to fly singing in ecstatic spurts upward and down again, heat waves distorting the horizon, that you see the way into the next world.

Its gate hovers before you, if you could only ride that far to reach it before sunset and urge your horse gently through. Or maybe as you neared your destination you'd get off and walk, holding his reins, leading him. The last step and he'd rear back, pulling the reins as they fall from your loosened fingers; you'd step through, the wind breathing softly in your ears. But your horse would choose to stay behind to graze forever in the wide fields of yellow grass.

PAMELA BANTING

Declining Orchids

Together they hike Cavell Meadows, the South Boundary Trail,
Indian Ridge and Wilcox Pass, keeping an eye out
for endangered orchids. When in an alpine meadow
he spots a group of northwest twayblades or blunt-leaved
bog orchids their Latin names spring to his lips:
listera caurina, habenaria obtusata [platanthera obtusata]

Because her presence allows him to speak
these words
he kisses her. The orchids are too tiny
and fragile for kissing, and besides
in the national parks they are protected.
He whispers the I love you.

Her ears scramble Latin and English
with the whistles of alarmed
marmots. He has long black hair
and a hero's mustache. Eyes brown,
narrowed with a certain shyness
and vulnerability. Cheekbones laid on
with a sculptor's trowel. And his thigh is cut
just so. He holds her and strokes her skin
all the livelong night until
even the birds can't take it anymore
and burst singing.

Horsing around in the Rockies.
One dazzling damned thing after another.
This love affair with sliding, with shale.
Harrowing and lucid beauty. A new ontology
opens onto the wide blue yonder.
A real-life sequel maybe.

Highway 22 North

Sunshine over my left shoulder, right hand
relaxed on the wheel, elbow out the window
cultivating a farmer's tan.

In the blue distance, a yellow
schoolbus burps three
ranchkids at their gate.
Screak of door lever
grind of first,
               second.

New green greening up.

Ditch grasses hula
with the breezes down there.
                         Dandelions galore!
Yellow lei
swinging with that swaying
                   grass
                       skirt.

Magpie perched on a black cow's back.
Black-white,
     black-blue, blue-
                   blue,
     black-black.

Clouds in a pile-up over Water Valley
rolling in like an Old Testament
prophecy, by golly, or Dolly Parton's
hairdo. One or the other.

Hawks atop fenceposts, giving every little stirring
their rapt attention. More hawks
preying from on high.
Wing   span.

Honey-dipped palomino grazes
pastureland. Cows also bend

and kiss the earth
chomp chomp chomp.

Trucks with horse trailers like silver
bullets wait to pull out
from every third sideroad.
Horses on the move,
caution to the wind.

Horses in the fields are looking good.
Barenaked athletes, muscles
mantled by the sun.

Highway 22 northbound.

Motoring.

Novice

You'd like to be the novice of a deer.
You'd do whatever it told you.
— Tim Lilburn, *Moosewood Sandhills*

I wouldn't want to be the novice
of a deer, do everything it told me.
I'd rather be another deer,
that one's mate. Surrender
my humanity, I think.
Rub off this thin
skin against bark
and grow a winter hide.

To be a deer, doe-
eyed, vulnerable
but strong in the haunches. Always on the lookout
over your shoulder to the predators,
who are many. Or so it seems
standing out in the open
watching your breath
poof the bright air.

Being a deer would mean nursing
my fawn. Would mean being
always nervous and mindful of danger,
twenty-four hours a day. But maybe for animals
alertness is not the same as fear,
as it is for humans. And twenty-four hours
might mean
something else.

If I were a deer, the wolves
might get the fawn, or me. But at least
I would have had it, and without being strapped down
on a delivery table, feet in the stirrups
with some man in a bloody white coat yelling at me
to be a good girl now, stop that, stop that
carrying on, do you want to scare the other
mothers? I'd have had it
in the bush, alone. Bite the cord,
swallow the traces, lick
lick the creature clean.
Let my milk down
and savour the tug, suck
and nuzzle. Graze
with the little one
poking its nose at twigs and new greens.

If I were to lie down
in the deer's bed.
If I were that one's mate.

ELIZABETH PHILIPS

Becoming Earth

Last year's garden and this year's garden meet this April day in the new poppy growing up out of rotting snow at the foot of dried stalks of Danebrog Lace. Even though the temperature is only plus four, I sit in a lawn chair wearing a parka, savouring the mild sun, its warmth almost tropical after the coldest winter in twenty-five years. Half-submerged memories of last summer's garden hover amidst the bones of yarrow and delphinium, flickering holograms of day lilies and marigolds, true lilies and sweet peas. I see four-foot-tall trumpet lilies nodding by the terrace, their huge yellow heads heavy with perfume. I see the fishpond plaited in water lily leaves, goldfish bunting the water's surface with greedy mouths. In reality, the garden is a soggy ruin. From the only dry corner I survey the gritty splendour of a prairie spring: the lawn brown and clotted with leaves, water, muddy footprints, dust and mold; the garden steeped in a mulch of fall leaves. I focus on the protected corner where a clutch of daffodil leaves are just greening up, all but the tips of the leaves still under mulch. In my eyes this is what counts, this flare of living green almost as pleasurable as the first King Alfred daffodil, or my favourite apricot tulips, or by midsummer the entire garden, a complex profusion inventing its own spectrum.

I've been in thrall to my garden for the last six years. Before that I had a passion for orchids, and then more recently a fascination with goldfish. I am only now beginning to step back a bit, to see what it is I have been doing while entangled with the fish and flowers in my care. I don't know, at this point, whether I have been captivated by them or they by me, but I suspect the energy between us flows more than one way. I do know that my obsessions become fodder for my writing (the word "fodder" brings to mind horses, the rinsed sweetness of hay, and I like that); that is, they become poems —

> Veiled in long fins, exaggerated, rare,
> the gold fish have been bred for splendour, spun from
> centuries of fish dreams, the human mind casting itself back
> into the sea …

My work as a writer is infused with images and ideas that have grown out of preoccupations so intense they have often left me entranced, beguiled. This spring I've begun to think of these various engagements as all one thing, a continuum of enchantment. My writing, I think, occupies a parallel plane, hovering above the ground, as my mind does during a season of thinking-while-weeding. Despite some nervousness about peering too intently at what has been a very pleasurable time in the garden, I want to play on the more interesting connections between my obsession with helping things grow and my fitful attempts to marry the earth with words.

Essentially, I wanted to rediscover my dependence on soil and sun. As a city dweller I turned to my back yard, where I could indulge my desire to look closely at plants and the patterns they form together in the garden. The urge to see has even permeated my dreams. In a prolonged, almost orgasmic dream I saw a succession of changing colours, and it was the act of looking itself that made the colours lift and bloom. I've also had recurring dreams of rescuing fish as the water drained rapidly out of the fishpond. (Passion and responsibility are entwined in the garden and in my imagination, two vines grown together.) I've tried to gain entry to the garden during moments of rest, simply by staring: into the eye of a fish swimming in a shaft of sun, into the glowing throat of a lily, through the trunk and up the veins of sap rising in the linden. I have wanted, above all else, to live a more layered existence, to heighten my awareness of the many ways to be in a garden.

> Say after me, *thou*
> *tree of life, tree of wisdom,*
> *tree of knowledge, tree of mercy.*

I fell head over heels for gardening, and like a sudden convert could see no other way but total immersion. An insatiable curiosity had me, in my first year-and-a-half as a gardener, taking *Perennials for the Prairies* to bed with me. I'd wake up in the morning and reread the entry where memory left off and dreams began. And I was in the garden as much as possible (I bought a laptop so I could write *en plein air*). My hands were never really clean that first summer, the fine grains of soil under my nails formed dark moons, talismans of rapture. As the great English gardener Russell Page says, a gardener learns "the ways and nature of plants and stone, of water and soil at least as much through the hands as through the head." I had instinctively chosen an honourable if well-worn path deeper into the garden.

Unfortunately, a Saskatchewan gardener can have her hands in the earth only five months of the year, or less if winter comes early or stays late. Her curiosity must often make do with books, or with photographs of the past season. Gardening where summer is short and explosive, shoots springing up at a frantic rate, I've been like someone with a mild fever, slightly crazed, driven to enjoy every moment of fine weather, and all the while struggling to learn to think like a garden.

> She bows her head again, and feels along her nape
> a cold spark, the first sepal of rain.

Digression 1. (Lines from various poems; earth references.)

Follow the body down, go slowly
and with deference to your place, some wild field,
and lie down
easy in your last bed of earth …

             … I have walked
without supplication, without paying fealty to the ground,
the still gorgeous earth …

… savour the elemental
taste, salt-

sweet of summer's blood
for this is the earth
made flesh …

… grass is the sun come down
to root in the earth …

            … You want to believe
that in the nature of the earth lies the light.

While I was mesmerized by fish, I spent free evenings reading about fish culture and staring into the aquarium. Eventually, I realized — while talking with a fellow poet, himself obsessed with deer — that I was trying to become a fish. One day I thought myself so deep into the water that when I came away from the tank and looked out into the winter street, I saw a giant plecostomus (a bottom feeder with a large sucking mouth for scouring algae off rocks) attached to the neighbour's elm. I began to think of water as air, as a medium I could breathe. Staring through the glass, in love with those red and gold and blue creatures and their balletic movements, I lost the difference, the distinction between water and air. Having been one with water, I now sought to become earth; I delved into the soil and its workings.

In the headlong freefall of obsession, I began to see myself, my actions, from a point of view a few inches below my own feet. As Shepherd Ogden, author of *Step by Step Organic Gardening*, has said, there are more living micro-organisms in two handfuls of soil than there are humans on this planet. Modern agriculture ignores most of those organisms, concentrating on three star nutrients (nitrogen, phosphorus, potassium), as if the earth were made for TV and the screen wasn't big (or deep) enough for a more complex picture. The organic gardener's task is to cultivate the depth and breadth necessary to understand the larger view — to know the soil as an ecosystem. She must imagine herself into those two handfuls of black tilth, to understand how microbes eat, breathe, excrete, interact with one another, plants, minerals, compost and other organic matter. As I turned the compost pile each week throughout that first summer, I saw how nature (with the exception of human nature) has no concept of waste. The life of the soil is rendered sweet out of decay. Everything that dies feeds the green world. (New theories in microbiology suggest that we ourselves are colonies of interacting, co-operative communities of microbes and enzymes, that we are the sky through which other worlds revolve.)

When I look into the earth and imagine the many blind but not insensate beings boiling with their singular desires beneath my feet, I know they are moving in a cycle through birth, death, decay, and that out of that decay will arise more life. When earthworms are killed or driven away by chemicals, the earth lets in less light, less air, and it is not itself. If the earthworm that struggles for life, moving like a blunt thumb through the soil, is part of the same cycle that confounds me, then I want it there. I want to turn over the earth while planting and see in my spadeful of humus a coil of worms dazzled by the sudden light. They are eating their way to heaven. As I am.

Digression 2. Garden Journal excerpts.

The keeping of a garden journal involves writing a few plain sentences each day. It can be a useful jog to the memory, a record of the success and failure of various plants and plantings, a log of ideas. Most importantly, it is a tribute to the dailiness of a life spent paying attention (even if it is sometimes scant attention) to the natural world — to the movement of weather systems, the garden's progress season to season, with the occasional more personal note woven in. The journal places significant events in the context of rain, snow, sun; the striking effect of a new planting of tulips shares equal space with more worldly successes. The death of the seasons and the death of a friend lie side by side, flat on the page. Yet these events will return, vivid and complex once more, when I come across them years later as I describe, on the same date, a fall storm or late lily.

> January 1, 1995. Cloudy. High -17 Low -22. Brought hyacinths out of cold room today. Not quite 3 inches tall, more like 2 1/2. Close enough. Begonia finished blooming — have to cut it back.

Writing in my garden journal has become an intimacy that stitches together other intimacies. Maintaining a spare account of when the crocuses bloom, of what small tasks were performed early in May, is a habit as domestic as turning the compost. Both gardening and keeping a journal slow the pace of modern life for a moment; they are both primal acts, the need to sow by hand, and the need to stop and make a memorial of that sowing.

Digression 3. Hands (Various lines from poems; hand references.)

> … how I love your hands, tucked into your jacket pockets cold from the journey across the beach …

> … Read the lines on my palms
> drawn by the feet of sparrows …

> … She shakes the fine black seed into her palm, sleeping cells of an articulate dust …

> … colour and form
> give meaning to her hand …

> … You watch the trees bud, and the buds unfold
> into leaves the size of your hands …

Last night I told you how, when I was a child of eight, I lay in bed holding my hands up to the light coming in the doorway. I tried to make my hands look strong, fingers hooked like fleshy claws. I was pleased with them then, their straight masculine lines, was even more enamoured with their shadows on the wall, enlarged beyond reason by the light. But in the day my hands grew small again, pale and weak and girlish. Only now, over twenty-five years later, have my hands come into their own. Though still small, they've grown wiry pulling weeds, throwing a spade into soil, hefting field rocks for a flagstone path. They have wind and sun on them, are scored with fine lines like the underside of bark.

I tell you this, you squeeze my hand, and we turn away from one another, to sleep.

> And my hand, so much smaller than your hand,
> moves toward the shadow of
>
> your belly ...

The focal point of my garden is water, a six-foot-square formal fishpond. Visitors are drawn to it, to the water turning in the heart of a prairie garden. Even the neighbourhood cats come, one by one, to stare at the fish and sit decoratively there, too satisfied with their lot to attempt fishing. It took one long afternoon to dig the pool, down two feet through topsoil and into clay. It was a warm May day. I left shelves along the edge of the excavation so some of the plants could be closer to the water's surface. When the hole was well roughed out, I sat down on the earth shelf and leaned back against what would be the north wall of the pond, sun on my sweating face. It was a good place to be, below ground. The slightly bitter smell of soil, my hands dry and caked with earth.

This will be the pond's seventh summer. The water irises that winter over in the pond are beginning to show green. I have ordered a tropical water lily, some oxygenating plants to help keep the water clear. Soon I'll clean the pond of the winter accumulation of leaves and muck. I'll bring out the goldfish, enjoying the moment of release, when the fish tip out of the bucket into the larger world of the pond. I'll put out the water lilies, beginning to grow again after their time in the cold room. These acts have become almost ritual, my labour flowing into water and earth.

Humans and other animals seem to have a craving for the sight and sound of water, for being out-of-doors, nothing between us and the sun. Sitting on the edge of the pond in summer, goldfish rising to the surface under my shadow, listening to the music of water over stones, it is possible to lose all thought, to become like the face of the water, empty of everything but sky.

Digression 4. (Various lines from poems. Water references.)

The fish become water,
water become fish.
I am also water, though this is less
than obvious …

… Water is the last stone, the only one
she cannot hold …

       … food
scattered like an offering onto the water …

… the lake and the mild light lie together, softness
on softness …

… the fish swim toward us
out of our own blood.

In his essay "The Eyes of Claude Monet," John Berger concludes this about Monet's water lilies, a series of large paintings done towards the end of the painter's life: "The painted lily pond was to be a pond that remembered all." Berger thinks the paintings were not only about Monet's garden at Giverny, a garden still famous for its beautiful colour combinations and composition, but about the memory of that garden. Russell Page has said that gardens are about moments in time. Both writers draw the connection between time and nature — nature as it is when harboured in the gardener's care, and time as it collects and refracts in the garden. A garden can act as a kind of private looking glass, through which the gardener has a very personal view of the seasons unfolding, of his or her own life passing. I have discovered that my garden is more than merely background, as the earth is more than a stage. Working this narrow piece of ground has given me sustenance when I needed it, sustenance for mind and body. My garden is small, but it is large enough, I think, to encompass all I hope to understand about myself as only one of the many animals living out a given span.

Gardens do build towards certain moments, but the moment when a garden is at its peak contains all the preceding days, when the roses had not yet opened or the gaps between perennials had not yet been filled by fast-growing annuals. A garden is about time past and time future, containing as it does the reminder of past and promise of future growth. A garden is primarily about the present, however, for nowhere are you so conscious of the season as it *is*, as you are in a garden. Spring is laid out at your feet in its delightful and dismal muck, summer is a burgeoning, a fullness, the ground that was bare two months ago is now covered, and fall with its red and gold, with its stalks of finished lilies and few last roses, contains the whole of the growing season within its borders.

In the garden, as elsewhere, time is mysterious. The morning-glories close by noon. The silky blooms of California poppies remain shyly folded if there is no sun to open their wings. The true lilies come on according to their own schedule, buds splitting to reveal luminous petals of red, ochre, plum. Even when the spring seems cold, the earth is warming at its own ineluctable pace. A late snow falls and stays for a day, but by the next morning is gone, revealing that more tulips have broken ground. I am delighted to be able to stand at the centre of such a complex unfolding and pretend I am in charge. When the garden is preternaturally splendid, and visitors give me credit, I nod, smiling to myself.

As a woman who may never have a child, I find in my garden the music of a reassuring fecundity, but also its opposite — the unexpressed, the unrealized notes and phrases. I pull out several cornflower seedlings so one may grow to its fullest. I leave out certain colours, favouring subtlety here, boldness there. The limey yellow flowers of nicotiana draw purple out of the campanula. The magenta of the petunias is deeper, more lustrous, when surrounding a grey-blue stone. I am tired of the beebalm because it is too big and sprawling and overwhelms the bed; I dig it out. I take out a peony because it is shrinking year by year, inexplicably. I remember its pure pink flowers, when it was still sultry, unstoppable. As a woman who may not have a child, I love the way the rhubarb breaks through in spring, its many pink heads crowning.

I move my chair closer to the red lilies, hoping to absorb their heat. I think of what lies in their chromosomes, the many unrevealed beauties of what it could be but is not. The garden in time makes sense of what can and cannot be. There are hidden forces at work in the soil, in the leaves of the Russian olive. The tree sheds its oxygen at night outside my window as I lie in bed, recounting to myself the virtues of trees, trying to understand.

I hold up the flower of my understanding, compare it to the leaning delphiniums. It may be a more elaborate bloom than what other creatures carry at the end of their brain stems; it may be our only real achievement, this ability to think over wide swatches of time. We may have little else to offer, our cerebral hum moving among the bees and butterflies. And so I keep trying, through poems, to gather a few of us together in the garden. We are still here, I want to say. We are not exiles. The cities so many of us dwell in, they too lie on the earth. Under the pavement, the land waits. Come into the garden, I say. Let us lie down here, quiet as daisies. Let us lie like children with our heads on the warm grass, listening for the many mouths at work. We can try, for a while, to see ourselves becoming earth. Look up now at the humans. They move over us so carelessly. They are like trees that have forgotten what it is like to stand still.

Sources

Line from poems quoted in this essay can be found in my books: *Time in a Green Country* (Coteau, 1990) and *Beyond My Keeping* (Coteau, 1995)

The Education of a Gardener, Russell Page (William Collins and Sons, 1994 edition)

Step by Step Organic Vegetable Gardening, Shepherd Ogden (HarperCollins, 1992)

"The Eyes of Claude Monet," John Berger, in *The Sense of Sight*, ed. Lloyd Spencer (Pantheon Books, 1985)

FRED WAH

Clematis Creek Humming

columbia virgin's bower: bell rue and horse
gate to the creek world above Crowsnest cut
off the clit or horns of heaven some pale
purple tree-river finally honing home and
the twig broken with meaning to sign pale
purple (chocolate on the trunk of the pine
tree) climbing climbing into you stem limp
at your musk to cop petals this tongue
pepper and the gorge in an outfall of brown
spring runoff the slope coal cloned to the
mat of this evening sepal delta deep touched
tooth your butter my cup

Nose Hill

Grass language knows
silent flower wind
no trembled flutter

north of joy
anemone mundi mound
emble hair scab

grace oat keel
none shingle sky
June naze puzzle

imported sweet awn
cope tribe discont-
but abundant thrill

never rough hooked
dream street springing
ocean grade panic

grammas gone north
thread-through-needle
spoke troop boat

w/ as ex hill
noon pond knot
having omph look

clusted node broom
first minute pendul
city locorice grazed

boulevard finger zome
tickled sweet pyramid
infloresce occur animal

then *gna* loop
feathered gravel home
new lawn river.

"nobody knows how to live off the land any more"

social action Hazel and I don't agree
savour the possibilities:
blueberry leaves, strawberry, raspberry leaves steeped to drink
fruit of pin cherry, mooseberry, gooseberry, chokecherry
build soup with deer, squirrel, muskrat, beaver
thicken with flour of fireweed, stinkweed, cattail stalk
toss in nodding onion, wild carrot, Indian turnip
steam spring plantain, tender dandelion, sweet lamb's-quarter
serve with sautéed nettle, mushroom, shelf fungus
pickle saskatoons, boil cambium of fir, poplar, pine
hull wild rice and wild oats for starch in your diet
bake pies of red currant, twinberry, bog cranberry
roast goose, gopher, fat caribou
toast grasshoppers
from the waters pull clam, crayfish, big jackfish, jumbo whitefish
string wire in the kitchen and hang lacy sliced moose meat to dry
pound elk or buffalo for pemmican
snare rabbit, raccoon imports, skunk (jakwas knows how)
nohkom favours duck soup, porcupine stew, fried bush chicken
salads show off rose petals, mallow sprigs, raspberries,
    cracked hazelnuts
yellow spring cattail heads taste like corn on the cob
dig below snow for red starchy bearberries
frozen rosehips are sweet and juicy, spit out the
seeds or you'll have an itchy bum
paper birch sap and Manitoba maple sap sweeten
tea of black currant leaves, sarsaparilla, black poplar buds
enjoy high bush cranberry compote
relax with a pot of muskeg tea

dehydrate your harvest in the sun
in a deep pit bury your booty under dirt to preserve its goodness
use your cash to *visit* the other culture

indigenous

the girl lies under a
loose-weave blanket of wool
blue mostly, green and yellow mixed in
from the light, through little squares
come four eagle feathers
tied to English words, four aliens
wave on wave of feathers and foreign words
language graft silences the mother tongue

the father prays, seeks guidance
to make his daughter one of them
the girl becomes the
bowl the father dips into
he holds up to the light
steel tools, Bibles, money
white sugar, university degrees, computers,
eye glasses, truck keys, political platforms
interac plastic, GST, history lessons

Euro mass culture packages the Holocaust
carries warnings of personal death and genocide
visible minority self-consciousness paralyzes the father
the danger crowds his mind and spirit
he opts for "getting along" and "following the rules"
he pays to carry a party card
the girl watches him usurp self, subvert her heritage

she lifts the bitter cup
becomes the new warrior
has fewer babies than her mother
she must turn back the English graft
to soften the Euro scars

HISTORIES

FRED STENSON

Bow River Expedition

Chesterfield House, 1822

One Pound One's winter house was only half built. Over the shell he had rigged a leather roof, making it into a kind of tent with wooden walls. The night of H.'s return from the Heron expedition, they sat in it without a fire, drinking rum.

Astride stump chairs and wrapped in robes, they had been at it, drinking and smoking, for hours. Getting drunk for no reason H. could decipher. All the others in the fort, save its guards, were asleep and H. desperately wished to be so too. Drunk as he was, his back and legs were stiff and sore from riding. Every joint announced its position with a flash of pain. He was cold to the bone.

The topic of Heron's expedition had been exhausted long ago. Not much to tell that Heron himself had not told First Officer Mack earlier in One Pound One's presence. Heron could have, and should have, handled the Indians better, but it was doubtful he would have gained any skins if he had.

That conversation had been finished for hours and it was hard to say what they were talking about now. From the leather roof, One Pound One had hung a candle made inside a buffalo horn, and the shaking light was like the shivering in H.'s core made visible. He wrestled with the muscles of his face to keep his teeth from chattering. If he could only sleep, his strength would return but One Pound One would not release him.

One Pound One tipped the rum keg over his mouth and took another black gulp, half of which ran down his neck. H. had never seen drink finish the Chief Trader, but it seemed like it had to tonight. His eyes were dim and swimming, his upper body wove circles around the base of his spine. Out of some monologue inside his brain, occasional mumbles surfaced.

— Murdering bastards …

To deal with the cold and the pointless waiting, H. tried to compose the face of Margaret. The image so available to him a month ago had to be struggled for now. What came to him instead was the sight of tramped snow jolting in front of his horse, or poplar trees gripping a woolen sky in dead claws. His every thought played against a background of Indian drums, even now when all was calm. Feathered tail fans brushed his face. Anklets of dew claws rattled the doors of his ears.

H. looked at One Pound One and hoped that the closed eyes and slumped posture meant he was unconscious. Then a hand came flinging that caught H. on the shoulder. The eyes startled open, glowing sulphurous in the livid face.

— I can't stop it! One Pound One yelled, as if it were the last angry bellow in a long argument. The bastard means to send you, that's all.

H. tapped his ear, meaning quiet, meaning there might be listeners.

— Goddamn them! I've been quiet too long.

The eyes closed, the liver-coloured face started to weave again against the light. The entire flesh shrugged and H. prepared to catch it. But again One Pound One jerked himself upright and reopened his eyes wherein all had turned to sorrow. H. had seen the pattern before, rage into maudlin affection, but never from this one. He watched as a hand came groping across the space and dropped dead-weight on his leg.

— Mack means to send you. He trades 'em guns and sends you down their middle. When he loses you, he'll say he tried and you're the proof it was impossible.

A thistle of fear pricked H.'s back.

— Where are they sending me?

— Fur Mountains. Missouri. Straight down at the Big Bellies and Mack's given 'em the stuff to shoot you with.

— When?

— Tomorrow.

— There's no fit horses.

— That's the worst. You go on foot. I tried to get him to pick Pambrun. I told him you're no fighting man. I even…

The words stopped and the whole being behind them went out like a snuffed lamp.

— Listen, John. Listen. I need to know what you know. Tell me what you know.

This time, One Pound One was gone. The flesh like flour in a sack was spreading over the edges of the stump, the eyes were closed and the lips slack.

The stem of the pipe slithered out of the mouth's corner, fell. The clay bowl split on the hard-pack, a greasy ball of tobacco stranded between its halves.

The Third Expedition, 1822

Thirty men and two Indian guides. Sinclair to translate. H. to lead. Trade goods of tobacco and rum. For weapons, they had fukes and HBC dags. For food, a bit of grease. Mostly they were meant to hunt their way.

South. On foot.

Mack rode out with them for several hours in the pale yellow sun that could not warm the day. During a rest, he saw Bourassa had no gun. He screamed at him and cut him across the face with his quirt. Bourassa said he had burst his gun on Heron's expedition and did not wish to go to the expense of another.

— Then get back to the fort. You are useless.

Bourassa surprised everyone by talking back. He would gladly go, he said, but he would buy no other gun. Nor was he going to stop at Chesterfield. He would leave this cursed expedition and take his chances on the prairie.

Bourassa walked away, back down their trail in the snow, the scrunching sound of his leather moccasins smaller until swallowed in the glittering air. From his saddle, Mack called weak abuse while the others stood by, faced in the direction of the escaping engagé. When Mack ran out of things to say, an immense silence descended and only two things to look at across the snow: Mack's equestrian shadow reaching and Bourassa's shrinking form.

The situation was oppressive and Mack had to escape it. Imploring God to take care of them, he cut his horse loose and galloped down the long v-shape of their footprints. The closer he came to Bourassa, the more tension gathered in the backs and shoulders of H.'s men.

The words Godspeed and good luck chimed in H.'s head. Godspeed, yes, if God walks his own prairie in winter loaded with weight. Godspeed, certainly, if the life flies out of your opened skull. I will come back, was what he said aloud.

Then the distance between rider and man on foot closed so tight one couldn't be made out from the other. A sound rose from the men, a grunt like they'd all taken a blow. But Mack did not cut Bourassa a second time. Only passed him by.

Directly after, H. called his men together.

— We must be smart, he said, if we want to get home to our forts and women. We'll look for beaver as we're told to, but in a way that gets us home. Sometimes you'll think I act strange. If there's Indians near, look at me anyway as if I were a great leader. Do that and we'll come home.

The men gave H. a loud hurrah for this. They began their walk with spirit in their legs.

That first day south, H. called the halt as the sun was coming plumply to rest on the horizon. They made their camp on the eastern edge of the valley, on a cliff commanding a broad view all round. They collected wood from the valley's shady face, and when they were settled for the night, H. made a strange announcement. He told them their chore was to drink every drop of the rum. If they could not drink it all, he would pour the remainder on the ground and break the kegs. They would do so here where there was no sign of Indians, before they took another step ahead.

It was the oddest night of their lives, those who could remember. Like New Year's at a big fort, except the rum never flowed nor the tobacco smoked as freely then as now. They had but one Jew's harp, but they sang and played and clapped and danced regardless until they were tired. The gambling and the dancing and the fighting went on long after the moonlight had waned.

H. got as drunk as the rest, but when two men in rum-roaring drunkenness drew knives, he was quickly between them.

— No dead men, he said. No half-dead men.

They posted no guard and slept how and where they fell, in and out of the robes and blankets they wore against the cold.

When next day's dawn came pink to the horizon, a foraging party of Big Bellies approached the camp from a long ways off, disappearing into the valley, then reappearing closer. Only H. was awake, grey-faced and eyes bloody. He let them come half the distance before he began to wake the others. He told his men to ready their weapons, to load them and point them but not to fire unless he expressly gave that order.

Himself unarmed, H. walked beyond musket range to meet the Big Bellies — boys, it turned out — and he stood without flinching as they came at a gallop, the robes around their shoulders flapping. They came shouting and waving their spears. Some had arrows on the string. Before this curious act of bravery, the Big Bellies skidded their horses to a halt in the snow. They sat on the winded mounts and stared mystified at the tobacco held out to them in the trader's hand. It was a mystery and probably a trap, and while the two leaders dismounted, the others stayed in their saddles, ready with bows and spears.

H. lit the pipe and offered it. After they had all smoked a couple of turns, he spoke the bit of their language he knew. He said he had a message and he would need another to come and translate it. He beckoned Sinclair, telling him to leave his fukes behind.

What he wanted said was that this little expedition was no stronger than it appeared. They should go back to their people and say how these white men travelled without horses and without rum, without any trade goods. He showed them the broken kegs.

— We're like cornered wolverines, he said, meaning that all they had left were their claws and the instinct to sell their lives dear.

The young Indians watched as H. wrapped a bit more tobacco in a red piece of cloth and tied it.

— Our last, he said, giving it to them. Now we truly have nothing.

The Fur Mountains, 1822

Dear Margaret,

You said once I was a fool to show my love for you the way I do. How more foolish you'd think me if you saw me at this letter tonight.

There is a big prairie here, close to the sky and level like a tabletop, coated with snow. The moon is so bright I don't need this fire for light, only for what heat it gives. On the plain an old tree has the moon in its branches. Right behind me it's all forest and I suppose I shouldn't have camped that way. Defence seems hopeless so I thought we might as well be close to wood. We announce our place each night with a giant fire. How else are we to survive this winter's walk?

When we came here this morning, there were buffalo on the plain. The wind was such they couldn't smell us. A Halfbreed covered himself in a robe and crawled among them. He shot a cow where she stood. We were starving and devoured much of it raw.

Now, another day's searching behind me, I am still sluggish with that meat. Did I find beaver? Oh, yes. Several lodges. My men would have cracked them, but I followed Heron's example. There are no beaver save these few, contrary to all the lies. Somebody else can kill the rest.

You see how I prove I am no longer quite a human man? Write my love a letter and I talk of buffalo and beaver. But I must try. Even as the other men are sleeping and snoring like saws, I will keep this poor watch and write this poor letter in hopes it will breathe life back into my memory of you.

I can say more in this letter than I could if you were here. I can say how I saw you that time picking stems out of berries on the river slopes at Carlton, the time I think of as the beginning. Hot day in late July and you had your skirts pulled up and tied around your legs to feel the breeze. You were bent forward poring over the berries, on the watch for worms.

Your legs were smooth and brown and the muscles tensed as you pushed onto your toes to hold the berries in the basin of your skirt and lap. There were wires of red where the thorns had torn you, and I wanted to kiss the places, run my tongue along them.

You looked up. I suppose I made a noise, and small wonder as I was never in such an uproar. I was helpless to move or shift my look. Sweet face and the bow of your lips smiling. I know it was amusement, but my heart was stolen anyway.

If it weren't for the books I read, I might not have any of these words. My books from England say love comes but once, the pure kind. I trust I have that kind for you.

Ever since then at every regale, every time you dance with a man, I can't stand it. Even though I know it's nothing to you. I knew it was different for us when I saw you looking for me during the brigade dance last spring. When I caught your eye, you weren't laughing anymore. That's why I went outside to wait. When you came out, I walked ahead through the back gate and down to the river. Where the sound of the river was loudest, you caught me up. I put my arms around you and the feel of the heat through your dress was like a fire. Your lips were the softest thing I ever touched.

We found a place soft enough to lie. You took off your dress and walked around me. You weren't ashamed. Then we mated. For all the men sniffing around, I was the first. That left me lonely until your fingers started tracing figures on my skin. I looked at myself, half expecting to see something there, maybe some kind of old writing.

That thought brings me back to where I am, this cold high place. The fire is down and must be rebuilt. No matter how we grease ourselves, this bitter cold is killing us by bits. If the warm wind does not come, I expect it will kill us soon.

I have no hope that anyone will read this letter, let alone read it to you. I only write it as a means of seeing you, in case I never see you again.

We could have been killed a hundred times by now. I keep that to myself so the men go on believing there's hope. Right this moment there could be loaded weapons in the trees. Why not? Much as I want to come home and lie with you again, why not?

That's enough said. I don't like to think how we're probably meant to die, and how I'm drawing these men farther from home toward it. One thing I do know is that, if I'm allowed somehow to return to you, no man living will take you from me.

GUY VANDERHAEGHE

Blue Horse In A Blizzard

(excerpt from *The Englishman's Boy*)

Even from such a distance Fine Man could smell their camp, the fried pig stink of white men. He took up a pinch of dirt, placed it under his tongue and made a prayer. Keep me close Mother Earth, hide me Mother Earth. It was light as day, the moon's bright face a trader's steel mirror, the grey leaves of the sage and wolf willow shining silver, as if coated with hoarfrost. Under a full moon, it was dangerous to steal horses — even from foolish white men.

One of the wolfers rose from his blanket and stepped away from the fire. The one with the ugly hair, red like a fox's, he stood making his water and talking over his shoulder. A noisy man lacking in dignity. It must be a poor thing to be a wolf poisoner, to be ugly, to eat pork, to hate silence. There was nothing to envy these people, except their guns and horses.

The red-haired one rolled himself back up in his blanket and lay like a log beside the fire. "Say goodnight to Jesus," said one of the other three men wrapped in blankets. They all laughed. More noise.

Fine Man felt Broken Horn's body relax beside him and knew Horn had been covering Red Hair with the "fukes," a sawed-off Hudson's Bay musket, the only gun they carried between them. Broken Horn was edgy. Fine Man sensed Horn no longer believed in the promise and the truth of his dream.

In his dream, there was heavy snow, biting cold. Many starving, shivering horses, coats white with frost, had come stumbling through the high drifts to crowd the entrance of Fine Man's lodge. There the grass of spring pushed up sweet green blades through the crust of the snow, tenderness piercing ice, and gave itself to strengthen the horses, even though it was the black months of winter. Fine Man read this as a power sign that somewhere there were horses wishing to belong to the Assiniboine. But Broken Horn did not trust Fine Man's sign any more, and Fine Man did not trust Horn with a gun in his hand.

Suddenly the white men's horses began to mill about, hopping like jack-rabbits in their hobbles. Powdery dust rose like mist, to hang swirling and shaking in the moonlight. Fine Man shifted his eyes to the fire. But none of the lumps under the greasy grey blankets raised a head, their ears were deaf. How did white men distinguish their corpses from those who had only gone to sleep?

The herd broke apart, horses turning and spinning, bumping one another like pans of ice in the grip of a swift current. A moment of complete confusion, rumps and heads bucking above the dust, then the strong current found a shape and stood alone, a big blue roan, broken hobbles dangling from its forelegs, teeth bared, ears laid back.

Lit by the moon, the roan was stained a faint blue, the colour of late winter afternoon shadows on crusted snow. Coat smooth as ice, chest and haunches hard as ice, eyes cold as ice, A Nez Percé horse from beyond the mountains which wore snow on their heads all the year round, a horse from behind The Backbone of the World.

When he saw him, Fine Man knew the promise of the dream was true and he rose from behind the juniper bush to show himself plain to the winter horse. Broken Horn's sharp intake of breath through the teeth was a warning, but Fine Man gave no indication he heard him, the power chanting in him. He stood upright in the moonlight, upright in his Thunderbird moccasins with the beaded Bird green on each foot, upright in the breechclout his Sits-Beside-Him wife had cut from the striped Hudson's Bay blanket. He gazed down at his hands, at the skin of his muscled thighs, at his belly, and understood. White moonlight was his blizzard, a blizzard to blind the eyes of his enemies who lay frozen to the ground in the grip of his medicine dream, drifted over by the heavy snow of sleep.

He edged toward the horse, addressing him in a soft voice, politely. Fifty yards to his left, the fire was rustling, hot embers cracking like nuts, spitting like fat. Behind him, Horn lifted himself to one knee, swiftly spiking three arrows in the ground near where his bow lay, and aimed the fukes at the sleeping body of a wolfer.

"Little Cousin," said Fine Man in a soothing voice, "Little Cousin, do not be afraid. Don't you recognize me? I am the man you dreamed, the man with the lodge of plenty. I am the man you led your brothers to." He stopped for a moment. "Take a good look at me. There is no harm in my hands," he murmured, displaying empty palms to the roan. Turning and pointing to Broken Horn, crouched with his musket levelled at the sleeping white man, he said, "That man there came with me to find you. Some of your brothers may choose to live with him — if they so decide. It is for them to choose." He stepped forward lightly, words rustling lightly. "Cousin, you are a beautiful being. I do not say this to flatter you. The white man rides you with steel spurs and a steel bit in your mouth. This is not how to sit upon a beautiful being — with cruelty." They were face to face now, he and the blue roan. He removed his left moccasin, the moccasin of the heart side. "Feel, Cousin, there is no harm upon my feet," he said, reaching up carefully to gently stroke the roan's nose with the moccasin. He pursed his lips and blew softly into the left nostril of the horse, who snorted Fine Man's breath back in surprise, shaking his head from side to side.

"Now you know there is no harm in my heart. Now you know that I am the good man who you dreamed. Tell your brothers," Fine Man coaxed.

Broken Horn was signalling him desperately to come now, leave this place, clear out, but Fine Man was making his way carefully and deliberately from horse to horse, showing each his knife before severing the hobbles. When he finished, he returned to the blue roan, stood at its withers, took a fistful of mane and walked it away, his legs matching its forelegs stride for stride. Hesitantly, the other horses followed the man and the blue roan, nineteen horses strung out in a winding procession through buck brush and sage, black shadows dropping sheer from their sides, edges sharp as a knife cut.

Without haste, they picked their way across the river bottom and to the feet of steep, eroded hills which, washed in the cold light of the moon, became reflections of moon's own face, old and worn and pocked and bright. Fine Man led the blue horse up the first hump of hill, the others filing behind, hooves daintily ticking on loose stones, gravel cascading loose and running with a dry sigh down the slope. He paused, his hands resting on the blue roan's withers; the string of horses paused too. Below, Fine Man could see an elbow of the Teton River poking through the cottonwoods and the tongues of the white man's fire darting, licking the dark. A sudden breeze sprang up and fanned his face, luffed the mane of the blue horse, stroked and ruffled the surface of the water so it flashed and winked in the moonlight like the scales of a leaping fish.

He and the blue horse began their descent then, down into the belly of a narrow coulee twisting through the scarred and crumbling hills. The other horses trickled down the slope after them, filling the coulee as water fills the bed of a river. One by one they dropped from sight, tails switching, heads bobbing, ghostly gleaming horses running back into the earth like shining, strengthening water.

The fire died amid the charred sticks, the moon grew pale. The stream of horses flowed north to Canada.

MARGARET SWEATMAN

1869

It is time for me to be born.

Imagine, heat. In the coupled loins of my mother (wearing wool pants and a heavy flannel shirt, and strangest of all, leather chaps, for he'd taken her while they chased a herd of thirsty cattle from the Wood Mountains to the Pembina Hills) and my skinny ardent dad. Hot as liquor, the juice that made me, on the night of August's showering meteors in a warm wind sweet with sage. Heat and the peculiar spin of their amorous sport upon the horse blanket. They are alone under cowboy stars that are like distant reflections of the embers of a camp-fire. They always laughed in their lovemaking. It was the laughter of the most successful practical jokers in all of Assiniboia. Their britches whisper as leaves in the breeze when they rustle and rub together. He thrusts inside her and she wraps her chaps round him and draws her knees up to his shoulders while the seed runs down, itching and hot. A woman in her precarious circumstances must deter coition at all costs and they were careful to spill, laughing. My mum and dad, in God's House of Lords, members of the opposition.

They'd been travelling with a half-dozen men, a sad bunch of buf-falo hunters reduced to driving cattle for a retired Company officer. They had spent a long month in such company under duress of my mother's disguise, feigning manly indifference to each other's earthy scent. It made them hot. And a little silly. And when the men had left them alone that night with instructions to return for the stragglers — a cow and her calf who'd been separated from the herd — they'd both shrugged and spat and threw down their bedrolls, grunting acquies-cence.

A lovely night, the stars above. Hunger from a long fast, constant temptation, and the arousal (perhaps you know of it) that comes from watching a lover's freedom or solitude — the aphrodisiac of the lover's mortal sovereignty, the face averted, the part that leaves you out.

She thought he'd come. Their catechism had reached that stage of exchange where one becomes another, pulse and tide for tide and pulse. Her own juice she mistook for his. She thought he'd spilled and that she was safely playing on pleasure's littoral. She was attune to her rhythms and knew she was ripe. So when she looked past his arching pounding shoulder and her own open legs and saw the lurid purple of the thunderhead cover the half-moon (while dad fought for an end to his need, pounding the walls of his beloved, seeking echo, seeking an end), when she saw the leader stroke of lightning — a brilliant ionized path stark white against the deep purple sky — and after a split second another stroke and the great intake of breath, dry as rage and bright as a path of quicksilver, she knew, she knew. The next stroke struck the ground at the centre of their diamond-shaped conjugation. The heat made their hair stand on end, my father's hair longer and scruffier than my mother's theatrical boy's bob. Twenty-five thousand volts.

My father was a compassionate man who would never inflict his needs upon his beloved wife. But I can't say for certain if he would have had the discipline necessary to have stopped himself before the fact that magic night. Anyone with the imagination to put themselves in his boots at that moment will forgive him the indiscretion of the fiercest ejaculation by a white man in the brief history of Rupert's Land. And though my mother was receptive, the voltage and the heat fired the seed, knocked her unconscious. She didn't stand a chance. They woke fourteen hours later, still coupled, surrounded by hailstones the size of turtle eggs. They smiled roguishly, knowing, and with blackened fingers combed each other's sizzled hair. It was two o'clock on the first afternoon of my life as an embryo. Father withdrew from mother slowly, very slowly, flesh welded to flesh, raw.

They would be satisfied for nearly a month. They helped each other stand and looked out at the barren trees, leaves pounded by the hail. The light was white as the inside of an oxygen tent. They buttoned their trousers. Horses gone. Cow and calf, vanished. They hobbled and sucked hailstones along the old trail marked by the wooden wheels of Red River carts. They held hands. They were glad I'd been tipped into the world, off a thundercloud like a huge tarnished tray, tipped like caviar into my mother's womb. And scorched there, the seed of a jack pine. The catalyst, a stroke of lightning.

My mother had come from Glasgow looking for the man she'd decided to love. My father-to-be was a tenant farmer from Orkney, sick of mud and poverty, who joined up with the Hudson's Bay Company and jumped aboard a ship headed for the New World. Sailing west sailing west, to prairie lands sunkissed and blest, the crofter's trail to happiness.

My mother was the only female student at the University of Glasgow enrolled in Theology, establishing the family tradition of studying passionately all things extraneous to survival. Dad had come through Glasgow on his way to the sea, and when mother saw his raw neck and smelled the grass in his hair, on the pretense of kissing his hands she gnawed upon his calluses as if long denied some vital nutrient.

She'd been raised a Wesleyan and took her faith through the telescopes of duty and intellect. At the time of his precipitous arrival, she'd been preparing for an examination on the methods of salvation. They met by accident in the stark sun of the college yard where she sat reading and he sat darning his socks. He had a freckled complexion. His Adam's apple floated under freshly plucked skin while he told my mother of free land and plenty in the Dominion. The effect upon my mother was a heartstopping reversal of foreground for background. She looked at the college which had long represented for her the keyhole to freedom, and she saw it as the funnel through which freedom poured itself into obedience. She looked again at the high-strung and thick-skinned fingers of the man beside her. He neither bit his nails nor cut them; he was worn down naturally through the effects of water, wind and soil. She saw a fly walk across his porcelain ear, unheeded. She saw the spinning possibilities for adventure and, always the lady, she chose to call it love.

She was wearing a Methodist gown. The book lay open between her knees which splayed, and her black-laced boots spread pigeon-toed, careless and ready. She said, "I have looked for God in all the wrong places."

There is no record of his reply, other than a simple and modest declaration of his unworthy nature.

Then he disappeared.

She made her way to London. She cut off her hair and put on a pair of trousers and got a job on a boat sailing for York Factory. She proved useful aboard ship and arrived with the reputation of a popular young lad capable of work that demanded more finesse than muscle. She was assigned to work the trade route to Norway House and joined a crew of traders with all the optimism of a wolf pup on her first hunt. She believed she was looking for her underfed crofter. It would be unseemly for a woman to be looking for liberty.

She found him at a buffalo post in Pembina. They were eventually assigned to the same quarters. He was greatly relieved to learn she was "the female from the University" (an epithet he reserved for her with all his ensuing affection and pride). He'd been compelled by the slope of her shoulders, her sway back and double-jointed knees that made him think of a little girl. She had hunted buffalo for two months without making known, even to her beloved Orkney, her true identity. She was a handsome, artless boy with a hoarse voice and brown eyes like a fallow deer. Such was my father's courage and tenderness, he didn't take his lust out in rage. He was, however, the only one willing to bunk with the boy because all the other men had lusted too and thought there must be something deviant in a lad who could inspire such passion.

They were better than lovers; they were conspirators. They signed up with a crew of hunters reduced to driving cattle. There had been only a few buffalo near the Red River Valley for several years, but the eminently retired Company officer was collecting a herd for private sport and he hired old hunters, my mother and dad among them, to drive them along with his domestic cattle over his vast tracts of land.

The hunters were tormented by the unnatural curtailment of their instincts. Forced to herd the animals they would traditionally slaughter, thwarted and confined in the new world, they watched with growing consternation the arrival of antipapist Anglophiles from Upper Canada. True, their outward circumstances had been altered but a little: they still rode horses over unfenced land, had no money, owned nothing, and slept on the ground. But the cursorial way of the Métis had lost its true function. They weren't permitted to shoot. Like the old ruminants they herded, the disarmed hunters chewed the cud of rebellion, squinting into the dust stirred up by advancing civilization.

My father was philosophical. Even here, in the brand new Dominion, a man has an overseer in the person of an aristocratic Scot. The retired officer would arrive with a gaggle of flatulent lords, three servants to a man, and they would bed the occasional Ojibwa, whom they said they found quite frisky if caught young. Buffalo proved better game than partridge or fox. The muzzled Métis hunters herded the buffalo within easy range, and before long Lord Hardy and Lord Finlayson and Lord Simpson would be sent back to Scotland sated, carrying hairy buffalo heads aboard ship and wearing elegant robes and hats. The New World was certainly wild. Returned from their excursion, they wrote poetry in the vein of William Wordsworth. They had known, in a biblical sense, Nature. And she was sublime.

But for my mother and dad, it was truly paradise to work hard and be paid a good man's wage and still — for they were both young and intelligent and easily bored — enjoy the fact that the expression of their lives was one extended double-entendre. They found themselves so amusing that everyone laughed with them, and they developed a reputation as a sort of travelling vaudeville in the camps. Then, as they say, lightning struck.

They left the employ of the eminently retired officer.

My dad had long since been depressed over his boss's speculations in real estate. He felt compromised. Walking gingerly toward the settlement at the Red, he confided to my mother that he felt the ground beneath them, the black-eyed Susan and dusty stalks of prairie orchid, the air full of sparrows and breezes like invisible thumbprints, the bountiful gifts of the Great Spirit, were changing shape as if to hide themselves from fate. He said he felt like someone witnessing a murder, and the victim was the land they looked on, there, in the innocent sun. The Garden of Eden had been sold to Eastern millionaires, and its beautiful limbs would soon be clothed in pinstripe and fences. And with tears in his eyes, my father said he was afraid.

Besides that, they couldn't find the crew of domesticated buffalo hunters.

They walked most of the way to St. Norbert at the junction of the Red and the Rivière Sale without seeing a soul. But for twenty miles of that trek, they hitched a ride in a cart pulled by an ox. The cart was home for a solemn young couple and their solemn-eyed baby who were wandering the trails of Assiniboia.

It was a hot afternoon and my mother and father had been walking for two days. They were still pretty tender here and there and they walked like a pair of hounds sniffing at the blossoms of Great Plains ladies' tresses. The air smelled sweetly of skunk, an aroma they both enjoyed. They told the urgent autobiography of paramours, needing to recreate themselves, now, with the lover arrived to heal the story into shapeliness, to make graceful the erratic gestures of a life. Occasionally one of them would drop out of earshot, distracted by the shriek of a falcon, ambling to catch up and beg for a recap, a clarification. "Your mother had a nice singing voice?" "You saw me in a dream?"

My father was terrible for mumbling into the breeze, turning his long skinny back, his voice nested in the hair of his chest. But my mother, still an earnest Methodist, would tell her life all in a breath, fighting for air, stalling the laughter. She was in the midst of a description of her family back in Glasgow, a long, loving history lasting at least an hour and a half, with her heart pressing her larynx and her eyes blind to the aspen stands and swift fox, her memory so full of the particulars of her lost family she was hyperventilating when my dad put his hand over her mouth and pulled her down into a low-lying stand of cattails. An inadequate hiding place, more a starting-line if they found they had to dash.

Two Red River carts, noisy as stuck pigs, rolled into view. Two oxen walked peaceably in an atmosphere of panic, seeming to exist in uncanny quiet while the carts screamed and tin cups rattled in the breeze. They were stacked with gear, a lantern swung tipping coal oil into the basket of onions and potatoes set upon a serpent's coil of hundred-link chains.

My mother and father hid while the first cart screamed past. In it there appeared to be five soldiers, though their uniforms were filthy and my mother had the impression they'd been lifted from dead bodies maybe somewhere in the south where American soldiers were battling the Blackfoot. But when the second cart rolled by, my mother moaned deeply, an old hunger suddenly recalled. There, seated between a red-haired man with muttonchops and a shining brass sextant, and holding a bundle of blankets to her breast, was a woman, the first woman my mother had laid eyes on in over four months. Blinded by a sudden grief, my mother stumbled out to the middle of the trail and stood helpless, her hands forgotten at her sides, her mouth open, a drop of spittle upon her lip. The driver was given no option. The cart came to a halt, dust floating in sunlight and silence thick as honey out of which recommenced the singing of birds. With her eyes fixed upon the skinny dress-up boy, the round mothering woman motioned them to climb aboard and indicated they could settle into the bale of straw.

They rode all afternoon in deafening noise, reluctant to speak above the din. The only words the young woman pronounced were in a language so foreign it sounded counterclockwise. Her partner didn't appear to understand a word she said, and he didn't appear to care, but he nodded affably, saying, "Yep" or "I don't imagine." Three times the woman touched his shirt sleeve, and when the cart stopped she handed him the baby, and waving my mother to follow, gathered her numer-ous skirts and disappeared into the bush. My mum was terribly anxious when this happened the first time. She was, you will remember, disguised as a man. But somehow the woman knew. She led my boyish mum into the bush. They were standing facing each other in green shade alive with the buzzing of mosquitoes. The woman put her hand under her skirts and withdrew a leather-bound volume of the Bible. It was in English. It was unlikely that she realized that it was sacred text from which she tore two pages, both from the Song of Songs, and handed one page to my mother. The paper was very fine, high quality. The woman squatted and suddenly her face was lit by a smile, her perfect white teeth and full red lips against a tanned face and blond hair. She smiled as if the common fact of bladders was a source of amusement infinite and humane. My mother unzipped and squatted too. They began to laugh while the fragrant pee ran in golden creeks between their feet, and they walked back to the wagon breathless and happy. The young woman took the infant from the militiaman and resumed her seat. She was, once again, solemn as an old photograph and just as gnomic. Thus they resumed their creaking journey.

My mother was a shameless voyeur. All afternoon she focussed her gaze upon the woman, my dad occasionally poking her ribs to make her stop. My mum would look away, embarrassed, but drawn like a dog to a buried bone, she would be back at it before long, fixing to understand how a woman with no English could be seated between a hawk-nosed Loyalist with muttonchops and a shiningly elegant sextant. She could at last not deny her curiosity a minute longer. Shaking off my dad's restraining hand, she crawled up to their seat and crouched there, a kid between two grown-ups. Dad couldn't hear the words she spoke into the man's ear (which was full of curly red hairs as if the muttonchops grew from that source). Without batting an eye, the fellow pulled a ledger from inside his shirt. Mum crawled back to dad, clutching her prize.

It was a surveyor's notebook. The land was sketched in pencil, artfully, bulrushes to indicate marshland, and stands of maple, poplar, pencilled as if the words themselves were drawings of trees. He'd traced the meandering of the Assiniboine River and identified each oxbow, the shifts in vegetation, "Oak, Elm & Ash" on the south side, "Elm, Maple, Willow" to the north. "Principally Poplar & Thick Brush" in the bend. And within the margins, his splendid sketches: a pair of mallards; a peregrine falcon, immature/mature, in flight/at rest; a burrowing owl with young (they looked like monkeys, but my mother didn't know that, having never seen a monkey). My mother could not have been more moved by the sight of a painting at the Louvre. It was the first time she'd seen her unkempt new country represented in artistic form.

She tried to share her enthusiasm with Dad. But my father's face was seamed with sorrow and he ran his worn fingers over the grid that lay upon the topography like a net, like a snare. My mother saw the land loved by an artist, but Dad saw the surveyor's scribbles as scars inflicted on his weary freedom. He pointed to the surveyor's remarks and watched my mother's lips move as she read: "*Little of the land has been cultivated, though the soil is rich black loam. The people who wander through it know nothing of agriculture and will not prove to be desirable landowners. It is my considered opinion, they will never give up their roving habits unless, perhaps, faced with starvation.*"

My parents descended for the last time at the first encounter with the Rivière Sale. The men nodded impassively as a pair of duellists, but the woman met my mother's eye and revealed a reservoir of mirth vast as a decade of rain. As the wagon rolled out of sight, my parents heard the untamed wheezing of a hurdy-gurdy and then the woman's mellifluous voice singing in her mirror-imaged tongue.

☞

They reached the Red. Already my mother was starting to feel the nausea that would plague her through the course of my gestation. She was that kind of woman. Within hours of fertilization. There was for her no gradual acceleration or nuance of trimester. Maybe they hadn't heard of trimesters in those days. Pregnant equalled pregnant. Full stop.

She tried to find a way to express to my father that radical change taking place within her. It was a mixture of joy and deep melancholy. She removed her hat and rubbed her head. She scratched her invisible balls. The freedom granted by her disguise was abruptly precious, now she was fated to lose it. She would never in her future life earn as much as she had earned as a boy. She would never enjoy a woman's labours as she had thrilled to the work offered a scrawny seaman, a novice trapper, or an unseasoned cowboy. The silver maples bore yellow seeds whose blades floated down on the early autumn wind. She scooped up a twig of seeds, hurrying to keep up with my dad, and with her nail she peeled seed after seed and put them in her mouth.

She searched her pockets as if looking for words, but found instead a spoon she'd brought from Scotland. It was the first in a collection of spoons she would harbour till her death. A worthless spoon, mostly nickel and crooked from riding in her pants, it was a King's pattern with an obscure family crest upon its stem.

The riverbank sloped like a woman's lap in a green checkered apron bleached by a dry summer. They walked through cutgrass and blossoming thistle toward the muddy shore. There was a wide clay shoreline of baked fishy mud, for the water was low. In the fissures between the clay tiles ran red long-legged spiders. They stood holding hands (in my mother's other hand, the spoon like something growing, urgent), looking at the pale waves on the wide river, a broad view of the Red's bend. Sweat formed on my mother's upper lip. Fish smell, and smoke. There, only fifty feet away, a bonfire. Tending it, a young Cree. He wore a wool coat and hat in the heat, handsome clothing, a tall hat. He looked at my parents over his shoulder as if they were insectivores, maybe a couple of plovers eating spiders and clams. Across the grassy slope toward him walked a woman carrying a baby in a papoose. Even from a distance, you could see she was beautiful. She, too, was dressed finely. She, too, threw my parents a brief diffident glance before joining her partner by the fire.

From her molars, my mother tasted a bilious acid, the flavour of rotten apples. She was throwing up, projectile vomiting before my father had time to turn around. It was a miracle because she hadn't had any food in four days. Copious. Things she'd never eaten, food not

available in the Red River Valley in 1869. Oranges and asparagus, arti-
chokes and lichee nuts. The future cuisine of the Dominion. I say again,
my father was the most compassionate man in the history of *Homo
sapiens*, and he leaned toward my mother and held his hand to her
forehead, supporting her poor head while she emptied her extrinsic
puke. The acid made her voice high pitched as a dog-whistle. "I need
… " she said. And Dad said, "Anything. Anything at all."

"I need a home," said my mother. And at once the nausea was gone.
She stood, clear-headed, wiping her mouth, ecstatic.

Dad was already walking toward the campfire. He had the wisdom
to stop halfway and sit down on a storm-fallen tree. My mum joined
him. They stared at the water for three hours. The two couples ignored
one another all afternoon and into the evening when a waning moon
climbed out of the forest in the south. Then my dad, looking at the old
moon, said, "This is good land."

The Cree nodded. The beautiful woman rocked to an unheard song.

"My woman is carrying a child," said my dad.

The Cree gave him a scathing look. It was in bad taste to speak of
one's good fortune to a stranger.

"We'll pay a dollar an acre."

The Cree's head went up. He motioned to the woman who produced a bag with a beaded string and handed it to him. The Cree
opened it, withdrew a piece of paper. "One-hundred-and-sixty dollars,"
he said. My parents were startled by his voice, startled to hear a French
timbre on the syllables.

My mother had the money she'd earned in her eighteen months as a
man. She'd kept it in her hat. She handed it to my father, who handed
it to the Cree, who handed it to his beautiful companion. The two men
shook hands. Thinking she might enjoy the privileges of manhood for
a few more months, my mother offered the Cree her hand, but he
looked at her with gentle ridicule. He said, "Your baby will have a long
life." His voice was soft.

Then he removed his hat and filled it with river water and doused
the fire, and soon my mother and father were alone in the dusk on one-
hundred-and-sixty acres of bush by the Red.

ELIZABETH HAYNES

The Great Unlonely Silences

Nari perches at the top of Healy Pass, looking at the yellow larches speckling the meadow below. She had come here alone, leaving the Sunshine parking lot — gondola cars creaking empty in the wind — climbed up the ski-out, then the narrow spruce- and fir-lined trail, skirted the ice-skiffed puddles, careful not to tread on untrammelled ground. The sky was full of shifting half-clouds. Other than a teal-Goretexed couple, she had met no one.

She lies back in the moss, imagines herself slogging through the bush behind panting, heavily laden horses, the squelch of hooves in mud and cries of "git on." She wonders if women came up here at all a hundred years back, when there wasn't a rescue service, trails, huts. She imagines herself the first white woman to accompany the expedition that reached this pass. Chosen for her mountaineering skills, honed in the Alps and Himalayas.

Yeah right. Women probably weren't allowed to hike back then, kept too busy sewing and cooking and cleaning and running after kids. And dying in childbirth. But what if you wanted to, loved the mountains like she did, couldn't stay away. What then?

Nari opens her pack, fumbles among water bottle and pile jacket and toque and mitts for lunch. She extracts a rather squashed peanut butter sandwich, bites, chews slowly, pushing the stuff from one cheek to the other. The clouds, darker now, obscure the last piece of blue sky. The wind whistles up the pass, carrying a faint sound of bells. Passing. She remembers a Christina Rossetti poem from school:

> *Who has seen the wind*
> *neither you nor I*
> *but when the trees bow down their heads*
> *the wind is passing by.*

She wonders if the teal couple will make it. They looked tired. You can always tell the tired ones by their sweat, their laboured breathing and grunted greeting (if they offer any at all) — and by their "look," one of irritation and determination, scowled at their not yet broken-in boots, a look that says "I came out to get to the top of this pass/mountain/glacier/scree slope, and I'm going to make it if it kills me." Which it does, sometimes. It. Mountains, rock, scree. Snow and ice. Elements. Elemental. Elementary, my dear Watson.

Nari studies Elementary Education with a specialization in Language Arts. Though the way Mr. Klein is cutting, it doesn't seem a good choice at the moment. She unglues a glob of peanut butter from the roof of her mouth, picks up *The Canadian Rockies Trail Guide* and reads:

> The pass offers an excellent perspective on the surrounding landscape. The block of peaks beyond the ridge to the northeast is the Massive Range, dominated by Mount Brett on the left and Mount Bourgeau to the right. Standing as a landmark to the southeast — nearly 30 kilometres distant — is the "horn" spike of Mount Assiniboine...the highest mountain in Banff National Park.

She has seen this all before, of course, on clear winter days, the sun waltzing across the snow, snow not wind-crusted or heavy or baseless, but light, so easy to carve turns, knee up, down, up, down the pass to Egypt Lake and the warmth of hut and fire. And she's seen it in summer, multi-coloured hikers spread over rocks, eyeing peaks and bagging rays. But not today. The sun must be at Larch Valley with the rest of Calgary.

The wind whips hair into her eyes. In her ears is the faint sound of bells — strange, the couple didn't have bear bells. She fishes out her jacket and toque, thinks she should leave, a front of some sort seems to be moving in. The larches a hundred feet down the pass are disappearing. A mist, grainy like an old photograph, settles over her. The teal couple likely turned back.

Yet she sits, still, her hands tucked under her arms, putting out of her mind the essay on Whole Language and Reading awaiting her back home. "Who has seen the wind neither you nor I but when the trees bow down their heads the wind is passing by." Language. The silence in the pause between words thoughts.

What would it take to become a mountain guide? There must be some female ones. Haaaaa, says the wind. What about Sharon Wood, the first woman to climb Mount Everest, she's a guide? And from Canmore, too. Hoo hooooo, the wind laughs.

A fog descends, enveloping the larch. The Ramparts materialize and dematerialize, once. Or did she just imagine it?

Time to go, she mutters, it's going to be an all-nighter on that essay, so the sooner I get home the better.

The bells again, louder, right behind her.

Nari turns. At the crest of the pass, a shape appears from mist, a person, woman, small, middle-aged, her dark hair wound into a loose bun at the back of her neck. She wears only a blouse and a long woollen skirt. Carries a big stick with bells on it and a sketch pad. Mist swirls around her feet as she glides up to Nari, smiles and bows her head.

"I'm sorry, dear, to disturb you," she says. "You see, I've lost my party. I stopped to sketch a very late *rubus parviflorus*, mountain raspberry that is, just off the trail, and when I returned they had gone. They were two, my friend Mollie and Chief, our guide. And our horses, Buck, Pinto and old Baldy, of course."

"Well, I, uh, did see a couple. In teal goretex."

"In what, my dear?"

"Goretex."

"Goretex, goretex," the woman mutters. "Horseback?" she asks hopefully.

"No, they were walking. They looked like their boots were hurting. They might've turned back."

"Oh, mustn't've been my friends, thank you anyway. I suppose they're just ahead. My, that wind is chilly and I left my buckskin jacket with Chief. Well, my dear, although I'd love to tarry awhile and chat (that is a most interesting pair of trousers you are wearing, very clever those large pockets at the knees), but I must be on my way. I expect we'll be stopping tonight at one of the lakes yonder. I understand there's an Indian encampment there, and perhaps my friend Mr. Beaver will be among them."

"Oh."

"Of course, if you've got nowhere in particular to go you're welcome to join us. The Chief makes an excellent cup of tea."

"I, uh, thank you, I'd love to, but I need to be getting back."

"Well good for you, exploring on your own, and without even a horse or guide, I must say, that is very fine."

And with that, the woman turns and hurries down the pass, mist swallowing her body bit by bit until all Nari can make out is a few strands of escaped hair, whistling, like the laughing wind behind her. Until all Nari can see is the top of a yellowed larch, a bit of goat's beard flitting in the wind.

Nari closes her eyes tight, shakes her head. C'mon, you're imagining. When she opens them, all is grainy, grey. Leave, she tells herself, before you freeze to death. They'll find you — *Student Dies of Overexposure* — publish a picture. Your face will be ghostly white.

Wind rattles her packstraps, travels the open space between jacket and toque as she hurries down the pass, into the warmth of trees. The snow trails her, stinging her exposed skin. The ice puddles on the trail are frozen solid now, don't even crack when she jumps on them.

The gondola creaks, empty.

Her car is a lonely mound of white.

Nari looks out the kitchen window at the flakes swirling out of the dark. She turned the heat way up when she came in and now she is hot, sweating. Knows if she turns it down, she'll freeze. Only two temperatures in this old building, hot and cold. She picks up her pen: In the whole language approach to reading, words are not broken down. A story's essence is conveyed through context. Snowflakes dance around the bare poplars. "Come out and play," they say, "the paper can wait." No, she whispers, work — and returns to the blank page.

Nari sits on a bench, huddled in sweatshirt and tights, waiting for the L.R.T. She dressed wrong again, the weatherman said sun, but the sky is grey and threatening. The train pulls in and Nari rushes on so she'll get a seat. The L.R.T. is full of students and businesspeople. A grim-faced mother pushes stroller and toddler through the doors. No one helps her. "This is a Southbound train," says the vaguely female mechanical voice. "Destination: Anderson. Please stand clear of the doors." The man in front of Nari snores against the window. Two boys are playing hackysack by the doors. The train jerks forward and she closes her eyes. No one talks here, but it is a silence of a different kind. Not freeing, like the other, at the Pass. No story in this pause. Or is there? She opens her eyes. A woman is standing beside her. A small woman in an elegant fur hat and long brown coat, carrying a leatherbound book. The woman from Healy Pass!

The L.R.T. lurches into Olympic Plaza. Doors slide open, the woman glides off. Nari fights through the lounging legs of teenagers and hurries after her, keeping the fur hat in her sights as it weaves between rushing office workers.

What are you doing, she mutters, the paper you slaved over all night, that is due by 10 a.m. today, one whole letter grade deducted for late papers? She crashes into some kids in school uniforms, mumbles a sorry. Damn the woman's gone. No, there's the hat, waltzing across four lanes of traffic, heading down the Stephen Avenue Mall.

Nari speeds up, almost running now, but the woman is faster, slipping effortlessly past throngs of workers. She turns into the Convention

Centre and Nari follows, opening the door just in time to see her vanish into the Glenbow Museum.

A smiling white-haired woman looks up as Nari rushes in.

"Why, you're our first visitor this morning," the woman exclaims.

The hat disappears into an elevator. "That will be t …," the woman calls, but Nari's taking the stairs, two by two, around the Aurora Borealis, past Nineteenth-Century Art, past Fur Trade and the giant tipi, past Firearms and Artillery and Edged Weapons, turning the corner just in time to see the woman glide off the elevator and into the archives.

The archivist looks up. "I'm sorry, the archives are only open to the public from…"

"The woman, where did she go?"

"Woman?"

"In the long coat."

"I didn't see a woman…"

"Yes! In an old-fashioned coat, with a large book, she just came in, you must have seen her."

Just then, Nari spies the hat peeking over a bookshelf in the next room. She rushes over. The woman beckons Nari with a gloved hand, her mouth is open, she seems to be speaking but Nari can't understand, the archivist is babbling something about the public and appointments. "Shhhh," Nari says. "Be silent. I can't hear."

The woman begins to fade, her boots first, then her coat, her lips, her whole face lightening, her hat losing density until she's only an outline, an image, like something caught accidentally in a photograph, behind the real subject.

The air is heavy where she was and presses Nari's hand down to a shelf with a leatherbound volume: *Banff — Mountaineering, 1900-1917*. She opens it and reads:

American Ladies Complete Four Month Packtrip
Two American ladies, Miss Mollie Adams, unmarried, of New York and Mrs. Mary Schäffer, widow of the esteemed Doctor and Botanist, Charles Schäffer, of Philadelphia journied, unchaperoned but for two male guides, into the mountain wilderness in search of the headwaters of the North Saskatchewan and Athabasca rivers. According to Mrs. Schaffer, they slept in the rough, forded raging rivers, climbed glaciers and studied rocks and flowers.

Below, a picture: her woman, Mary Schäffer, smiling at the camera from the top of a pass, from the back of a horse.

Mrs. Schäffer told this reporter she loves the outdoors and encourages women to explore it, as travellers and, in the future, she hopes, as guides. She ...

"Come along now, Miss."
A security guard takes Nari's arm and escorts her out of the museum.

Ten thirty. She sits in the W.R. Castell Library, reading *A Hunter of Peace*, about Mary Schäffer Warren, explorer, artist, photographer, botanist, a Quaker woman who married her guide, Billy "Chief" Warren, in 1915 and settled in Banff. Nari reads this:

> There are few women who do not know their privileges and how to use them, yet there are times when the horizon seems restricted and we seem to have reached that horizon, and the limit of all endurance, — to sit with folded hands and listen calmly to the stories of the hills we so longed to see, the hills which had lured and beckoned us for years before this long list of men have ever set foot in the country. Our cups splashed over. Then we looked into each other's eyes and said: "Why not? We can starve as well as they; the muskeg will be no softer for us than for them; the ground will be no harder to sleep upon; the waters no deeper to swim, nor the bath colder if we fall in," — so — we planned a trip.
>
> We learned the secret of comfort, content and peace on very little of the world's material goods, learned to value at its true worth the great un-lonely silence of the wilderness.

From her seat by the window she watches the lunchtime mob thronging out of city hall, rushing along sidewalks. Cars rev at intersections, afraid of stalling in the cold. Her essay, "Whole Language and Reading," lies at the bottom of her pack. If she leaves now, she can be in Banff by one. If she leaves now, she can watch the articulation of needles — yellow/orange/green — hear the sibilance of snow, feel the glide of ice on mud, the plosion of cold air in lungs, the friction of wind on neck. She can be silent. She can speak.
She signs out the book and goes.

GEORGE BOWERING

Parashoot!: Diary of a Novel

The Nicola Valley runs as beautiful as can be, especially now that the main highway runs elsewhere, from Kamloops down to Merritt, in the high plateau country. If you were an Indian in that country you would probably speak words from a number of languages, and after a while some of the languages would be white people's languages. If you were an Indian in the Nicola in 1879 you would talk the way the Kamloops people talk, and the people up the river, too. You would know how to talk Okanagan and Chinook. Your talk would be injured by English words and French words the fur traders brought in. And then there were still some of the other words, the strange words the oldest Nicola people still had to use when they were telling their stories.

The old people would tell their stories, filled with those strange words.

"Yeh, yeh," you would say, and look serious, but some of those words would be words you only had to know for these stories.

Some of the stories were the truth and some of the stories were stories. Well, that was the way. The smartest people were the oldest people, and when they got to be old and told stories they no longer cared if you said what is the truth and what is a story.

I wrote "By noon he was a corpse" in someone's cabin up on Tod Mountain, closed the little writing machine, and got into my Volvo.

That is, there is somebody writing all this. I was not going to mention that, or at least not often, meaning not to skew a reader's attention or even pleasure, until the following story happened.

It's a forty-five-minute drive from Tod Mountain to Kamloops. There, if you are going to town instead of the Secwepemc Centre, you cross one of the bridges over the Thompson. I crossed the main bridge, and instead of heading for an artery I took the quick right turn, a truck route. River Road, it said. Big machines clawing at the riverbank, dust in the air, detours. Now this is more like it, I thought.

Around a detour, across from a beer bottle deposit, there was a little square park with a grass surface, elm trees on three sides, some kind of European pines along the fourth. A sign proclaimed Pioneer Cemetery. I stopped the Volvo and got out. In one corner of the park there is an

L-shaped monument, old gravestones set side by side horizontal now in concrete. I looked at the grass again. There were rectangular patches of different-looking grass. There were slight depressions. Different colours. A peaceful looking place, and deserted, only a few blocks from a mall filled with smoking teenagers.

I decided to see how many names I recognized in the L. There were some nineteenth-century storekeepers and their wives I knew. Hello, I said. Often there was information that the person was from Scotland. The names all sounded quite European.

Then I went for a little walk across the grass. Immediately I came upon one grave all alone in the grass. There was the usual rectangle of stone or plaster or concrete — something hard, in any case — in the middle of the grass. And there was a flat horizontal grave marker. Here is what it proclaimed:

> "In Memory of John T. Ussher — 1844-1879
> — Killed by the McLean Bros."

Do you have a son about fifteen years old? What if a man with whiskey on his breath put a black bag over his head and then put a thick bristly rope around his throat, fixed the thick knot under his ear, and pulled the lever that dropped the trapdoor under his slippered feet?

Whenever I pass through dry country, big stones, few trees, maybe sagebrush and cactus, the thought comes to me that this is the way landscape is supposed to be, or this is the way God meant the world to look like. Growing up in that kind of country, though, I read the Bible and other such books, and there it was, God's original plan, the garden of Eden. When Adam and Eve and all the rest of us got thrown out, it was into a kind of desert they got thrown. All through the Bible, whenever people are thrown out somewhere it is always into the desert. Of course, where the Bible was written just about all the country looks like the desert.

Where I grew up it looked a lot like the landscape in western movies. We played western movies a lot, with sixguns and all, but no horses. It helped a lot to be able to crouch with your sixgun behind a clump of real sagebrush. We wore neckerchiefs all the time. When we wanted something, we pulled the neckerchiefs up under our eyes.

I didnt think of it as landscape. It was just the Valley and especially the hills. There were a lot of plants I didnt know the name of, but I recognized them. I knew where there were caves. I knew what spoor was, from the books I read after I got home in the dusk. I knew what coyote shit looked like.

The Overlanders acted out the most famous story of courage in the history of white people in the Canadian west. These were people who had the nerve, in the middle of the nineteenth century, to travel from Ontario to Winnipeg, pick up some livestock there, and head for the middle of British Columbia. In Fall of 1862 the Overlanders were travelling down the North Thompson River. They hadnt had anything to eat for several days. There was food all around them, but they did not know how to see it. They needed Indians to stay alive.

So they were really happy to see their first Indian village. They grinned in their scraggly beards and shouted to each other as they brought their heavy rafts to shore and caught them up against the urgent water. They could not see any signs of life around the village.

So they walked up to the tipis and looked inside. They looked inside all of them. All they saw were dead bodies lying on the ground inside the tipis, lying next to one another, all ages.

The Overlanders did not even look around for food. They got out of the village as fast as they could.

Farther down the river they saw another Indian village and came close to the shore, but they did not see any signs of life in the village. They continued down the North River. They did not look at the Indian villages.

When they got to the South River they found some white men. Luckily they found some Native women, too, because the day after their waterlogged craft fetched up on Fort Kamloops dirt, Mrs. Schubert had a baby. Mrs. Schubert was the only woman in the company of 220 men. She had three little children with her. At Fort Kamloops there was no doctor and there were no white women. The Native women showed Mrs. Schubert how to have a baby on the high plateau. In a few days her husband and his fellows would begin to look around for useful land.

They thought all the Indians would disappear, and at least that sticky problem would go away. In places such as Victoria, people thought it was too bad, but perhaps the best thing overall, in the long run.

Many of the Shuswap people thought they would all disappear, too. They were filled with sadness. They were too tired to go out far into the mountains to bring back food and skins. The Shuswap people wondered who had sent the white people.

The Cheyennes had a saying: "A nation is not conquered until the hearts of its women are on the ground."

The white men needed furs and food at first. Then they needed land and women. The white people kept sending their men across the ocean and leaving their women at home. The Shuswap and Okanagan men did not want to go across the ocean and help themselves to the spare white women. But the white men wanted women to do the kinds of jobs that seemed more like work than adventure. While they were at it, the white men also wanted someone other than each other and their horses to stick their penises into. But in the Shuswap and Okanagan communities there was not all that much time spent on war, so there was not a significant surplus of women.

It was a problem in arithmetic.

One day in the late 1860s, a group of young Okanagan men arrived at a fairly new ranch at the north end of the big lake. All the wranglers were out in the hills, rounding up four-footed property. The Okanagan men went into every building and gathered every Okanagan woman in sight. They did not take anything else. They did not break anything or burn anything. They did not leave any feathered lances on a forty-five-degree angle in the dirt. There was a table with a nearly full bottle of Hudson's Bay whiskey on it, and they just left it there. The dogs barked and snarled all around the feet of their horses, but they did not shoot any dogs. Hundreds of blackbirds were walking all over the manure on the vegetable patch, confident and industrious.

The Okanagan men put the Okanagan women on their horses. They made them leave all their cleaning utensils and sewing kits behind them. They wouldnt let them make the beds. The women did not make any noise. One of them was carrying a baby on a board at her back. Clip clop. That's the way the horses walked back home, clip clop.

While the Shuswap and Okanagan people were negotiating their confederacy and scaring the pants off the more recent occupants of the area, the Nez Percé people a little to the south were at war with the

United States Army. This happened because white people located some gold in the Salmon River and the Clearwater River on the Nez Percé reservation. And wherever there is gold there is timber, so in came the settlers, business as usual on Indian ground.

Chief Joseph and his soldiers said enough is enough, and so in 1877 they declared war on the United States. This scared the pants off a lot of USAmericans, because Chief Joseph's 250 soldiers fought to a draw with 5,000 bluecoats. A lot of bluecoats and a lot of Nez Percé women and kids lost their lives in Chief Joseph's war.

In Kamloops and Victoria they were reading about the Nez Percé war.

Most people thought that eventually smallpox and other European diseases would turn the Indian people into history. But in the meantime you didnt want Indians on the warpath.

The United States government reached an agreement with Chief Joseph and his soldiers. The Nez Percé should have known better. They thought they were going back to the little bit that was left of their reservation. But the U.S. government sent them to settle some malaria country in Oklahoma, the former Indian Territory.

They read about that in Victoria.

☞

It was getting harder to find skins for the Hudson's Bay Company, and it was getting harder to find salmon for the people. Sometimes when a Shuswap person went to the river to find fish he would end up in a courtroom. He was guilty of trespassing. They told him what they meant by trespassing, but who could understand this language when the words in it did not mean what the things were? They said the cow people now owned the land beside the river. Sometimes they only leased the land in case their cows wanted to walk over there. If a Shuswap fisherman walked on that land to get to the river he was guilty of trespassing.

It was as hard to understand as the sin. The priests came to the village every year and talked about the sin. They made a bad smell and a bad noise and talked in their language about the sin. They did not explain trespassing. They wanted fish, too.

When the priests made their buildings they took water into them, and they took Shuswap babies into the buildings and put water on their faces. Water which the salmon had passed through. They did not know what they were doing. When the white people made babies inside Shuswap women, they did not know what they were doing.

It was not trespass or sin, because they did not wind up in a courtroom and they did not have to give things to the priests and their buildings.

They did not see some Shuswap people walking across cow country to paint pictures on stones.

The guards were used to fighters and even killers in that cell block. There were a lot of USAmericans in the Province. There were a lot of Indians who got whiskey from the USAmericans in exchange for furs and secret stories about valuable stones. There were far more men in the Province than there were women. If badly shaven men find themselves in such a country, they have to do something with the whiskey in their veins. So they fight. Sometimes they kill. Sometimes they just bring blood to the surface.

But the guards did not remember anyone like the McLean brothers and Alex Hare. They were not USAmericans. They were not Indians. They were something else that had come down from the country no one here could imagine. They were a species. There werent even any stories about this kind of person.

"I wonder if there's a lot of them up there," said one guard.

The two guards were smoking poorly made cigarettes under the protection of an eave. It was not raining, and it was not snowing. Solid wetness was coming down. It slid on the ground. It slimed the bare branches of a catalpa tree.

"They look something like Indians," said the second guard.

"They're no Indians. They're something else."

"They look something like Indians. Except that little one. He's got light hair. Looks around thirteen."

"He's a killer," said the second guard.

"I seen killers before now."

They stood back as far out of the dreadful falling wet as they could. They pulled out the makings and fumbled and produced two more badly made cigarettes. They leaned their backs against the whitewashed wall.

"Well, people will be taking a good long breath now the Indian uprising isnt going to happen," said the first guard.

"They ought to have a look at these here halfbreeds now. People wouldnt worry so much."

"Well, the oldest one."

"Yeah, he'd make me a little nervous, I have to admit. I mean if he wasnt chained to a wall. Even with that hole in his side."

"Can you understand that language they're always talking?"

"Probably Indian."

The wind shifted and sent a gust of mushy wet stuff into their faces. They turned to face the wall until the wind went off another way.

"Another thing I cant understand. If there was going to be an Indian uprising like they say, how come these kids was supposed to be the big troublemakers? How come the Apaches or whatever didnt come swooping down out of the hills? These guys aint Indians."

"Are they white boys?" asked the second guard. He threw his crumbling cigarette into the goo on the ground.

"Hell, no!"

"How many more of them kind you figure they got up there in the country?" asked the second guard.

"I hope to hell there aint too many of them."

"You said it."

"Have to hang the whole works of them, reckon."

The lawyers stood the way they always stood. They made all the gestures they were used to. Holding spectacles to eyes while bent to read aloud from a thick volume. Striding tall enough to strain their waistcoat buttons as they used all the frugal space in this little outpost courtroom. Raising an arm on which a cloak hung nicely as they indicated four objects of the Crown's scrutiny.

The jury waited for all this language to finish so that they could get to the hanging.

The witnesses from ranch country were wearing their best outfits. Their hair was slicked back from their foreheads. They said that they knew all about the McLeans and Mister Hare. Some of our Breeds are good hard-working individuals, they said, and some just dont know the meaning of property.

The lawyers worked in the blur of history, and they wanted to make this trial as much like a trial in a big city in England as was possible. They were working in a small building beside an icy river that most people would think too far west to picture. But they were in the middle of the place their lives would be given to. Following their deaths they would have streets and lakes and towns named after them.

Look, said the lawyers. The Government allows these sons of two races to drift loose, keeps them outside the school and the church, stands idly by while they learn to take other men's horses and cattle and whiskey. Then all at once the Government changes the rules and sends an armed posse to their mountainside campfire. Who among even our luckily educated youth could respond with cool sanity in such an event? Look, said the lawyers, you have heard from the highest voice in this courtroom that our society is responsible for the error-filled path these lads have taken. We know where true guilt lies.

Listen, said the Crown's lawyer, every act of the prisoners showed that they had entered on a systematic opposition to authority.

The jury waited.

It was an interesting trial. Some day an author should make a court-room drama out of it. All the material is there. It will break your heart.

Newspaper readers in Victoria and New Westminster and Kamloops and Toronto loved it. They belonged to a culture of words set in type. They liked to tell stories to their children and neighbours, but words set in type were like words cut into stone. Except that you could hold the newspaper in front of you, open the pages, snap the paper and commence reading, anywhere you wanted to. Words set in type could lay iron tracks across the mountains. Words set in type could not be mistaken, or modified. They were not stories. They were not true stories or legends or family property. Words set in type were the end results of centuries of civilization and serious consideration. They precipitated solid facts out of the fluid of the day's confusions. In parts of this frontier there were flagstones where once there was mud. Words set in type were the flagstones of history. People who could set words in type could go anywhere in the world and make order out of rough country where the unorganized natives had only passed their short lives gathering available berries and slaying unfortunate animals that had wandered into their ambit.

When I was a boy in the Okanagan Valley I looked around a lot. Never knew what I was looking for. Never found arrowheads or ancient Spanish coins in the dust. Found a skeleton once and put the rocks back on top. Found a little pistol once and kept it till it disappeared on me. Found a necklace made of Dutch money. But no one ever told me what to look for.

I was scared of McLeans from the rumours I had heard, and I kept an eye out for them. Kenny McLean wasnt in my school anymore. I started to wonder whether he was a ghost that came and sat in my classroom for part of a winter.

When I was a boy I was not told anything about the Okanagan Valley, but I learned a lot about the James gang and the Daltons and the Clantons. All those wild and dangerous brothers from Missouri, where my grandfather had been a boy. But what about the McLeans? Did they escape? Did Archie McLean escape? Is that a true story about the Kanaka hangman and the severed ropes and the quick horses?

When I was a boy I knew that the James gang and the Daltons were buried deep in history. But I kept my eyes out for McLeans. I kept my eyes open for McLeans whether they were a gang of gunslingers on the vengeance trail, or peaceful men living out their lives in the hayfields, or ghosts. I did not believe in ghosts, but I believed in God. Still, if there was a God, there was a book about him, and in that book there were a lot of stories about things that can happen even if they are hard to believe. You have to want to believe such things, I had somehow learned.

I still want to believe some things that are hard to believe. There are no gravestones for the Wild McLeans, so you had to wonder whether they were dead, or whether they had ever lived. The field where they were buried no longer exists.

Who would hang a fifteen-year-old boy?

In the beer parlour in Lawrence there is a *karaoke* machine in one corner, but no pool tables anymore. Now the tables do not have ciga-rette-burned terry cloth on them. Now there are framed pictures of famous locals all around the walls. If you look at the pictures it will not be long until you find a photograph of Windy Bone. Windy Bone is the most famous Indian in Lawrence. I dont know how old he is, but what-ever his age is, he doesnt look that old. I have never heard anyone call Windy Bone an Elder. If you keep looking at the framed pictures on the walls in the beer parlour, you will keep on finding pictures of Windy.

It is afternoon, and Windy Bone is sitting at a table in the cool shade of the beer parlour. He has a glass of beer in front of him, but he isnt drinking it. Windy says he doesnt drink beer anymore, but he likes to sit here with a glass. Before they closed the two pool halls in Lawrence, Windy Bone was the best pool shark in town. Bang, the eightball would be gone, and Windy wasnt even looking when he shot it.

He is wearing his hat, a black stetson with silver conches making up the band around it. He is wearing strong riding boots that were pol-ished not too long ago. He has a handsome nose and slightly puffed cheeks now. He slouches in his beer chair. If you are not too shy he will tell you stories. He does not usually tell you the legends you might expect, or the true tales you might expect. Windy has a sense of humour that tells you that you had better be content to be a white man surrounded by irony. A lot of white people in Lawrence say that Windy's a "character." They mean to be comfortable and patronizing. Boy, are they dumb!

Here is Windy Bone's account of the Indian method for catching wild deer.

An Indian rides into deer country and leaves his horse tethered to a tree. Then he finds himself a nice spot in the shade and waits for a deer to show up. Indians are very silent and patient. When a deer shows up the Indian waits for a while. Lets the deer get over his anxiety and start cropping grass. Then the Indian begins his stalking. He is very quiet and extremely patient, making very small moves, stopping after every move to blend in with the scenery. Once in a while the deer lifts his head with the antlers on it and sniffs the air. But the Indian is blending with the scenery and he is downwind.

It takes a long time, but the Indian is slowly sneaking up on the deer. Now he is just a few steps behind him, blending in. Now comes the hardest part, and this part is what makes an Indian different from a white man. The Indian has to get right up behind the deer without the deer's noticing. Now there is nothing to hide behind.

The Indian makes a careful step and stops. The deer doesnt see him. The Indian is right behind him but the deer is looking in every other direction. Now the Indian is right behind the deer. He can reach out and touch him if he wants to. In one patient and unseen motion the Indian raises his right arm. His first finger is pointing right at the deer. The deer's tail is up. That's the way deer are. In one movement the Indian puts his finger right into the deer's hole. Quick, before the deer can move, the Indian crooks his finger.

Then the deer moves. Well, most people have seen how a deer can move. He can go from standing still and maybe quivering a little, to jumping through the forest in no time flat. You cant see him warming up. He is just gone.

This is where the Indian pays for his deer. The deer is jumping over rocks and under pine trees and between cactuses. The Indian maybe weighs just about as much as the deer, maybe a little less. He's hanging on for dear life, his finger crooked. Every time the deer comes down, the Indian comes down, on rocks or cactuses or greasewood. Every time the deer jumps again, the Indian's arm is nearly torn off, and he has to concentrate all his attention on his finger. All his body's strength has to keep that finger crooked. When the deer is coming down, the Indian tries to get his feet on the ground, take a few fast steps. But then he's off again.

The deer is hauling somebody that's just about his own weight. The jumps get shorter and lower. After a while the deer's taking a few steps between the jumps, and the Indian can get on his feet and run for a while. Now the deer is just walking fast. He cant jump any more. Pretty soon he cant walk either. This is when the Indian congratulates the deer for a good run, and then he has him. If he hasnt lost his knife along the way.

"That's the Indian way of deer hunting," says Windy.

"I never knew that."

"There's only one thing to look out for."

"I would have thought there were a lot of things to look out for," says the white man.

"Only one thing to look out for."

"What's that?"

"That deer, if he suddenly decides to take a quick left turn, all you've got is a brown finger," says Windy Bone, looking at the full glass of beer on his table.

When they talked about revenge, the priests said that only God was permitted to take a life, and only God was allowed to take vengeance.

"There are other gods with other ideas," said Allan McLean.

"There is no god but the Lord," said Father Chireuse.

"Is this Lord going to get even with Mara for what he did to our sister?"

"There are many Maras and many sisters," said the priest.

The priest sounded as if he had rehearsed wisdom. Allan could not talk that way.

"Will our sisters avenge us?" he asked. He knew what the young priest from France would say.

"Women are the vessels of the Lord's love," said Father Chireuse. He did not know whether the *demi-sauvage* mind could understand the spirituality proposed by human flesh.

Allan looked at the young man in the black skirt for half a minute without speaking, though it was obvious that he would speak. He was going to tell a story to the priest. He wondered whether the priest would know exactly what he was hearing.

COWBOYOGRAPHY

ARTHUR SLADE

Jesus Busts a Bronc

So I'm at the Shaunavon rodeo sittin in the stands and it's a typical small town day flags waving clowns laughing hot dogs sizzling and damn if these trumpets don't play a loud glorious note and a voice on the intercom announces *the next rider is Jesus Christ* and I doubletake twice saying *Jesus Christ* and this man in funny robes beside me pipes up with yeah, *Jesus Christ Almighty and he's pretty good I've been following him for about two thousand years* and so I sit back in my seat and wait and wait and wait cause there's all this opera singing first and a smoke show and angels performing some mystery play and my attention starts to wander so I turn to the guy next to me and ask *so what's your name anyway buddy* and he answers kinda sad *it's Judas*

So finally the music's over and there's this commotion in the arena you see they've just wheeled out this stall with a dark dark one-eyed stallion inside and he's kicking up dust and snorting fire and his name's Mephistoffily or some such long-winded thing he looks evil mean and I know this horse comes from *hades acres* the big burning ranch down under then another trumpet sounds and in walks Jesus or the holy cowboy as we call him in the west and he's wearing the slickest snakeskin boots rawhide chaps blue jeans a white T-shirt a big texas hat and a leather glove on his right hand and he bows to everyone then swings himself over the fence lands square on the bronc grabs the rigging nods to the gatekeeper and the crowd takes a deep long breath

do you know who I am Judas asks me right then and I get kind of annoyed but I remember something about thirty pieces of silver and a kiss and him stringing himself up and I mutter *yeah yeah yeah* and he says *everyone remembers me for that one day* then he shuts up cause there's this noise like trees snapping in two and the bronc busts outta the open gate his back end bucking his body twisting in the air and that white hat Jesus was wearing goes shooting straight towards the heavens up there with sputnik I guess and the bronc hits the ground and the earth shakes and sparks explode off its hooves lava shoots skyward and somehow through all this fight and fire Jesus is hanging on and I can see he's grinning too

Judas kinda sighs saying *I never really knew what I was doing you know it seemed like the right thing at the time betrayin' him to the elders an them chief priests* and I think why of all the people in the world do I have to sit beside Judas Iscariot then there's this crack of thunder that silences everyone you see the stallion has leapt so high that he actually blots out the sun and angus-black clouds have darkened half the sky and the bronc kicks and bucks in the air like he's not ever gonna come down again then Jesus lets out a *yippe yi yay doggie* and lightning strikes them both lighting them up like those bright flashing signs in the city and the horse and Jesus plummet to the ground

and the crowd is going absolutely crazy bananas clapping and hooting and saying *right on Jesus* though for a second I think I can hear crying or sniffling beside me but then Christ digs his heels into that bronc's side and it gives its final burst of rebellion breathing fire twisting bucking and shaking like he's caught in a giant invisible paint shaker then he spins around so fast he looks like a tornado and you can't see a thing but dust smoke and ashes a moment or two later it all clears and there's Jesus smiling away his arms in the air and that bronc is whinnying and neighing and trotting backward and forward whichever way Jesus wants and the crowd cheers so loud they hear it in Ottawa

then the apostles come out and surround Jesus like bodyguards and the intercom announces *that's the end of the show folks* and people start lining up to meet the star performer and I see Judas beside me just staring like he's a kid looking through a glass wall at a prize he could never ever own and I get this kinda almost sad ache and so I ask *why don't you go down and talk to him you know he's got this rep of being a forgiving guy* and Judas just shakes his head and says *naw he said it would have been better if I was never born he doesn't ever want to see me again not after what I did to him* and for the first time I look right at Judas right at his face and he looks just like me or like my uncle or like someone I knew a long time ago then he pulls up his hood turns and he's gone away from the crowd out the back of the stands and I watch as he disappears into the great wide open space of the prairies

I look down at the people gathering around Jesus asking for autographs or blessings and Jesus is waving his hat and everyone's laughing and laughing and people are kneeling and the sun is bright and I feel my face cause there are tears in my eyes and I cannot tell if in this very moment I am feeling joy or sadness

JIM GREEN

Another Tall Bear Tale

Colin Hedderick told Dad about the time
he and his partner stumbled onto a bear,
it charged, Colin ran, then tripped,
dropped his rifle and kept running,
running round and round and round
a runty little clump of scrub willow.

The partner got hisself all in a lather,
being somewhat new to bear country doings
so every time the two of'm come around
he'd jack another cartridge outta his rifle.
No shooting mind you, just jack another
full round out into the crisp fall air.

About the fifth or sixth go-around
Hedderick was getting just a tad winded
so he hollered instructions to buddy —
"You run for awhile and I'll shoot."
So that's what they done. His partner
took the relay, Hedderick shot the bear.

Dad had his doubts about it at first too,
but Colin had the hide on the cabin floor,
a full head mount including the teeth
that Dad stumbled over on midnight trips
to the outside biffy, so what the heck,
with that kind of proof, it has be true.

Scotch and Soda

Jean Charles mentally measured the distance from his saloon chair to the coat rack. No problem. He carefully calculated a course that would carry him from the coat rack to the door. It could be done. Tipping his head back, he delicately drained off the last of the scotch, placed the glass carefully on the table, snugged his hat down onto his forehead, nudged his chair back and slowly rose to his feet.

Nodding his smiling regards to friends and neighbours, Jean Charles meticulously navigated his charted course out through the door of the Alberta Hotel, descended the three steps to the street with a slight rolling motion, set a new course for his mare at the hitching post.

Untying the reins didn't present any untoward difficulties and Jean Charles managed to get the reins over her head on the fourth attempt. He reached up for the horn with his left hand, shifting his weight in deliberate preparation to lifting his foot to the stirrup. His hand encountered the back of the saddle. Well now, that was a fine how-d'ya-do. He stood there smiling, trying to work it through, eventually concluding that he must be on the wrong side.

Walking around the other side of the mare, sure enough, Jean Charles found the saddle horn alright, but darned if he could locate the reins or indeed the mare's head, so he went around the other side … After several go-arounds, he finally found himself mounted, desperately clutching the horn with both hands lest it disappear somewhere off into the night again. But when he reached out for the reins, all he could find was the mare's tail. A perplexing turn of events to be sure.

A raucous cheering section had gathered in the street by that time, so the organizers of the event gently pulled the old gentleman off the mare, kept him chatted up while the saddle was switched around and cinched tight, remounted him, handed him the reins, turned the mare in the right direction and gave her a slap on the rump. She knew the way home. It was just another Saturday night in town.

Milk and Honey

Not milk and honey
for all of them,
not by a long shot.
Out east of here
on the open prairie
forsaken homesteads
hidden in coulees
roofs slumped in
tired walls leaning
vacant window holes
door frames askew
attest to failures
of those who left
and inside one
testimonial relic
desperate letters
scrawled in wood
FROZE OUT
DRIED OUT
BLOWED OUT
STARVED OUT

SLIM DAVIS

Clearwater Country

There is a little piece of country and it lies a long way back,
There are no roads or highways, and you always have to pack.
A skeletal forest spikes the sky, high up in the pass,
Vales and hills are covered with a rich and virgin grass.

In the valley horses are feeding in grass up to their knees,
A wild horse stands and switches flies beneath some ancient trees.
In the dusk of evening the Coyotes yip and howl,
High up in the bruley, the Grizzlies skulk and prowl.

At night the boys ride into camp, line the pan with biscuits, put on
    the coffee pot,
By the time they've settled down, Supper's good and hot!
After they have finished, they sit and roll a smoke,
They talk about the mispent life of many an old cowpoke.

They talk about the weather, and why packing doesn't pay,
Then unroll their blankets, and are glad to hit the hay.
One dreams he rides a salty pony, of pitching down a hill,
He grits his teeth and kicks his heels for fear that he might spill.

Another dreams he's running a wild band, along the glacier ice,
He wonders if his pony stumbles, will he see paradise?
They are up in the morning, sometime before the sun,
They talk about the packing and where the wild bunch run.

They put their saddle on some pony, and head into the wood.
So why not go out packing, the life is plenty good!

Monty

Monty was a saddle horse, his coat was shiny black,
If I was chasing horses he would never lose the track,
I rode in the Mountains and in Valleys far away,
He would always bring me back to camp at the end of day.

One day I found a big pack horse, he had been gone a year or two,
I threw my rope to catch him, it came down good and true,
He began to jump and pull when he felt the noose,
He did not want to get caught and he tried to get loose.

He pulled Monty down in a hole, Monty fell on my leg,
The hole wasn't very deep, it was shaped like an egg,
Monty's feet was on the bank, he was on his back,
The old pack horse would roll him up when he took up the slack.

Every time he rolled him up, my leg came further out,
So I waved my hat at the packhorse to make him jump about,
Two Ravens came by and in a tree they took a seat,
They knew that if I did not get loose, they'd have lots to eat.

I finally got my leg out and stood there on the ground,
I knew I could get Monty out if I could turn him round,
I tied Monty's feet to the packhorse and made him pull back,
He turned Monty around when he took up the slack!

I took the rope off Monty's feet, he got up with a bound,
The old packhorse was snorting and Monty looked around,
I looked at that old packhorse, I said "You're wild as any Deer,
I guess you've earned your freedom, I'm going to leave you here."

There never was a dull moment with Monty, take him to a creek
    to drink,
He would try to dump you off, just for the fun of it, I think!
If you stood on a cutbank to see what you could see,
Monty would try to knock you off, if you didn't grab a tree!

Monty was a good pony, he always done his best,
I rode him for many years, all over the West!
Life is like a campfire, you start out warm and bright,
And as the years slip by, you burn out in the night.

Trail from Red Deer to Pine Lake

The road from Red Deer to Pine Lake was a very bumpy ride,
It went through Willowdale and over the Divide,
It ran southeast along the ridges, hitting every rock,
Sometimes a wagon got stuck in the mud and made the horses stop.

There were mudholes in the Spring and frozen ruts in the Fall,
Often in the Winter, you could not see the road at all!
The road ran along a ridge for nearly a mile,
You had to let the horses rest every little while.

You came down off the ridge at the end of Schrader's Lake,
There is a grassy meadow where you can unhook and take a break,
If the day is getting late and the sun is out of sight,
You just set up your camp and stay there for the night.

The horseflies have gone to sleep, they've been biting all day,
And as the darkness gathers the mosquitoes come out to play.
You have to build a smoky fire out of a rotten log,
The mosquitoes don't like the smoke and go back to the bog.

As the moon comes over the treetops, the Coyotes start to howl,
This is joined by the hooting of an Owl,
From there the road ran through little hills, as crooked as a snake,
When you came out in the open, you could see Pine Lake!

The storekeeper was there to help unload the freight,
He said, "That ain't too bad, you're only one day late.
Turn the horses in the pasture, and stay a day or two,
Then go back to Red Deer if the sky is blue!"

DORIS BIRCHAM

The Prolapse

the sky is a dark quilt
stitched above our heads
where night has hidden the stars

we turn the light on inside the calving shed
watch a four-year-old heifer give a final push
see the calf's hips slide through the opening
behind its head and shoulders
the cord snaps
hind hocks and hooves
partly hidden inside the cow
are last to leave their dark world
the calf wet, slippery
lifts its head, draws its first breath
the cow struggles to stand, heaves
and in as little time
as it takes a star to fall
her womb turns inside out
like a sock   her womb
wrong side out
with placenta attached
hangs almost to her hocks
a ball of flame
pulsating

lariat halter disinfectant
she could hemorrhage
die in seconds
we work quickly together
place her in the *frog* position
knuckle her front knees beneath her
pull her back legs out straight behind
I drag her calf up close
where she can see it, smell it
talk to it, where it should help
distract her from the urge to push
I straddle her back

face backwards, feel the warmth of her
the dampness of her hair
I reach for her tail
hold it taut
while two pairs of hands
begin to undo the afterbirth
its velcro-like attachment
gently, one button at a time
mustn't let the placenta's weight
tear a blood vessel
a torn button, an artery throbbing
a ribbon of fire running wild

seven buttons remain
before the placenta is released
from its lifeline hold
the last one undone
the lifeless jelly of the afterbirth
falls to the straw

we wash the inside of the womb
hold the fiery ball
in blood-stained hands
slowly ease and push it back
inside the cow
the flame extinguished

next the suture tape
the long curved needle
stitches through the vulva
pulled like a drawstring
and tied

at our urging
the cow stands and her calf
encouraged by its mother's murmurs
makes a first floundering try
to get to its feet

we leave the newborn calf
nudging its mother's flank
leave the cow, her quenched fire
the secrets hidden deep within her

we step out into the dark
where the stars are buttoned
to the wrong side of the sky

Equinox Storm

At Coffee Row on a March day
warm with sun when winds are quiet
the conversation of retired ranchers
circles tables, one says
a storm front's movin' in
from the west, another recalls
the night he found twin calves
stretched flat out in a snow drift
tells how he warmed them
in the bathtub, saved both

The following three days
and nights, snow comes in sheets
tattered by wind, cold
fills every empty space

Flashlight in hand
ear flaps pulled down
looped twines in my pocket
I push through the dark
towards the corral
where cows stand bunched together
backs clumped with snow, icicles
stitched to their chins

Ear tags are no use now
I've learned to know these cows
by the fullness of the folds
beneath their tails
the tightening of udders
I look for uneasiness
listen for soft murmurs

The old lined-back cow
stands at the edge
of the herd, my eyes search
for a softening of the depression
beside her tail head
she follows my moves
head in the air
she skirts the herd
I flounder in a drift
try again to ease her
towards the shed
where there's a bed of straw
a wall against the wind

On the way back to the house
snow needles my eyes
wind has erased my tracks
the same wind that carries the sound
of the train whistle
from Piapot, seven miles
to the north

I re-set the alarm
ninety minutes to sleep
before the next rounds

The morning after the storm
half-tons line up outside the coffee shop
I knew it would be a bad one
one oldtimer says, *a couple of days*
before it hit, my saddle horse
spent most of one day lyin' down

his friend says, *back in '67*
I lost eleven calves
snow never let up
for three whole weeks

the stories they share
fill their morning hours
years roll backwards
as cows come alive in memory
rise up out of storms

ANNE SLADE

ghost story

marjorie's been living on her own
for half a century
on the old harrison place north of town
with her herd of crossbreds
and strip of oats along the creek

when she's lonely
marjorie saddles her mare
rides to the neighbours to borrow sugar
or exchange books
always needs some excuse
like she shouldn't take time for herself

she's a storyteller
everyone in the country has heard of her ghost
shimmering
between the barn and the well
searching and calling
charlie   charlie   charlie

marjorie says as how charlie homesteaded
on her place and when his wife took sick
in the winter of eighteen
he rode through a blizzard to fetch doc miller
holding the heat from her forehead
tight in his hand
till the cold leached it away

next day they found mrs charlie
out by the well
still
in her nightgown
her shawl wrapped around her shoulders
and the dipper frozen in her sculpted hand

they're buried together
in the municipal cemetery

but she searches for charlie like he isn't beside her
drifts from the barn to the well
calls
thin as the wind whispering through the loft
charlie   charlie   charlie

Company's Comin'

I got up at six, there were lunches to fix
for my man and the kids going to school.
Combed hair, tied shoelaces, wiped sticky faces
found swimsuits to take to the pool.

Gave each kid a hug, then picked up my mug,
sipped coffee as I waved from the door.
Looked at my list, and noticed I'd missed
a few of my last-minute chores.

We were gettin' guests, their first time out west,
they'd never been near a ranch,
I wanted things right, planned day and night
wasn't leavin' a thing to chance.

I'd baked homemade bread, made sure they'd be fed
home cookin' and ranch-raised beef,
pickles and jam and country cured ham
with a chokecherry wine aper'tif.

My man comes back in and he starts to grin
'cause I'm plannin' and I'm still not dressed.
He says,"Man, what a life, this bein' a wife!"
I tell him to give it a rest!

I can see by his face, he's got some place
he wants me to go, so I take a stand.
"I can't leave home, they're s'posed to phone."
He insists that he needs a hand.

"Oh, come on outside, no, this is no lie,
it'll take a few minutes, that's all.

No, you won't have to wait, just close some gates
you'll be back before they call."

I pull on tall boots and start in to root
for a jean jacket near my size
so if I'm sittin' down, and someone comes 'round
my nightie is somewhat disguised.

Pete stopped for a chat, an' I'm grateful that
he didn't notice I wasn't dressed.
Then I followed my man, and his gate plan,
and wondered about my guests.

You know the story, sure he said he was sorry
but it was an hour or more.
I whipped into the yard and hit the brakes hard
'cause the company's there at the door.

It's hard to describe how I felt inside,
'cause outside my nightie was blowin'
you see, it got caught in that gate up on top,
there was more than just flannelette showin'.

Here's a lesson hard-earned, each ranch wife should learn.
Sometimes your man has to wait.
Ease off on your stress, say "No" steada "Yes"
let him close his own doggoned gates!

ROSE BIBBY

Tales from the Hayshaker's Wife

This is a series of poems depicting the learning, the living, the loving and the laughter that keep the rural couple on the land.

For those who have ever wondered what it takes to keep the place and the partnership together when you have a husband and wife working together on a daily basis, I can tell you. It takes Love, Commitment, and a Sense of Humour. It also takes Learning, and for some of us the learning started early.

School of Farm Wifery

I was just newly married to a farmer
      and was confused about his machines
I only knew about planting and cleaning
      and canning and milking and fixing his jeans.

The tractor loomed like a monster of steel
      the binder and thresher were scary
And when he told me I'd have to drive that John Deere,
      I agreed, although I was wary.

I didn't know much about steering and clutching
      but the crops still had to be cut
So when he perched like an eagle on the old binder seat
      he must have had nerve — and lots of guts!

I soon realized that the seat of that tractor
      was not where I'd rather be
And by the time we got about halfway around
      I was gettin' a little bit SLEEP-y.

Then the tractor wheels hit a dead furrow
      I rocked through it lickity split
He flailed and bounced on the old tractor seat
      but managed to hang on to it.

I thought I heard some unusual words
    and vowed to pay more attention
But on coming around, I hit it again —
    the language was louder, and too bad to mention!

On the third round that fool thing surprised me again
    but by now I knew my mistake
So when the tractor wheel hit that dead furrow,
    I promptly jumped onto the brake!

He came off that seat like a shot from a cannon
    and ended up down in the binder
But I still thought, being a new hubby and all,
    his *words* could have *been a lot kinder*.

We've managed to partner for thirty-five years
    since that day my schooling began
But I guess I'll never earn my diploma
    because I just *can't* cuss like that man.

Some folk just seem to know more than others, and the Old Hayshaker will tell you that this is some advice he wishes he'd had a long time ago. He hopes it's not too late for some young farmers to take heed.

Testing ... Testing ...

The farm boy goes out searching for to find himself a wife
Someone who'll come and share the work and worry of his life
He likes that she is pretty, kinda rounded, not too lean
But he never seems to check out how she is around machines.

Then he puts that girl behind the wheel on baler, rake or plough
And his patience is a tested in so many places now
Soon you'll have that girl a backin' up the trailer on your hitch
Jackknifin' and a spinnin' tires, not knowin' which way's which

Or comin' down the hill into a granary on the yard
The brake and clutch are smokin' and the box is leanin' hard
And sometimes you have to watch the loader she's manipulatin'
It jumps and jerks, the hoses pulse and yer nerves just git to gratin'.

Then she's tryin' to get a corner with a pounder and a post
This is the sad manoeuvre that tears you up the most
The hitch is bent and battered and the far wheel's off the ground
The PTO is squealin' and the steering's come unwound

And she sets up there a dreamin' and a schemin' in her mind
How this damn machine is takin' up and wastin' *her* good time
And just when *you* are thinkin' that this surely ain't no fun,
She looks at you and grins and says, "How'm I doin', Hon?"

So to all of you young farmers, here's I think some good advice
When you're lookin' for a partner who's to be your new farm wife
Just check a little farther than the cut of her blue jeans
Try her out and see how she can handle your machines!

Being more or less forced into it, the Old Hayshaker will tell you that
this is the best way he knows to describe his wife.

How to Describe My Wife

She won't learn to swim and she won't learn to ride
  Though I've tried my damndest to teach her
She wants to argue when I know I'm right
  She's a charming, but obstinate creature.

She can't seem to get the hang of machines
  Especially my pull-type post pounder
And when she's out there helping to sort out the calves
  Confusion just reigns all around her

But she's pretty good natured, she laughs a lot
  She likes people, sunrises and roses
Still she's hard on the head and hard on the nerves
  And Hell on hydraulics and hoses!

I suppose he always thought that he could teach me everything I ever needed to know, but then, that's just like some of his other theories. He has theories about a lot of things, one of them being that women think differently than men, another being that women will try to reason their way out of any situation. So I just call this …

Sink or Swim or "A Woman's Reason"

He used to try to teach me to swim
     I hate water, the bathtub scares me
But he has this theory that women are built
     with extra air sacs roaming free
Inside their skin and parts of their body
     so they just naturally float.
I've never completely swallowed this line,
     I don't swim, I must tell you folks.

And he's tried to teach me to ride,
     to give'er up there on a horse.
He says that the reason I can't learn to ride
     is all in my head, of course.
So I got to thinking about air sacs and bodies
     and floating and all that he said
And started right in to comparing
     this reasoning to horses instead.

Now if women are built with extra air sacs
     floating in their hips and buttocks
And think of the air bags she's carrying
     on her body up close to the top
Add some cellulite just for good measure
     now with fat cells I'm having to cope
Just think of the buoyancy I'm thought to have
     when my horse takes off on a lope.

Picture me with my shoulders thrown back
     feet jammed down in the wood
Tummy tucked in, buttock sucked up
     and my grip on the line real good
Then my horse moves out and my mind starts to work
     so I grab the horn on the saddle
My nerves start to quiver, I shimmer and shake
     when those cells in me start doing battle.

And do they make clothes for well-endowed riders?
    picture shirts with little, wee snaps
Jeans with their tidy, tight waistbands
    and bras with elastic stretch straps
I've tried riding in tights like equestrians wear
    to girdle-in air sacs and flesh
And sport bras that crisscrossed my back like a vise
    and flattened those bags to my chest.

But it don't seem to help my dilemma
    in stretch, in sweats, or in jeans
Those fat and air pockets, like two pigs in a blanket,
    are battling it out at the seams ...
So Darling, I know that you think I can swim
    with what I have hidden inside
But the very same reason I can't sink in the water
    is the same one why I can't ride!!

Even the Old Hayshaker wonders how a guy is supposed to argue with that! So I just say:

Who's Perfect?

I never could handle a cheque book
    and by now I guess there's no hope
Tidy is not one of my strong points
    with neatness I never could cope

I beg to offer resistance
    in discussions about horses and cows
Instructions just seem to slip by me
    it was ever so bad, it's worse now

I'm forgetful about dates and engagements
    can never find the place that I wrote it
Have projects galore that I've started
    hundreds maybe, don't quote it

I'll do anything rather than housework
    and think up elaborate schemes
To put it all off till tomorrow
    so I can follow my dreams

I'm not really great around horses
    the equestrian way's not my bag
And over the years it's apparent
    that parts of me've started to sag

There might have been a Miss Perfect
    if you'd spent longer lookin' there Hon
But I can't believe being perfect
    Ever could be this much fun!

I guess, like people in all lines of work, we sometimes sit back and ask
— "What if?" What if we had not followed our dream and found other
lines of work? What if we hadn't made it work and had to leave? What
if …? Those are the days we sit up, take stock, and the Old Hayshaker
will tell you what …

The Good Things in Life Really Are…

There's a few things I've sorta got used to
    that I kinda like in my life
Like fresh coffee brewed in the morning
    a good-natured, hard-working wife …

Like two auction marts close beside me
    I go there to B.S. and look
Like the market report at the noon hour
    three girls and a wife that can cook …

Fresh air and space all around me
    land without too many stones
Cows grazing where I can watch them
    a warm fire when I come home

True friends I know I can count on
    a good horse that ain't testing fate
Good fences to keep down the worry
    and a woman who'll open the gates

But of all the things I'm enjoying
    I'll tell you there's none quite so fine
As snuggling close with my darlin'
    in sheets that's bin dried on the line!

I guess some of the very best things about the fact that we chose to live and work on the land are the appreciation we have for those who came before us, the appreciation of what the land has to offer us, and being able to laugh about the daily adversities that the job sends our way. One very good thing for me as a writer is that I am not only inspired by our surroundings, our work and our relationship, but also by the personality and support of my Old Hayshaker. As long as he keeps providing material, I'll keep writing the poems!

HILARY PEACH

Outlaw Girls

Honey hit the open road
with her gun still smoking

Honey was an outlaw
she was a wanted poster
she was a photograph
on every lamppost
in her eyes

Honey was an outlaw
she had no time for anything
she had a way with women
she was a wayward woman
she was a churlish thing
with a girlish disposition

they say she was too emotional
and they say it was all hormonal
and today they can treat these things
they say that she was moody
but she was only mad
and they say
that she was crazy
they say
that she was crazy
but she was only mad
she was an old woman
in a young girl's soul

The night that Honey pulled into town
she looked like a wildcat she'd been
driving all night through a craziness
that left her ragged and tornup
she was escaping the remains of a nasty
little love affair with a cancan dancer
just driving the backroads from town to
town with her memories devouring her

mind's eye like locusts and her heart so
near to breaking that every cloud or
tumbleweed or lone coyote caused her
to gasp and stumble until her own tired
lonely spirit was forcing her over to the
side of the road

The night that Honey pulled into town
all she saw was one more nameless ugly
little smalltown barroom full of bourbon
and nameless ugly little cowpokes soaking
their daily fears and longings in big glasses
of watery beer

She ordered two shots
and drank them
without breaking eye contact
with the bartender
he was later heard to remark

     it was like i had locked eyes
     with something
     completely wild
     which is something
     i have never
     locked eyes with before

Billy was ten times meaner than any alleycat
and not nearly so handsome

He spent his spare time fucking, dodging bullets
and thinking up new ways to die
he was on his 28th beer and couldn't get drunk
he'd spent the day shooting the heads
off dandelions with a singleshot .22
and now he was waiting for night to fall
so he could go driving

When he saw Honey something broke
inside and he had to ask her
     are you waiting
     for somebody?
Honey had a mean streak that ran

clean through her and she was in no mood
she said
> if you want
> to meet
> in the street
> and slap leather
> then get your gun
> but don't be slinging
> me insults
> or pickup lines
> I'm in no mood

Billy levelled his buckshot eyes and said
> because if you're not waiting
> i thought maybe
> you'd like to lock antlers

that was the first of thirteen
solid days and nights of lawlessness
they drove out along an abandoned
dirtroad with a bottle between them
and just before they got to the railroad bridge
they stopped the truck and Billy
pulled out his crossbow
they attached sticks of dynamite
to the arrows, lit them and
fired them across the river
in sparkling arcs
that sent up sudden
and feathery explosions
of sand and water
on the opposite shore
that deafened and flashed
in their laughter

Honey smelled like a cloudy day
and dragged him across the desert
he buried her in wildflowers
she snapped him
like a dream on a line
he fired her like a pistol
and she read him like a sermon

that night they were a herd of buffaloes
stampeding over a mountain and
they were a skyful of black clouds
and they were criminal

they were behaving like hound dogs
and they fucked like alleycats
and like rabbits and then like elk
(Honey kicked him square with her split hoof)
they fucked like timber falling
out of the sky and like a tsunami and
like a particular frail moonrise

they fucked like a housefire
the flames screaming up
from the inside out
and like a snowstorm
billowing huge banks of snow
against the riverbank
and they fucked quiet and solemn
as the inside of a chapel at dusk

when it was over
when the sun was
throwing its saddle
over the horizon

Billy lay still

Honey shook herself down
like a wet dog getting out
of the pond and she saw
that they were two
of the same brand
they were both outlaws

the next day
they packed up Billy's Ford
and toured the land
they ate only in diners shaped like
gigantic food — they lived on
Gourmet Burgers and Homemade Pies
and coffee drunk from over-thick cups

they filled the glovebox with snackfoods
named after baseball players
and collected pens that had things in them
that slid from one end to the other
they listened to country music tapes
stolen from gas stations and sought out
long-forgotten roadside attractions and asked
strangers to take their photographs

and when they were too tired to sleep
they pulled into the nearest motel
and fucked on the foldout bed
and only used novelty condoms
that always broke

for thirteen days they
slammed arrows into the sides
of nightmares committed small
political acts with short-fused
explosives stampeded in rainwater
rolled in honeysuckles and undid
their own misgivings

and on the thirteenth day
Honey woke up on a hotel roof
with all the blankets from all the rooms
of the fourth floor piled up around her
and all the constellations reflected
against Billy's shimmery side

She looked at Billy then
sleeping all streaked in
saltwater and honeyblossoms
and she realized for the first time
that she had tied herself
to a crazyman
she had tied herself
to a man who was a river

but worse than this
Honey realized
that she had tied herself
she had tied herself up

she had tied herself up
to a runaway train
she had tied herself
inside herself
she had tied herself
inside herself

Thirteen days of landbased adventures
and now she was slipping him
her honeylacquered absence
She was restless
she could hear the Chevy
stomping at the side of the road
and it was just too much
the way Billy had started looking at her
as though she had
walked out of a storm

all the nights
stretched behind her
like the broken ties
of a railway line

she was
caught in time
she was blinded
she was hungry
and angry

O Honey

she picked up her gun
and she reached for
her clothing
and she put it on
and she reached
down in the pocket deep
down in the pocket
for that handful of bullets
and she pulled out one

and she loaded her gun

Billy was sleeping
so still and so cleanly
there was no trace
of meanness
about him

and she loaded her gun

O Honey

Honey bent down
over that sleeping outlaw
and her lips were gun-barrel cold
she pressed them against the ear
of that crazy river and she said

>   i will love you
>   over and over
>
>   i will love you
>   over and over
>   and over and over again
>   and again
>
>   just because we've done
>   the things we've done

and she loaded her gun

>   i will love you
>   over and over
>   and over and over
>   again
>   and again
>   and again and again
>
>   again and
>   again and again
>
>   and she was gone
>   she was gone
>   and she was gone

Billy woke up
and she was gone
Billy woke up
and cussed himself out
and she was gone
and he was furious
and he threw everything
off the roof

and then he lay back down
he was tired
and his eyes
were on fire
and there was
nothing he could do

Honey hit the open road
with her gun still smoking
and that blackeyed devil
still hung inside her
that Billy still hung in her
eyes like a star

Honey drove into the underwoods
like a traveller of dreams
in her rusted out Chevy
she thought about Billy
and his brand new hearse-black
fuelinjected Ford F350 longbox kingcab
and she was sad and regretful

she drove into the mountains
where the catroads and dirtracks
snaked through the slash like a
handrawn map of all her veins and arteries

and when she ran out of road
she drove straight through the alders
keeping it slow and even
remembering her way from centuries before

and when she could drive no further
Honey got out and walked

deep into the underbrush through
salal and huckleberry and when
she had climbed all the way up
she climbed down and down
through the razorgrass and skunkcabbage
and dropped down into
the pocket of the mountain
that held her most sacred dreams

there was a stream
that turned a corner perfectly
cutting deep and shady
trout hideouts into the riverbank
there was a fork in this stream
and at this crossing (the tow downstream,
legs against the mountain, the wider
body broken at the hips) there was a pool

Honey could see
the brooktrout there
cutting lazy figure eights
against the gravelbed
circling and conniving
in its roughshod consciousness
she could see her own reflection
over the surface of the pool
her image intermittently broken
by descending midges
and dragonflies

and as she leaned back
and gazed into the mountain
an image wound its way
into Honey's vision
the way a brooktrout
will flash its scaly side
slowly back and forth
under the pondwater

and in the vision Honey saw Billy
her sometime lover and sacred friend
with whom she had committed glorious crimes
and he was laughing and he was tangled up

he was all tangled up with that same
cancan dancer who'd broken Honey's heart!

Billy was as crooked
as a snake in a cactus patch
and Honey wasn't having
her haunches spurred
by any rustler

the truth was upon her:
she, Honey, was alone
and all the cancan dancers
and cowpokes in the world
weren't about to change that

but before Honey could be overcome
by the icy shadows of this grave insight
a second vision came sidling up
came sliding through the afterwaters
of the first and Honey started to see shapes
just under the pondwater and these shapes
changed and collided there in the troutpond
until Honey could make out what they were

and what they were
what they were
they were other outlaw girls
and Honey realized that she was alone
but all over the country there were thousands
of outlaw girls just like her and some of them
carried guns and some of them didn't
and they all drove pickup trucks
Chevys and Fords and Fargos and Mercs
and Internationals and even Dodges

the truth flashed its scaly brooktrout skin
that day under the shining water and now lay gasping
in the open its silver gills choking and its scaly sides
shining on the surface of that sunlight afternoon

and when Honey climbed out
and saddled up the Chevy it wasn't
her jealousy spurring her inward

it was nothing other than her own
lonesome soul and deepdrawn hunger
driving her and driving her

and when Honey lit out
on the highway that day
her hair restless with salal
and her skin streaked
with screaming amanitas
she couldn't stop thinking
about all the other outlaw girls
covered in hornets and sorrow

and as she drove
along that dusty road
she started seeing them
everywhere rolling naked
over the heartland

THE GEOGRAPHY OF HOME

HAZEL JARDINE

Jumping Jehoshaphat

The church was hot. Sunlight streamed through St. John who solemnly balanced his halo in the stained-glass window beside me. The band of colour stretched to the blue carpet and was filled with specks of dust drifting aimlessly. A thin round-shouldered man, turning his tweed cap in his hands, crossed the beam to sit in the row ahead of me and the specks became frantic, like the bees when disturbed in old Mr. Wilkes' hives. Then they settled again, floating lazily back and forth with the responses.

"Oh God, make speed to save us."

"Oh Lord, make haste to help us."

I shifted the top of my bare legs where my dress had pushed up. The skin was stuck to the pew and I leaned one way and then the other to peel it away from the varnished seat. But I didn't really care. We would be off to swim at the dam after the service.

Dad had been tinkering with the engine of the car that morning when I left for church with Mom. The yellow stripe around the squared-off body of the old green Essex had gleamed and the sun had glanced off the hood folded back on one side of the engine. The crank had been sticking from the front, and greased pieces of the car lay along the running board. Mom had sighed. "I hope he gets it back together in time. I hate it when he takes things apart."

The curate had moved across to the lectern to read from the book of Kings, all about Jehoshaphat and how he destroyed all the Asherahs, whatever they were, and how God seemed to like that a lot. I poked Mom and mouthed "Jumping Jehoshaphat" because that was what she always said when I'd tell her Blackie was off again to that spaniel behind the McKinnon Block. I listened carefully to the lesson but he didn't jump at all, just kept asking to be saved from the Moabites, Shunamites and Mosquito-bites. But I still liked the way Reverend Wood rolled out the words in that English accent.

"And Jehoshaphat saith to the Lord, `We do not know what to do but our eye is upon thee.'"

Then he moved the green cloth marker to the next lesson in the huge Bible open on the back of a golden eagle. I didn't remember eagles in the Bible, but then I never saw anything about moose either, and there was a plaster one with a slot in its back downstairs on the Sunday School table.

The second lesson went a little faster and the collects turned out to be spectacular. Old Canon Bryan was helping out. I'd never seen him smile and he had the weirdest voice, like he was holding his nose all the time. I don't think he was, but then you couldn't see the ministers too well when they were kneeling behind the roodscreen.

When he had finished reading, Canon Bryan stepped back from the prayer desk to sit down. I guess he wasn't used to our church and how there wasn't any chair right behind him to sit on. You could just see his bald head above the screen and then it was gone. It was really quiet for awhile. Then there was a ripple of throat clearings and people were staring very hard at the organ pipes. His shiny head popped up again further back against the wall in front of the high carved back of the chair. The church breathed out and kneelers banged up but I thought I'd better keep looking at the pipes until the singing got going.

After the hymn, the lights were dimmed and everyone settled down for the sermon. Dean Smythe could paint pictures with his voice, pictures that flashed around on the rough stone walls and shot up to the high arched ceiling. Once I was so full of those pictures I told God I'd be a nun, but later when I talked to Mom she just smiled. But I really meant it, especially after Mom said why Mrs. Brown shouldn't be having a baby because her husband had been overseas for two years. I had it figured out that you got married and prayed and God sent you a baby. But when Mom told me, all embarrassed, *what* went into *where*, that's when I knew I had been called to the habit. I would pull a white pillowcase around my head and then my black taffeta circle skirt over top with the waistband tight across my forehead. I'd pull out a bit of my curly hair around the edges, until Bernice said at Youth Group that you had to be bald.

I liked to stare at the minister with half-closed eyes and watch the lights shimmering off his head, like he was an angel. Maybe we're all angels if we could just see ourselves that way. Maybe even animals, even dogs like Blackie. He would always come tearing around the garage to meet us when we came home from church. Back and forth across the lawn he'd whip and then he'd drop down panting beside the running board of the car and stay there until we left. Mom would hand me the brown wicker picnic basket smelling of apples, the blackened pots, towels rolled up with bathing suits hanging from the end, the piece of red checkered oilcloth, and a couple of *Leader-Posts*.

I would hop with Blackie into the back seat and grab an apple from the basket. Dad would bend over the crank at the front. Around and around and then one more time and the car would shudder into action, like the Black Beauty on the Shadow, only ours was the Green Hornet.

Then he would jump in behind the wheel, slam the door and drive off. This was always my cue to scream, "Wait for Mom!"

He would shout back over the *hrumph, hrumph* of the engine, "We don't need her. Let's go." And Mom would come out of the front door carrying the blue plaid car blanket she'd won the summer before throwing hoops over glasses at the fair. She'd shake her head and smile and Dad would back up for her.

In the back seat I would squeeze the metal clips at the bottom of each blind, pull them down over the side windows and enjoy the *rrupp* sound it always made. Then I'd lie on my back in the dimness and rub my hand back and forth on the olive green velour, raising the nap to a darker shade and smoothing it light again. Soon I would feel the car jerk to a stop at the corner, then swing to the right off Prairie Avenue and into the dust rising from Government Road, rolling me back against the roughness of the seat.

A sudden movement of white surplice on the uplifted arm in the pulpit waved me back and a cascade of words spilled over me. Then I was back in the car, the town dropping behind me out the back window and we had passed the Weyburn graveyard. I would whisper to myself, "If I should die before I wake, I pray the Lord my soul to take." But I crossed fingers on both hands like Bernice and I always did when we talked about death. I would zip up the blinds, crank down the window and hold my face to the wind, watching the ditches moving past with their orange cowslips and tumbling balls of weeds. I would see the great flat stone where Bernice and I always picnicked from the brown paperbags clutched all the way from town against the rubber grips of our handlebars.

If I looked deep into those ditches I could see a whole world of rivers and bluffs, cliffs and mountains. I would fly over them, gazing so intently that I would feel dizzy from the height. And if Dad had to stop to add water to the sizzling radiator, I could see bugs moving just like cars through the valleys.

I was startled to my feet by the world rising around me full of coughs, the scraping of books from the racks and the clatter of kneelers flipped up, one after another, against the seats ahead. The organ inflated the church, blowing in more and more sound until, if I clenched my teeth, I could feel the vibrations in my silver fillings.

> Not ours to mourn and weep
> In life's first joyous years,
> How shall we strive the fast to keep
> With better gifts than tears.

As the church again settled to its knees, I closed my eyes and wondered how you strived the fast to keep, but was soon back in the car. By now we would be passing the old schoolhouse with its boarded windows and collapsing fence. There was a huge poplar tree in the corner of the yard and lots of chokecherry bushes. Sometimes we went here instead of to the dam and we would play baseball, all of us, Mom and Dad and a couple of air force fellows she had gathered up after church.

But today weren't going to play ball at the school. We were going to the dam instead. There weren't any trees there, except little ones planted along the road, but there was water and that was enough for me. It had been blowing dust for so long, biting into my face, gritting in my teeth, but now the rain had come, the sidewalks were covered with frogs and salamanders and Mom was always running up shrieking from the basement.

There were crayfish at the dam, all frantic legs and claws when you held them up by the middle, and a million stones to chuck and silvery schools of minnows to catch in Mom's embroidered hanky. Dad would build a fire and then settle on a warm rock, and I'd sit beside him and lean against him while we ate apples and looked at the water. Mom would bustle around, boil the kettle, warm the chicken stew and then lay out soda bread on the plates on the oilcloth. I could still smell those apples and the chicken gravy right there in the church.

The kneeling benches clattered through the church and I swayed to my feet for the *Venite*, intoning from my confirmation prayer book. "When your fathers tempted me — " I saw Dad's rear sticking out from under the lifted hood. "And let him remember where the pieces go...," I sang quietly under my breath.

When I looked up the last hymn it had seven verses. I slumped down in the pew. But maybe the minister was thinking of driving some place too because he cut out a couple. I threw myself into the *amen* so loudly that Mom looked kind of hard at me.

When we turned the corner by the lilac bush and pushed open the creaking gate, Blackie was nowhere to be seen. The engine hood was still up and parts of the car were strewn on the driveway. Mom took a quick breath and hurried up the steps and I followed her through the porch, suddenly not wanting to go in.

I heard a door bang and a sliding thump like when the bag of potatoes had tumbled off the shelf in the cold room. Mom was pushing on the bathroom door.

"Dearie, dearie. Are you all right?"

Then they came down the hall, Dad leaning heavily on Mom, his arm limp around her shoulders, and he dragged his foot sideways across the hardwood floor. She stumbled with him towards the couch, knelt on one knee and let him roll onto it.

I hurried past them down the hall into my bedroom and dropped to my knees by the Winnipeg couch. "Oh God, make speed to save us. Oh Lord, make haste to help us. Please, God, you can't let him die. I know you won't let him die." And then I heard Mom calling me and ran back to the living room.

"Run, dear, over to MacFarland's and get the doctor. Hurry. Your Dad's real sick."

I ran all the way down the block and hammered on the door of the sprawling yellow house on the corner. I'd never been there before but had often seen their retarded Lisa skipping by herself in front of the house. She answered the door and at first looked blankly at me from her red-rimmed eyes.

"Lisa! I need your dad real bad. Please, Lisa!"

Tears were streaming down my cheeks. She turned and ran inside. I waited and twisted my embroidered handkerchief as I leaned against the doorjamb until the doctor shouted down, "Who is it?"

"It's Kathy Byron. It's my dad. He's real sick. Please hurry."

"I'll be right there when I get my bag together."

When I ran home and into the house it was very quiet. Blackie lay under the table with his head between his paws. Mom turned from the couch, her face twisted, and I could see my dad. His mouth was wide open and his eyes staring. Mom came to me and tried to put her arm around me but I moved away.

"Don't cry, dearie. It will be all right."

Then she took a deep breath and said, "I want you to go to the Red and White store and phone Reverend Cole and tell him."

I stumbled down the back steps, ran along the lane and into the small store behind our house and then had to line up to use the phone. Mary had been standing behind the cash register joking with a red-haired salesman and they smiled at me, and an old lady at the counter nodded. When I got to make my call it was suddenly very quiet in the store.

"Reverend Cole? ... Oh ... Would you tell him when he comes in that my dad just died ... Kathy ... Kathy Byron."

I heard myself talking like I was standing beside myself. Someone gasped, Mary began to cry and I dropped the receiver and ran outside.

I raged through the ditch along Government Road and ran forever down the highway to the mental hospital grounds before I fell and lay howling halfway into the caragana hedge. The sun was hot on my legs when I got up, brushed off the leaves and walked home.

⌒

The monstrous peonies almost covered the polished coffin, and when we had left the house it had been filled with them, on the piano, on the kitchen counter, even on the floor. Ants were crawling in and out of some of them and a heavy, sweet smell lifted from the masses of pink petals and choked me. I glared at the flowers pushing themselves at me and thought of Mrs. Brown, fat and rouged and smelling of perfume, squeezed into the pew beside me on Sundays. I pulled a prayer book from the rack. It opened to "A Table of the Movable Feasts for 100 Years" and I started to flip the pages. Mom reached over and found "The Order For The Burial Of The Dead."

The choir came down the aisle in a flutter of white surplices. Reverend Cole walked behind, his black stole flopping at every step. Mom nudged me gently with her elbow and I stood up but leaned against the pew ahead, my knees suddenly weak.

I stared ahead until the singing was over, then dropped into the pew so hard I felt the jarring up my back. The minister crossed to the lectern and began to read.

"O spare me a little that I may recover my strength before I go hence and be no more seen."

"Hear my prayer, O Lord, and with Thine ear consider my calling; hold not Thy peace at my tears."

Please God, you can't let him die. You won't let him die.

Reverend Cole moved down the red-carpeted stairs and stood beside the coffin. He held his arms extended, palms upward.

"Forasmuch as it hath pleased Almighty God, of His great mercy to take unto Himself the soul of our dear brother."

I tore the page out slowly, one small tug at a time, and down beside my leg, away from Mom, I crumpled it into a tight ball. I dropped it to the floor and kicked it toward the wheeled trolley and the flowers.

I let out a long slow breath. Then I looked at Jesus in the window above the altar and his eyes smiled at me, like they always did when I looked up while everyone else was praying, and I remembered Jehoshaphat talking to God.

"We do not know what to do but our eye is upon thee."

So I kept looking at Jesus until his face blurred into a wash of reds and purples.

When I walked down the aisle beside Mom, I passed Jeannette from school, sitting right on the end of the pew. She's always been my sworn enemy, and there she was right beside me. Tears were streaming down her face and I felt all mixed up.

Blackie was tied outside. Mom had decided that I shouldn't go to the graveyard, so I unclipped him from the fence and sat on the ground letting him lick my neck and ears. Then I got up and we walked home.

It had started to rain when I turned into the driveway. Parts of the car were lying around and I saw that the plaid blanket was still folded on the trunk. I spread it out on the ground and carefully set each of the greasy pieces into the middle and wrapped them up.

I carried them into the back seat of the car, pulled down the blinds and in the dimness cradled them. I could hear Blackie whining and scratching at the running board and there was a gentle pattering on the roof.

I had begun to shiver when a car crunched over the gravel of the driveway. I could hear people calling me but I pressed tightly against the green velour, breathing in the smell of the apples.

ROBERT HILLES

A Career in Farming

1.

My father always wanted a career in farming. When he got his 120 acres from old man Smith, he did everything possible to try and work the land as the government required. Seventeen acres had to be cleared and then cultivated for five years in order for him to acquire the deed for all 120 acres. The Trans-Canada Highway runs right through the small field he did manage to clear. Not the entire seventeen acres, only five, and one year he planted potatoes and they came out fine. But by next summer he'd lost interest in potatoes and couldn't come up with another crop, so the land remained fallow. All summer long he'd sit out back of the house with a beer in his hand and stare at those five acres growing nothing but weeds. It would have been okay if he'd planted something the next year, but the brush came back year by year after that. He never did clear the seventeen acres and he lost the land ten years into the contract. Now the Trans-Canada Highway goes right through his little field, and the last year of his life, he wouldn't return to look at it no matter how hard I coaxed him. He said there were too many memories and left it at that, his hand around a beer as his eyes fought back the tears. Across the room of his apartment, the TV blared some commercial. We turned away as the TV's glare spread across the otherwise dark living room like a searchlight.

2.

In one of the few pictures I have of him, my father is on the Smith farm where he was raised. In the photograph he appears quiet, one hand visible, the other hidden by Mrs. Smith's arm. Her hand is held straight out, tense. Only my father is looking directly at me, as if in the centre of the camera he could see me even then. He looks so strong as he stares into the camera unafraid of the future. His pitchfork is planted in the ground just behind him like a shy friend. Mrs. Smith looks most secretive, her thoughts carefully protected. Her brother, Rube, beside her has his eyes covered by his hat and a cigarette stuck to one side close to the child he holds, her face turned away from the smoke towards the black dog on the ground beside her. They all appear exhausted from work, even the two young children, held up to the camera as if promised a day in heaven. Only my father looks strong and freed by his labour, his life on the other side of the camera. The way he stands explains a time when labour taught the body important lessons. What he laboured for was neither inside his body nor his mind, but in the world itself with the ache of day's end. His sleeves rolled up tight to his shoulder, his arms strong and tanned, the hair on the top of his head wild like mine was when I was a boy. And it's the missing hand I'm drawn back to, as I imagine it, holding all kinds of things. Perhaps a cigarette, a pair of well-used gloves or the hat he should be wearing. Standing beside him, a marked distance from the others, is Royal Smith. His left hand tightly grips his pitchfork. His broad hat covers much of his face and he is looking at the ground in front of my father as if he's lost something there. He looks lost as if the camera contained death. Behind them there are piles of hay marking the progress of their day. The camera has no interest in the hay, only in capturing this small group. Once the camera was put away, they must have turned back to the piles of hay. For me, the picture is a secret part of my father's life given to me, carrying across time an image of his work I'll never forget. Perhaps that is the reason he is the only one looking at the camera. Perhaps what the moon, sun and wind perform makes no sense without some notion of that reality.

Last summer at the house of the boy in the picture, I discovered the photograph and finally found my father's youth. I handed him the image and he looked at it from old age and smiled. I suddenly realized, as my father fought cancer, that there was so much about him I didn't know.

Through his open shirt I can see the pronounced nub of his collarbone making him even more human, more alive, and I could stand next to him, my arm around him, joining the picture. No one would notice how I'd look straight into the camera just as he does, as he has taught me. Then we'd both resume work, walking wordlessly side by side, finding in the quiet steps and the gentle rustle of the hay something our bodies fit carefully inside. We could stay there forgetting the camera and all those cut off from this perfect day in late summer when the wind picks up and dies, while the log house waits behind us with a steady stream of smoke from the chimney, even on such a hot day. Inside, Mrs. Smith continues to bake pie after pie.

As we work in the killing heat, our thoughts fill with the image of pies, and we work in silence, stopping now and then to watch each other's movement, smiling confidently to ourselves, knowing our bodies make this possible. All of this. Our minds as careful companions. And I feel loved by him within this imaginary day. As I am loved now even though he is dead and I lose those years between when I always wondered. But as I work, I begin to feel a hidden future pulling me free from my father, and when he turns to me I am gone.

Only in the picture itself are his thoughts as clear as that day which holds them. I could look at that face for hours, discovering in the minute details all the clues a son could ever need. It must have been Lloyd Smith, the small boy's father, who took the picture. I wonder why it is only my father who is intently focussed on the camera. And as our eyes meet through the discomfort of time, I know he can see me caught in the camera's lens, looking out as he looks in. His son, a product of light, who years later writes him these words to fill his loss. And I know we both have been lost in a world too big for either of us, and those around us sing through the day as if filled with some glorious god-abandoned spirit. But he and I don't sing. Rather we stand a little off from the others, not out of bravery, nor fear, but because we are both made shy by the light and what it reveals. It passes before we can catch a hold of it. Still, it's what fits the hand that we can take with us into death, our lives caught tenderly in an open palm. Like light or water or rain it soon passes from our grasp and we close our fingers in joy knowing even love as big as we can make it, slips free. Like his, my mind is a mystery fitting in the dark skull like a caged animal. Now and then I look to my open hand, hoping what was lost will be there waiting. I wonder if that day in the photograph came back to him as he entered death. If it did, how bright was the sun as it filled his head with all death can offer? I put down the picture and I go to the other room where my own children are playing. I touch each one softly on the cheek.

3.

My father built the house on his farm when I was five years old. He would take me out with him on weekends to help him with the construction. He was often bathed in sweat as he scraped the bark off the logs. When the house was finished we moved in, calling it The Farm. My father referred to it as The Farm for the rest of his life, even though he lost the house and land over thirty years ago in 1964. The house burned down and the government moved in to reclaim the land for back taxes and because my father failed to clear the lot as specified in the original deed. My father was never one for understanding paperwork. Too many words. Too many signatures.

I don't have a single photograph of the house my father built. They were burned as well by fire in 1964. It's as though the house consumed itself and any evidence of its own existence. The fire ended my father's career in farming. For the rest of his working life he was employed putting up signs for the Department of Highways in Kenora. He never went back to the site of the fire, though I have, many times. I liked to stand in the heap of ash and imagine where my room had been. Now all I can see is the high bedroom window with my bed below it, the moonlight spread there like a sheet, and I am in the doorway looking for the little boy who is gone. Living in a home built by love, it is easy to believe that the rooms themselves bear that love and so each time you enter a room, more of that love rubs off on you.

4.

My father wasn't that good at farming, losing interest in the work after a couple of years. When he was younger, it was easier for him to find the work inside him, to breathe as it breathed, and he became each thing the work taught him. On the Smith farm everything was done by hand or with the aid of horses. My father learned to look up from the middle of his work and find the world around him taking a shape. They grew a lot of hay and a few vegetables. The hay was grown to feed the cows and horses. They owned two Clydesdale horses, five cows, two-hundred chickens and ten turkeys. Not much of a farm by today's standards, but it was what my father once dreamed of having. When he was a boy, he thought he and his future sons would live life as farmers. But things changed. Partly he changed and partly the world changed. My brother might have been a farmer, but I never would have been. It's not that I don't like physical work, it's just that I prefer what goes on in the mind. What my father saw when he looked up from his labour would have scared me in ways I couldn't tell him.

At night his hands would sometimes bleed from blisters and he'd lick the blood, liking how it tasted in some way he could hardly explain to me, his old eyes accustomed to the sun. In the late afternoons in summer, he'd often crawl under the shadow of a stack of hay and take a nap, so cool there it was easy for him to sleep away from the heat. When he'd wake, the sun would have found its way to him and he'd rise without ache.

5.

My father didn't lament the end of his career in farming. By then he'd learned that things ebb and flow like the wind, always in flux and difficult to hold. It was me who regretted his having left his career with the land, as though I'd wanted my father to stay true to a single dream. It was me who didn't want change. Change meant learning love all over again. The clearing my father made has overgrown with trees climbing to heights beyond forty feet. Some nights I pretend that one day I'll clear that land again in order to reveal both the small piece of earth and the secret to my father's life. When I look back at the picture of my father in the open field, I see that he didn't give up on purpose. It was just that what he loved had changed. The world, for him, must have been what it is to all young people, powerful, full of unexplored, unnamed hope. As if a different part of him were nurtured by each new career, my father changed, I suppose. I think of all the careers he could've had and I could've had and all the different men we could have been. But it was the farming that gave him his beginning, that made him a man I could love, whose photographs I can look at every day to find something new.

Life is neither memory nor record. It is something of our own making that slips through and disappears. A remorseless wind merely lifts and carries us where we might have gone otherwise, given the chance.

SUSAN HALEY

The Outhouse

It was duck-hunting season and Robert's whole extended family would soon go to their camp at Joker Lake for several weeks for what was by all odds the best season of the year: the fall. They would dry fish, shoot a moose if they could get one — or a couple of woodland caribou — and dry the meat, pick cranberries and blueberries, and eat gallons of delicious, thick, rich duck soup. It was a time for taking boats out onto the lake, for lazing around in the last of the sunshine before winter brought the dark; a time of gourmet eating. This was the cream of life for a hunting and gathering people, and the abundance of food was a cynosure.

Robert was going to go hunting with his family this year; he usually did not go hunting because of the demands of his poker-playing schedule. But as he was no longer playing cards he had a lot of time on his hands and he was restless for some kind of activity. He was intending to go out with his mother, since he had gambled away his boat and motor some years before. They usually went to the camp by boat through a complex of lake and river systems travelled winter and summer by their ancestors for thousands of years.

But in the three days before he departed he wanted to make everything shipshape in what was beginning to look like his permanent home — or at least, his home for the coming winter. The fish shack. It needed an outhouse.

He had spent all of one day and part of the next scrounging materials and tools: lumber, plywood, a door of some kind, hammers, a saw.

Another task was to get Haga involved in the project. He would be needed to help with the digging, but Robert was too wise to mention this. Instead he had entrusted Haga with five dollars to purchase some nails at the store the previous day.

It was now early afternoon and Robert had come home with the picks and shovels he had managed to borrow. He made a fire in the stove and boiled the billy for tea. Then he munched on a piece of bannock, looking at Haga, who was still asleep, lying on his back and snoring without inhibition.

"C'mon, get up. We've got an outhouse to build," he said

Haga slept on, snoring now a little ostentatiously.

"It's a nice day."

"Look, it's something to do," he said in desperation. "Don't you want to do something?"

Etiquette forbade anything much more forthright than this. Robert tried again: "As soon as we get the hole dug we're going to need those nails you bought."

Haga sighed and rolled over to face the wall.

"Get up," commanded Robert. He took hold of the foot end of Haga's sleeping bag and hauled the whole thing down on the floor, Haga inside coming with it. Haga hit the floor with a good-sized thump, then sat up indignantly.

A moment later he got out of the bag and bundled it up on his bunk. He was fully dressed; Haga wore everything except his boots to bed usually.

"Well, now you're up," said Robert.

Haga went to get himself a cup of tea in dignified silence.

"You can't stay asleep all the time."

Haga added sugar, sipped experimentally, then added more sugar.

"Look, winter is coming. You're going to like having that outhouse just as much as me."

Haga had begun his usual early-morning throat clearing routine; it was his only ritual of personal hygiene, for he never shaved, washed, changed his clothes, or as far as Robert could tell, even took them off. Sometimes, irregularly, he combed his hair, using Robert's comb.

Throat clearing for Haga started with a prolonged snuffle, during which he seemed to draw his vocal chords up behind his tonsils, an expression of pained surprise appearing on his face. Then he let go in a full-throated hawk, which was designed to propel the accumulated ball of phlegm up onto the back of his tongue. He would savour this for a moment or two, rolling his eyes, as he checked it for size and viscosity. After that he went to the door, hawked lingeringly once more and spat the giant blob in a satisfactory and aesthetically pleasing arc onto the moss.

For a moment he lounged in the doorway, cleansed and ready to start a new day. Then he sighed, yawned, belched slightly and said to Robert: "All right, let's see what you got."

Much relieved at being forgiven so quickly for taking peremptory action, Robert followed him outside into the clearing. It was a wide opening in the bush, now slowly filling in with willow and poplar, but with a good prospect of the lake. A ruined tipi stood in the graceful frame created by beach, lake and bush.

The fish shack was really a sort of lean-to attached to a much larger structure, the fish packing plant. About fifteen years before, the packing plant had been rendered obsolete by the arrival of more modern means of transportation bringing food from the south and by the fish marketing boards, which set prices too low to export. The building had been allowed to fall into decay: little boys broke the windows with stone, teenagers used it as a place of assignation, then it was robbed for lumber by homebuilders such as Robert. There was not much left except the bare structure with the lean-to hanging off its back.

Robert had scavenged most of his lumber here. Then he had unofficially borrowed some large scraps of plywood from a Housing Corporation construction site and found half a roll of roofing at the dump.

Haga inspected the accumulated trove of materials.

"Got tools too?"

"Borrowed them from Herod." In addition to his positions as Mayor and Justice of the Peace, Herod McCrae ran the Department of Public Works depot, which meant that he drove the grader and operated the only mechanical workshop in town.

Haga had moved on to inspect Robert's best find: the door. He had come across it on the beach, where it must have fallen down the bank off somebody's junkpile. In a town as off the beaten track as Prohibition Creek, people were in the habit of collecting all manner of odds and ends and keeping them for a rainy day. It was a full-sized wooden interior door in good repair, and it had two perfectly straight hinges, still with screws in them.

Haga was avoiding the main issue: the shovels, the pick and the crowbar. He looked at the pile of things, his hands in his pockets.

"You got the nails, right?" said Robert.

"Nails?"

"Well, I gave you five dollars for that yesterday, remember? To get nails at the Coop."

"Oh yeah."

"So where are they?"

"I don't know. The store was closed."

"Closed?" Robert exclaimed. "On Friday afternoon?"

"Well, I was busy. You can't expect me to do everything." Haga was evasive. He was also uneasy. He turned away from Robert.

"So what did you do with the money?" Robert confronted him, and Haga again turned away. "I guess you spent it."

"I gave it to a person in need."

"A needy person with a brew pot," said Robert in disgust.

He stared at Haga's back and kicked the pile of digging tools. After a moment he put his own hands in his pockets and turning away too, began to whistle. There was no point getting upset about things like this. He could go into town for a game anytime and win the money for a bag of nails. Or a bottle of booze.

He was not going to do that, though.

A truck came jolting toward them in low gear along the rough track through the undergrowth. It was a red one — Herod's Ford. He pulled up and jumped out, puffing. Herod was a very fat man; he never walked anywhere; he needed his truck to get around, keeping his finger on the pulse of Prohibition Creek

"Hello, Robert. Haga." He nodded at Haga, who was staring in surprise.

"I heard down at Housing that you boys were going to build yourselves an outhouse," he continued, "so being that I'm the mayor, I thought I'd bring you the paperwork."

"Paperwork?" said Robert, startled. Herod was handing him an application form.

"Yeah, we've got a zoning by-law now. Means that you've got to apply. Now this is a commercial use here, since it's the old fish store, but I figure the council would let an outhouse application through. After all, the employees have got to have some place to go."

"The employees?" said Haga.

"That's us, I guess," Robert told him.

It was a three-page form, calling for *"an architect's drawing, including floorplans, of the proposed structure."*

"We were just going to do this ourselves — no architect," protested Robert.

"Well, if she's only an outhouse ..." agreed Herod. "I guess they'd let you off that. Just write down how many holes she's going to have."

Robert took the pen Herod offered him and sat down on a fallen log to read the rest of the form.

"Describe relationship to any nearby buildings indication position of water, sewage and electrical lines," he read. He looked around at the clearing, full of the golden leaves of autumn, at the hulk of the old fish plant, at the little lean-to clinging to it crazily, the stovepipe coming out of the roof. There was probably an old electric line somewhere, and perhaps there had once been tanks for water and sewage — no one knew where they were any longer, though.

"All bathroom and kitchen facilities must conform to minimum standards set by CMHC," Robert read.

If the Canadian Mortgage and Housing Corporation regarded an outhouse as a bathroom, then by their regulations it probably couldn't be an outhouse. On the other hand, if it was not a bathroom ...

Haga was displaying the tools to Herod. Herod was looking gratified; they had all come from him in the first place.

Robert read: *"Outbuildings must preserve a forty-foot fire separation from existing structures."* Forty feet: that was about twenty steps — a long way to go in winter.

"I was just wondering if you'd happen to have any spare nails," Haga was saying.

"Did you boys run out of nails?" Herod inquired.

"You might put it that way," said Haga.

"Well, sure. I guess I can spare a few nails."

They got up on the back of the truck and began to rummage for nails. Surprised and impressed that Haga was taking some initiative, Robert went back to his reading.

"*Specify type of heating and indicate position of chimneys, exhaust systems or provision for venting of fumes.*"

It was the first question he had been able to answer. He wrote in "The Great Outdoors" on the top line of the space.

Herod had found a whole box of nails in the tool chest on the back of his truck.

"Gee, thanks," Haga was telling him.

Robert gave back the application form and pen. "I did my best with this, Herod. There were a lot of spaces I had to leave blank." Aside from his name at the top of the front page, the form was almost entirely blank.

"I guess they're used to that in Yellowknife," said Herod

"What's Yellowknife got to do with it?"

"You don't know? The Department of Local Government made up a town plan for us last year. Now everything's got to be approved by headquarters."

"Why the heck did you let them do that?" said Robert in disgust.

Herod sighed and sat down beside him on the log.

"To tell you the truth, I don't know the answer to that one myself," he said. "Seems as though we're always doing something that ain't in the town plan nowadays."

"It's the same old story," said Robert. "Look at this — white man even wants to tell me where I can shit next winter."

"Well, the council here isn't going to turn you down, Robert, that's for sure."

"Yeah, but what about Yellowknife? The Department of Local Government sure won't think much of the way I filled in that form."

"Local Government's supposed to come in and have a big meeting at the end of the month. I don't guess they'll look at the paperwork till then."

"This outhouse has got to be finished before that. I was thinking of going to Loker Lake with Ama at the end of the week."

"Well, you could just come to that meeting."

"Yeah, I think I will. I might have a complaint about this," said Robert

"I guess I might have one too," said Herod with a sigh. "Anyway, you can kind of explain your application to them."

"So they can go ahead and make us install running water and electric lights?"

"I'd kind of like you to come to that meeting anyway, Robert. We're going to talk about the airport too."

The Prohibition Creek airport had been a running sore for years in discussions between the local councils and government. A dirt strip situated in a firebreak, a mudhole in spring and summer and full of snow all winter, it was notorious among the local airlines for its accident potential.

"Sometimes I get mad at meetings like that," Robert remarked.

"Well, maybe that's why I want you to come."

Robert was surprised to hear this. He liked Herod and he knew that Herod liked him, but in terms of local respectability they were almost at opposite poles.

"I always like it when you begin talking in that high-falutin' way of yours," Herod explained.

Someone else was using the Complaints Department for its proper purpose.

Herod got up off the log and lumbered to his truck.

"You boys all set up to go now?"

"Sure. Thanks."

"Yeah. Gee, Herod, thanks a lot."

The red truck rattled and bumped its way over the rough wood road out of the clearing.

Haga had picked up a shovel and was attacking the ground right where he was standing.

"I guess it's time to get started on this thing," he said.

Robert stared at him in astonishment, putting his hands on his hips. Haga paused to grin at him sheepishly, then fell to again.

"Got some nails, did you?" Robert began to swing the pick.

"Yep."

They were working in rhythm, Robert in the hole with the pick, then Haga tidying up with the shovel. The ground was hard and rocky, beginning to freeze already.

"Well, that was good," said Robert.

"Borrowed 'em from Herod."

"Lucky he came by."

"Well, we weren't going to get nowhere without nails." Haga spoke censoriously, and Robert looked up in surprise.

The work in the hole was too hard for them to go on talking. After about an hour, going at it steadily and dislodging several boulders from the layers of frost, they had a hole wide and deep enough for their purposes.

Robert was cleaning the earth off the tools. Haga belched, spat, squinted at the sky, then started to go into the shack.

"Hey, where are you going?"

"Time for lunch," said Haga.

"Lunch!"

He came out again a moment later, grinning, with a bannock in his hand, and sat down on the rotten board that constituted their doorstep.

"Oh. Okay." Robert sat down beside him. "I was just worried that by the time you finished lunch it'd be suppertime, that's all."

Haga continued to sit for a while after he finished eating. Robert got up and wandered restlessly around. As usual, Haga was operating on a timetable of his own.

"C'mon, Haga, I just want to get this done before the snow comes, okay?" he said at last.

"Okay," said Haga. He stood up. "But just remember, without me, this whole thing would have been a disaster," he continued.

"What do you mean by that?" demanded Robert.

"I got the nails," said Haga. "You can't put up an outhouse without nails, Robert. And I was the one who got 'em. Just you remember that next time you get the itch to pull a fellow out of bed."

LORNA CROZIER

Joe Lawson's Wife

The woman who pounded on our door
came out of the wind, hair wild,
voice thin and broken. Philip
drove with Dr. Bird beside him,
I sat in the back with her,
Joe Lawson's wife, both of us silent
and staring straight ahead
though there was nothing to see
in those two beams of light. How
to comfort? When we got to the barn,
Philip was awkward with the rope.
The doctor pushed him aside,
climbed the milking-stool
the man had kicked away
and cut him down. Joe Lawson,
though it was hard to call
what hung in the barn
the name — the rope had cut into his neck,
his face blue and bloated.

I kept my eyes on his hands.
They were what you noticed
when you first saw Joe. Big, solid hands,
as much a part of the land as the stones
ice heaves from the earth every spring.

It was a minister they needed
not the doctor, but Philip hung back.
Dr. Bird was the one who told me
Take her to the house
and make some tea. She wouldn't leave,
but covered her man with a blanket
that smelled of horse, then sat
in the dirty straw, his swollen head
in her lap. By then her sister had arrived
and the neighbour with a wagon.

The sun was rising, its splinters
from the cracks in the walls
fell around her.

At last she let the men
carry the body from the barn
but still wouldn't go.
She pulled the wooden stool
to the stall and milked the cow,
its udder heavy, barn cats
coming out of nowhere at the sound.

There was no pail,
milk streamed out and hit the ground,
pooled around her feet,
the cats licking and mewling.
Her sister stood helplessly beside her
and motioned us away.
There was nothing to do but go,
above her head Philip mumbling
something I couldn't hear.

At home, he clung to me
as if his feet were swinging through the air
and it was I that held him up.
How to comfort. We bring so little
to each other. Later, after we had slept
he went into his study and I followed,
watched him from the door.
So upset, he left it open.

He tore the drawings he had sketched
last Sunday, his parishoners
as he had seen them from the pulpit — all
alike, his pencil strokes relentless,
pinning them and their piety to the pews.

Everything would change for us
if he could draw
that woman on her stool, her simple
act of courage — or was it resignation?
The shadow of her husband still

swaying from the rafters,
milk puddling at her feet
and between the cracks,
the sun's bright nails pounding through.

Country Dweller

Paul, the school teacher
who drops by to see us
now and then, tells me
pagan means *country dweller* —
that's where we've gone wrong.
We've tried to tame the wild gods
and make them one.

Maybe even Philip
could believe in them.
A horse god. Among the reeds
and rushes, a wind god.
In aspen leaves, a god of light.

The smallest, the most slender
is the god of rain.

I tell Paul she must be
female, a four-legged animal
with soft paws and swishing tail

for that's what we hear
when she comes near us
for her green communion
with the grass.

Dust

Rags stuffed under the doors,
around the windows
as if they were wounds
that needed staunching

yet the dust
settles everywhere,
on my skin, my hair, inside
my sleeves and collar.
I feel old, used up,
something found
in the back of a cupboard.

I cover the water crock
with a tea towel
embroidered with a B,
turn the dinner plates
upside down on the table.
When we lift them
two moons glow
on the gritty cloth

and in the mornings when we rise,
the shape of our heads
remains on the pillowslips
as if we leave behind
that part of us
that keeps on dreaming.

DI BRANDT

This land that I love, this wide wide prairie

It is impossible for me to write *the land*. This land that I love, this wide wide prairie, this horizon, this sky, this great blue overhead, big enough to contain every dream, every longing, how it held me throughout childhood, this great blue, overhead, this wide wide prairie, how it kept me alive, its wild scent of milkweed, thistle, camomile, lamb's-quarters, pigweed, clover, yarrow, sage, yellow buttercup, purple aster, goldenweed, shepherd's purse, wafting on the hot wind, hot clods of dirt under our bare feet, black, sun soaked, radiating heat, great waves of heat standing in the air, the horizon shimmering, flies buzzing endlessly, wasps, bees, cicadas under the maple trees, dripping with sap, the caragana hedges brushing the air lazily, heavy, golden with blossoms, the delirious scent of lilacs in bloom, hot pink begonias, marigolds, sweet peas, spider queens, wild yellow roses, crimson zinnias, baby's breath, the cool fresh smell of spruce, jack pine, elms gracefully arching overhead, asparagus, cucumber, radishes, onions, peas, beans, corn, raspberries, strawberries, chokecherries, gooseberries, blackberries, yellow currants, red currants, rhubarb, wild yellow plum, crab apples, Japanese cherries, canteloupe, watermelon. It was heaven, the prairie was, the gift of its bounty accepted easily by us, her children, running barefoot all summer, through the garden, the fields, our feet hating the constriction of shoes in the fall, the return to school desks and books and sweaty silence. The hot dry smell of wheat during harvest, the sexy smell of our own skin, bellies, thighs. The call of crows, killdeer, sparrows, kingbirds, barn swallows, robins, orioles, nuthatches, woodpeckers, blue jays, mourning doves, the surprise of toads, little frogs, earthworms after rain. The bellow of cows, the cool wet nuzzle of calves' noses, the grunt and snuffle of huge pink sows wallowing in dirt, the squeal of newborn piglets, soft newborn kittens in the barn. How I loved you, how I loved you, how I love you still.

This stolen land, Rupert's Land, Métis land, Indian land, Cree land. When did I first understand this, the dark underside of property, colonization, ownership, the shady dealings that brought us here, to this earthly paradise? Our thousand acres of prime black farm dirt, waving with wheat, barley, flax, oats, corn, alfalfa, and later, sugar beets, buckwheat, yellow rapeseed, corn. Our many fields patched together painstakingly, passionately, laboriously by our father, with devoted help from our mother, field by field, bank loan by bank loan, from a single field and two-room shack in the 1940s, shortly after the war, into a large, modern farm in the '60s and '70s, debt-free, fully mechanized, flourishing. Was it the time our mother searched through our winter drawers for underwear and stockings to give to the Native woman who walked across the fields from her camp, with outstretched hands, to our door? Who was she, we pestered our mother, where did she come from? Why does she need to ask us for things? Was it the time I read about our Canadian history, in Grade Six, where I first heard about the Hudson's Bay Company, Rupert's Land, the Selkirk Settlers, the Métis Rebellion? And later, in Mennonite history class, I heard about our own arrival as a people, a contingent of Mennonites a thousand strong, from Ukraine, by ship and the Red River wagon, to what became known as the West Reserve, near the U.S. border, in the newly formed province of Manitoba in 1875. (Was it then I began to doubt the purity of our fathers' pacifist stance, refusing to fight in the war, choosing instead to go to CO camp in northern Manitoba to cut timber, or even, in some cases, enduring imprisonment, a betrayal of our *Privilegium*, our Charter of Rights granted by the Governor General of Canada in 1873, which included "exemption from any military service" [Zacharias 30], our fathers refusing to defend the land with their bodies, their hands, yet clearly benefitting from the territorial struggles that created Canada?)

It was something else, it was something unspoken, invisible yet tangible, in the air, in the vibrations of the rich black prairie soil under our feet, a memory, lingering in weeds, in grassy ditches, on the edges of fields, a wildness, a freedom, faint trace of thundering herds of buffalo and men on horses, whooping joyfully, dangerously, reining them in for the kill, unbroken prairie, sweet scented, rustling, chirping, singing, untamed, unsubdued, stretching to the wide horizon, women and children sitting around a campfire, the smell of woodsmoke in the air, the incessant beating of drums. There was no getting hold of this memory, this ghost, this whiff of another world, another way of life, no way to see it or understand it, and yet it was there, in the wind, calling to us, plaintive, grieving, just beyond the straight defined edges of our farms, just outside the firm rational orderliness of our disciplined lives. I spent many hours during adolescence following its scent, alone, escaping the house and yard, tracing its outline, its beckoning shadow in the clouds, in bushes, in forgotten bits of prairie near creeks or bogs, in our twenty acres of pasture out back behind the yard, still unbroken grassland, buzzing with crickets and grasshoppers and flies, redolent with wildflowers and cowpies and sage.

There was another memory, too, hidden in my blood, my bones, that sang out from me sometimes in that place of newly broken prairie, an older memory, of a time when the women of my culture had voices and power and freedom, and their own forms of worship, across the sea, out on the green hills under the moon, in the Flemish lowlands of northern Europe, a sturdy peasant life, deeply rooted, before the persecutions, the Inquisition, the burning times, the drowning times, the hanging times, before we became transients, exiles, hounded from one country to the next, seeking refuge from wrathful authorities who couldn't stand our adult baptisms, our democratic communities, our disloyalties to the Pope and king. Before the violence of the persecutions got internalized in our psyches, before we began inflicting them on each other, the same violent subjugations of body and spirit the Inquisitors visited upon us, only we did it secretly, in our homes, we did it to our young children, so no one would see us, we did it to our adolescents, with ritual beatings and humiliations, so they would have no voice, no will, no say of their own, we kept the women bound with rules of humility and obedience, as servants to the masters, their husbands, who owned all the land, owned everything, who went to church with head held high, proud in their democratic brotherhood, proud in their tyrannical lives at home.

The first time I participated in an Aboriginal ceremony near Winnipeg, a few years ago, in the bush, under the full moon, I had such a strong sense of recognition coursing through me. I remember this, I remember this, my body sang, I remember when we gathered, my women ancestors, around fires like this one, surrounded by trees, not so many centuries ago, before we were made to tremble under the wrath of God, the vengeful One, and his long-armed, heavy-handed privileged henchmen, our bishops and fathers. I remember when worship meant laughter and dancing and lovemaking under the moon, carelessly, instead of sternly remembering the torture of a god, and fearing the night, and obeying our husbands, and sitting still in church.

This man's land, owned and ploughed and harvested by men. And the women kept as servants and slaves. When did I first understand this, that the women had no place, no voice of their own in the Mennonite farm village economy, even though they worked as hard as the men, keeping huge gardens, and weeding and canning all summer long, and cooking and sewing and cleaning year round, for us all? Was it the time my father ostentatiously brought out the black farm book, where he kept his accounts and his field notes, after dinner, and announced it was time for our brother to begin learning about how the farm was run, and my sister Rosie and I crowded round, full of curiosity, and he sent us to help our mother do the dishes instead? (Was it then I began to hear the hypocrisy of our fathers' endless talk of religious community and anti-hierarchy and brotherhood?) Was it the time we joined the 4H sugar beet club, and our dad said, no, only boys can grow sugar beets, and he sent us to pull weeds in our brother's acre all summer instead? (I always loved the weeds more than the cultivated plants, they were prettier, wilder, they smelled nicer, I admired the way they kept coming back, insisting on their right, their place on the prairie.) And at harvest time our brother had a record yield and made a lot of money, several hundred dollars, and when we complained about the unfairness of it, our dad ordered our brother to pay us for our labour and he gave us each a dollar. (It still sticks in my throat.) Was it the many times we watched our mother swallow her disappointment, her disagreement, her own wishes, her needs, in deference to our father? And later, there were calves, entire fields, a series of new motorcycles and trips across the country, a half share in a new pickup truck for our brother, and for us, five cents a pound for picking raspberries and strawberries all morning in the summer heat, if there were customers for them, which came, on a good day, to thirty-five cents in our pockets. And strict rules about how we could spend it and where we could go. And eventually, a half share in the entire farm for our brother. And for us, disapproval, endless disapproval, for our women's bodies and dreams, going off to the city to find our own lives, with no parental support.

When the Governor General Lord Dufferin visited the Mennonite settlements on the West Reserve in 1877, two years after their arrival en masse from Ukraine, he found, as historian William Schroeder tells it, a beautifully decorated arbour in which three young Mennonite girls in lace kerchiefs were serving hot lemon-seasoned tea, surrounded by flower bouquets wrapped with poetic lines of welcome, in German, hung on little pine trees. After listening to the Mennonite bishop's welcoming speech, His Excellency addressed the gathering of a thousand or so new immigrants thus:

> Fellow citizens of the Dominion, and fellow subjects of Her Majesty: I have come here today in the name of the Queen of England to bid you welcome to Canadian soil ... You have left your own land in obedience to a conscientious scruple ... You have come to a land where you will find the people with whom you associate engaged indeed in a great struggle, and contending with foes whom it requires their best energies to encounter, but those foes are not your fellow men, nor will you be called upon in the struggle to stain your hands with human blood — a task which is so abhorrent to your religious feelings. The war to which we invite you as recruits and comrades is *a war waged against the brute forces of nature*; but those forces will welcome our domination, and reward our attack by

236 FRESH TRACKS

placing their treasures at our disposal. It is a war of ambi-
tion — for we intend to annex territory after territory —
but neither blazing villages nor devastated fields will mark
our ruthless track; our battalions will march across the il-
limitable plains which stretch before us as sunshine steals
athwart the ocean; the rolling prairie will blossom in our
wake, and corn and peace and plenty will spring where
we have trod. (Schroeder 104-5; italics mine.)

Schroeder does not specify how the Mennonites received His Excellency the Lord Dufferin's speech, so liberally sprinkled with military
metaphors. I imagine they grimaced and recoiled from this language,
reminiscent as it must have been of recent persecutions suffered at the
hands of the Russian military, and other military persecutions before
that. Still, the weird, contradictory combination of warfare and hus-
bandry, conquest and cultivation of land (and convenient blanking out
of its earlier inhabitants), the schizophrenic attitude toward the prairie
he articulated is a deadly accurate description of Mennonite farming
practice in Manitoba as I knew it, growing up in Reinland.

How come, I remember asking my dad, if the wheat is poisoned by
the red stuff you've sprayed on it before seeding, to kill bugs, poisoned
enough so we can't taste handfuls of it anymore as it gets poured into
the seeder troughs, how come it won't poison us later when it grows
new plants, too? Every year throughout the '50s and '60s (while the U.S.
and U.S.S.R. were building bombs) there were new pesticides, new
herbicides, bigger machines, fancier equipment to disseminate them
more quickly, efficiently, every year the chemicals became more
poisonous, as the weeds became hardier to withstand them, as the
pesticide companies and seed companies grew larger to sustain and
control this burgeoning market. My father scoffed at safety measures
against pesticides. He remembered spraying DDT all over his bare arms,
before it was banned, to ward off flies. And look at me, he'd chortle,
healthy as an ox. He was annoyed at new spraying restrictions as they
arose. He died of cancer at age sixty-one. My brother, who is forty-
seven, recently quit farming and left the community in desperation due
to environmental illness, surely caused by exposure to pesticides. (And
that was the end of Elm Ridge Farm, my father's thousand-acre dream
that we sacrificed so much of our lives for, his carefully stitched-together
playing field, so unsolid after all, scattered back into the hands of
strangers.) Here is how Harvey Janzen, my brother, describes his
symptoms in a recent letter from Calgary, Alberta, where he is being
treated by a doctor specializing in chemical sensitivities:

My weakened body had begun to react to fumes besides farm chemicals like automobile exhaust, commercial cleaners, fabric dyes, glues, ink, paint, perfumes, and scented personal care products. My body reacts instantly when exposed to these. Different fumes will cause different symptoms to occur. Fatigue and exhaustion is usually the end result. I have done very little driving during the past year due to fatigue and loss of muscle control. Driving is also affected by loss of vision due to cataracts in the lenses of both of my eyes.

In a little more than a hundred years, my fellow countrymen and women, we have managed to poison the land and our food sources and our own bodies so drastically as to jeopardize the future of all life in this country. The birch trees in the Pembina Hills close to our farming village, which we used to visit every fall to admire their flaming orange colours before the onset of winter, are dying. The rivers are being choked with reeds and fungi because of fertilizer run-off into the water systems. Many, many people in south central Manitoba, in the heart of Mennonite farmland, are dying of cancer, MS, pneumonia, leukemia, all of them victims of damaged immune systems and, indisputably, environmental pollution. There are very few birds now, very few frogs, toads, gophers, foxes, deer, very few wildflowers and prairie grasses left. It is the same in other farming communities across the nation. And elsewhere in this province, the forests and lakes are being ravaged by the pulp and paper and mining industries. It is the same in other provinces and countries across the globe.

In all those years of listening to preachers preach to us, every Sunday, in the Mennonite village churches, endlessly exhorting us to repentance, to a more ethical life, not once did I hear a single one of them talk about the land, except to pronounce gleefully that we "shall have dominion over it," a special permission, a decree from God, though, on the other hand, paradoxically, we should not go to war to defend it. Not once, in all those lists of sins, fornication and lust and desire and whatnot that we were endlessly warned against, did I hear one of them talk about an ethical practice of land ownership or address in any way the politics of gender and race, the politics of chemical intervention, the dangers of pesticides and herbicides and chemical fertilizers, and later, the implications of genetic manipulation of seeds and livestock for the land and the creatures in it and our own bodies. (When I became a vegetarian at age twenty and began cooking organically, my father said, "You're trying to sabotage my farm.")

This is why I weep, sitting on my wooden veranda in Winnipeg, not far from the Forks, where the Red and the Assiniboine Rivers meet, on a beautiful tree-lined street canopied by great green elms, on this beautiful July evening, in this prairie landscape that is still heaven, still paradise on earth, despite the volatile weather, the bugs, the mosquitoes, the endangered earth and air, because I remember, somewhere my body still remembers, when it wasn't so, when this beautiful land was unconquered, unsubdued, unbroken, when the people of this land tried to live in harmony with its shifts and rhythms instead of in violent conquest over it, when the creeks and ditches were filled with frogs and meadowlarks and red-winged blackbirds and butterflies and wild clover and bees instead of sprayed grass, when the fields were grazing grounds for wild herds of buffalo and antelope and deer instead of straight hard rows of chemically altered grain.

There is regret in me, regret I feel deeply, sharply, here in my belly, sometimes, so I can hardly breathe, for this slow dying prairie, how she lost her stupendous wildness, forever, around the time my great-grandparents came to settle the dispossessed Native territories, to break them, to plant their rich farms and gardens, that I am so grateful for, so sad about. It is why I cannot write *the land*, because I am torn inside over it, my helplessness in the face of such massive destruction, my ongoing love for the prairie, how her beauty still catches my throat, her power, majesty, so much bigger than we are, there is still time to turn it around, to save the land, undo its massive poisoning, the scent of prairie on the hot wind, calling out to me, my love, *eck lev dee*, *ni-mi-ta-ten*, I'm sorry, *ki-sa-ki-hi-tin*, I love you.

Sources

Schroeder, William. *The Bergthal Colony*, revised edition (CMBC Publications, 1986)

Zacharias, Peter D. *Reinland: An Experience in Community.* (Reinland Centennial Committee, 1976)

Cree translations by Emily Munroe

SHARRON PROULX-TURNER

sing your song

your children are strong

we are métis

when I was a kid, I thought the dictionary was a story book. my granny gave me a dictionary for my fourth birthday. she'd look in there and she'd see a word and she'd tell a story long as your arm. sometimes she'd just look at that big book the whole time she was telling. sometimes she'd tell me these two stories back to back. she called these stories, the meek and the weary.

now, the word meek comes from middle english and old norse. it used to mean compassionate and kind, but that meaning's now obsolete, which means that's not what meek means any more. now it means having a patient, gentle disposition while at the same time it means lacking in spirit or backbone, weak and spineless. the weak and spineless shall inherit the earth, eh?, hee, hee, hee.

first is the story of narcissus and echo, which is the meek part. the dictionary says that in greek mythology, narcissus is a youth who causes the death of echo by spurning her love. that a goddess named nemesis causes narcissus to fall in love with his own image in a pond and pine away for himself until he dies and changes into a flower, the narcissus.

thing is, the dictionary lies about this story, is what my granny says. first off, the love that's here is clearly lust. it's important not to confuse the two. and echo's not a person, she's a nymph. a nymph is a female spirit with little power or importance. see, the greek culture was very sexist. I guess that's why the white christians got into it so much, eh?, hee, hee, hee.

anyway, narcissus is a handsome lad of sixteen. he's the son of a nymph named leiriope and a river god named cephissus. narcissus, as it turns out, is courted by many would-be lovers of both genders. echo is after him, it's true, but so is this guy whose name's not mentioned. this guy prays and prays that narcissus feel what he's feeling, which is unrequited lust, which is lust that's not returned. the goddess nemesis hears and answers this guy's prayers.

nemesis is the goddess of retribution and it's her job to make sure that people are made aware of their shortcomings. she doesn't actually cause narcissus to fall in lust with his own image; this he does all on his own. what she does do is arrange for him to walk by a pond on a nice sunny day and see himself reflected back like in a mirror.

see, narcissus won't date anyone because he thinks he's too good for them all for some reason. as for echo, she's already been altered by the bad medicine of some cruel older goddess. echo's still a young girl in her teens and all she can do is repeat the last few words of whoever she's listening to. pretty hard to let a guy know you're interested in him when you can't speak your own mind, eh?, hee, hee, hee. at any rate, echo pines and pines over this boy and ends up being that voice you hear when you're in the mountains or in an empty building or whatever.

at any rate, narcissus sees himself in the pond, falls in lust, and dies there. he dies there because he refuses to leave this guy he's in lust with, which is his own reflection in the pond. I guess he starves to death and then he turns into a flower. it must've been sunny and there must've been a bright moon for a lot of days running. hee, hee, hee.

now, this is a very famous story by western european standards. they made up a new meaning for what narcissus did and called it narcissism. narcissism means excessive admiration for or fascination with oneself. the experts on child development say it's the stage when you're a baby in which the self is the object of your erotic, sexual interest or lust and also the persistence of this stage into later years. the idea here, and it's one that's popular in patriarchal circles, is that wee toddlers are sexual towards themselves.

my granny says the truth is, sex is a matter for sexual maturation and individual choice. children who are not raped need feel only the pleasures of holding and touching their own bodies. any sex a child experiences is from an adult or another kid who's been raped, and either way, that's rape. who tells the complex unconscious infant sexual phantasies to the experts on child development who insist that babies are into sex? the infants themselves?

her second story is short. this story's the weary part. weary means worn with exertion, suffering, etc., tired, bored, disconnected or vexed by continued endurance. in this story there's a young white man who thinks his stories are greek and his culture's canadian. he's actually a celt but he doesn't know this yet. his mommy's from the crow clan and his daddy's from the wolf, which makes him crow but he thinks he's canadian. this boy spends a lot of time in his in-fill house in front of the mirror. he's a city boy and he likes to do the bars. he plays pool pretty good and he likes to watch hockey on tv. he reads the paper, jogs on saturdays and spends his sundays with the folks. he has a car, a job, and he's thinking about getting a dog. that crow boy, he's goin places.

my granny says that crow boy's a gem. his people made contact with ours almost as far back as our stories can remember. we shared things. sacred things. you'd never know it now.

one time I met a guy from overseas. this was a few years back. he talked like he'd talked to my granny. he was young, early twenties, and here because he was a political refugee, kicked out of his country because of his politics. he'd served in the army over there and his best friend was killed in a battle. died in his arms. this young man had lots to say about the men his age in canada. he said they seemed immature and bored and their talk was empty of meaning. he said he should've known something was up when he drove through this city for the first time. he said if he didn't know better he could swear that for calgarians their god must be in the shape of a house and their god's heart had to beat to the rhythm of a hockey puck on the big tv. beer must be free up there in showhome heaven and their god must've swilled a few too many during the first period.

I was glad I'd met this guy and as it happens, he was glad he'd met me too. I told him my granny's weary story and he laughed until his belly ached.

laughing's sacred. it's medicine. laughing, land, love, language. four of the sacred l-words is what my granny says. she'd go through four a's, four b's, and so on to four z's, and then she'd start again with four new ones again and again. some words were in the four a lot. like circle and grandmother and sacred and respect. but her four r's were never reading, riting and rithmetic. the essential elements of a primary education is what the dictionary says. those words laid out like that are lies and poison is what my granny says.

english dictionaries are good for lies and poison. one time I heard this woman talk about that. she talked just like she'd talked to my granny. she was giving a speech on the barriers for aboriginal women in universities. at first I didn't really know what she was talking about because her voice was flat and soft and she was using academic language, words so big and sentences so long I couldn't be bothered trying to figure out what she was getting at. then just when I'd lost interest completely and was looking around the room to check out how many people I'd have to knock knees with to get out of there, she starts drumming and dancing and half-chant-half-song very loud and strong and clear and to the bone. my eyes my breath my ears my self filled with her rhythm, floated in her words. her movements pulled at my eyes until she slid behind a podium, stood stock still, and started reading from a large open book.

bachelor: one who has taken his first university or college degree; an unmarried man; a young male fur seal kept from the breeding grounds by the older males.

master: one who has received his second academic degree; a degree which is more advanced than a bachelor's but less advanced than a doctor's; a craftsman or worker whose skill or experience qualifies him to practise his craft on his own and to train apprentices; a male teacher.

she looks up from the book. she says, this is a brand new dictionary of the english language. for my people, the métis people, and for aboriginal people, language is sacred. my language, michif, does not appear as a word in this dictionary. language is our mother. like the drum, the song, the dance, language allows us to express truth. this english language is full of lies. an aboriginal woman or any other woman goes to a university to become a white man? your language hates women. your language says a squaw is an algonquian word which means woman. this is a lie. squaw is a white man's hate word which means whore, slut, pig, piece of shit female indian. with that, she closes the book and walks away from the podium and out of the room.

that mostly white male audience gives this woman a standing ovation. they are entertained. during the question period they all talk at once. they say they didn't understand why she sang in a language they didn't understand. they didn't like being called the white man. they didn't understand why she was still so hostile, considering the number of scholarships that're there just for the natives and most of them go to waste and then perfectly deserving non-native kids can't go to university because they can't compete for those unused scholarships. they didn't understand why she took dictionaries so seriously. after all, they didn't. who in their right mind would?

the woman takes the floor. she says that the white men are monopolizing things and they haven't even asked one direct question. then she speaks passionately in michif for a short time and walks out of the room.

I didn't actually meet that woman because how she came to me was in a dream. but I can say that that day my eyesight changed. my vision cleared. when I got up that day, I pulled out the piece of paper I'd gotten from the elders with the métis nation of alberta. it reads like this:

métis nation of alberta
oath of membership

I am métis

as a métis
I honour with pride the blood of both my
mother and father.

as a métis
I acknowledge the rich history of my
people and the courage and dedication of
our leaders.

as a métis
I pledge to preserve the spirit and enhance
the identity of my people.

as a métis
I confirm my commitment to my
family, my people, my nation.

as a métis
I accept my responsibility to put service to
my people ahead of self interest, and to
honour the spirit and the letter of the written
and unwritten laws of [creator] and the métis nation.

and that day something else happened. my throat opened to my eyes. my hands opened to my throat. my spirit opened to my hands. my heart opened to my spirit.

that same day I make my first flight as a writer. I leave calgary in the morning. it's cold and snow and winter still. in vancouver it's an hour behind and so I get there at the same time. in vancouver it's full spring. pink blossomed trees and very warm. the grass is long and green. yellow lion's tooth and sacred cedar. ocean in the air. and crows. crows at the airport too. both airports.

it's crow that taught folks how to fly, in the air and on the ground.

makes sense when you think about it. that's why crow hangs around highways and airports. crows like to be where people're movin is what my granny says. you pay attention to them crows, ma petite. you've got crow on both sides of the family. crows all the way back into the sacred pines and crows all the way back to europe. them crows they like the pines. cedar's pine's sister. crows hang around cedar too. they know a good thing when they get you there. hee, hee, hee. got lots of heart, that crow. tries to get folks to come and remember. to heal. thing is, crow's moved into the city too, just like the people. crow knows cities aren't so bad. they're good for lots of things. got lots to say, that crow.

talks people talk too. they say that crow's a tattletale. a gossip. gets you into lots of trouble. keeps you honest. shapeshifter too. plays tricks on folks all over the place. eats carrion on her days off is what my granny says. watch what you carry on that plane, ma petite. hee, hee, hee.

my grampa was a celt. one of the crow clan. they called him old crow. he liked to pop in on folks just so's he could say, carry on, carry on. he said that crow she's sacred. big job. job so big she'd split herself up sometimes so's she could do a few things at a time. kept people on their toes. crow goes right back to the start of things and crow goes right out and to the end of things too. only thing is, it's not a straight line she's swingin on, it's a circle. crow's creation is what she is. big job. creation's a paradox you got to understand. a paradox don't make no sense is what you got to understand. most people don't get it, see?, so they say that crow's a death-bird. but that crow, she changes with the wind and if you can't take a joke you shouldn't ought to've joined up in the first place is what my grampa says.

I almost miss my flight back home. I get to the airport early, thinking to take my time. I stand in line. the line is long, very long, with zig-zags made from ropes and poles to keep us like a garden. I pull the ticket out to make sure I'm in the right line and then I see the time. I run to the front of the line, run to pay some new airport tax, run to the run-way.

they've overbooked the flight. no one's boarded. I hand my ticket to a very sweating looking agitated flight attendant. several people are talking at once to several flight attendants. actually, everybody's yelling so they can hear each other. the room is hot the people are hot. the attendant yells at me, this flight's overbooked. you're too late. you can't get on. I yell, well, do your best. I'm pre-booked and I know it's late, but it's not departure time yet and here I am. oh, and by the way, see if you can get me a window seat, will ya? the person looks up, right eyebrow raised, mouth open. hee, hee, hee, I laugh real loud, just kidding.

I get a window seat in first class. first time. actually, I've only been in a plane a few times and I've never had a window seat. it's not that I'm afraid to fly or anything like that. flying's a real rush to me. can't afford to fly places is why.

when I was a kid I had this theory that moving at high speeds can lengthen people's lives. because of the adjustments you have to make in time so's not to have everything rushing by you like when you look straight down at the highway from over the edge on the back of a pickup truck that's clipping right along. I got this idea from reading about how if you travel at the speed of light I think it is, you wouldn't age, you wouldn't get any older or something. so I'm sitting eating salted almonds, which are free, looking out the window, feeling absolutely thrilled, thinking about what a waste it is that the middle seats're made into tables up here in first class, thinking about how when I was flying to vancouver I had an aisle seat and a dusty dense blue curtain in front of my face to keep me from seeing the backs of the heads of the first-classers. it was very claustrophobic so I read the whole way there.

I look out the window the whole way home. at first I'm very excited. I see the round of mother earth. I feel the awe of the ocean. the mountains make patterns on the round. it takes a while before I notice something's wrong. the mountains look like farms. there's squares and squares. triangles. rectangles. I want to laugh and cry at the same time. it's so beautiful. it's so horrible. we're flying through a hole in the ozone. from the hole you can see what's making it.

I'm silenced. silenced by the beauty. silenced by my fear. not a cloud in the sky all the way home. next day it rains. it rains the next. the next and then the next. then there's the floods. the silt. the patchwork silt. rich mountain topsoil litters southern alberta.

mountain is crying
prairie is sighing
air is dying
willow is crying
pine is sighing
cedar is dying
river is crying
lake is sighing
ocean is dying
salmon is crying
dolphin is sighing
eagle is dying

crow is painting
in a circle
mother's words
crow is writing
in a circle
mother's words
crow is singing
in a circle
mother's words
crow is dancing
in a circle
mother's words
caw
caw
caw
caw

A SENSE OF PLACE

BEN GADD

O Canada National Wilderness

Probably it should be in the Rockies.

Yes, it definitely should be in the Rockies. I'll bet that if you went across the country asking Canadians what they thought of when they heard the word *wilderness*, lots of them would say, "The Rockies, of course." So that's where we'd have O Canada National Wilderness. In the Canadian Rockies.

Picture it: Lake Louise, surrounded by ice-covered peaks. In the foreground there's a Mountie astride his horse in front of an imposing hotel, the Canadian flag snapping smartly in the glacial breeze. Downright patriotic, this place. You can almost hear the national anthem.

Ah, but wait. That's O Canada National Park, not O Canada National *Wilderness*. O Canada National Wilderness would be all this minus the Mountie, the horse, the flag and the hotel.

Just the lake and the mountains.

Here's what it would be like to go to O Canada National Wilderness. You'd take a deep breath and step across the boundary. Then you'd look back at what you were leaving behind: the parking lot, the car that brought you there (smell of hot motor drifting across the invisible line), the large warning sign:

> Entering O Canada National Wilderness
> No services next 50,000 square kilometres

Instead of a paved trail leading to a bridge over the first creek, you would see a simple path. That path would have been established many millennia ago by moose and elk and bears. They would have waded the creek, no problem. You, being a water-hating primate from the African savannah, would teeter across on stepping stones, getting one of your feet wet. If you had arrived an hour later, the glacier upstream would have poured another five cubic metres per second into the channel and you would have had to swim like the moose.

But still, the farther you went through windfalls and boulder fields and bogs, the more you would smile. You would smile because of all that would *not* be there. There would be no motorcycles or 4X4s or any of those nasty little "quads" (currently the conveyance of choice for serious wilderness abusers). No machines would be allowed in O Canada

National Wilderness, period. Not even mountain bicycles, one of which I own and love.

Nor would there be any pooping, mudhole-creating horses. The moose and the elk and the bears would have pooped some and churned up the trail a bit in wet sections, but their effect on the land would be nothing like the effect of horses.

No helicopters full of tourists would buzz your campsite, because no scenic overflights of O Canada National Wilderness would be permitted. You would see no spent cartridges in the woods or discarded fish heads by the streams or snarled monofilament line on the lakeshores. Nor would you take a bullet in the back from some hunter who had made a mistake. No killing of anything bigger than a mosquito, not even a fish, would be permitted in O Canada National Wilderness.

You simply wouldn't have to think about these things. You would know that O Canada National Wilderness was what the sign said it was: real wilderness, the nation's best, in which the normal human activity of wrecking everything was suspended. Any human entering O Canada National Wilderness would have to do so benignly — that is, self-propelled and self-provisioned, without motors, wheels, axes or guns. You would enter with little more than your ingenuity. But on the other hand, you would get to see grizzly bears, because lots of them would live there. You'd see wolves and wolverines and golden eagles and many other species.

No nicely prepared tent site in a designated campground would await you at the end of the day in O Canada National Wilderness. You couldn't light a campfire except in an emergency. But you could go anywhere you pleased and you could camp anywhere you liked.

Nobody would be looking out for you except the other people in your party. If you chose to go alone, no one would be looking out for you at all. Warden patrols would be few, and only wardens would have radios. Or maybe they wouldn't.

Scary, this. But spicy and strangely desirable. We have an archetypal craving for such a place. After all, the conditions there would be rather like the conditions under which our species lived for all but the last 10,000 of our 200,000-year existence. The conditions would be primitive, in the best sense of the word. Humans are first-rate primitives. We evolved to be full-time professional campers, travelling about in little family groups through vast, primeval landscapes. We're not particularly happy in our impossibly overcrowded world, with its impossibly reduced turf. For us, going into the wilderness is like going home.

Of course, we couldn't stay at home for long in O Canada National Wilderness or we'd start wrecking it. So we'd have to be visitors, eating out of our packs and heating up our coffee with fuel we carried in on our backs. We'd be obliged to suffer a bit. Given the rigours of O Canada National Wilderness, most of us would get our fill fairly quickly.

And given those rigours, the number of people willing to reach the very heart of O Canada National Wilderness would be few. Those people would have to struggle through the torrents and stagger over the high passes and claw their way through the untracked green hells.

Well, okay, the high passes of the Rockies are typically beautiful, green hells are uncommon, and every valley has its natural trails. But all except the most persistent humans would be filtered out. And even if there were fully committed humans bent on laying waste to the wilderness, there would not be enough of them to wreck this place.

Are there any O Canada National Wildernesses on earth? At the moment, none that I know of. None quite like this. But we could have one. This one, in the wildest place in the world. It's even wilder than Antarctica — they allow snowmobiles in Antarctica — yet climatically a whole lot more pleasant.

Would it work? Hard to say. The wilderness would have to be very large, and it would have to be isolated. Where could we find a place like that?

Well, we already know that it has to be in the Rockies. The northern end of the Rockies, the part between the Peace River and the Liard River, is practically untouched. It's also big — 67,000 square kilometres — and it's still pretty isolated. Good. We could establish O Canada National Wilderness there.

But what if too many people decided to go?

Okay, we'd have to restrict the numbers.

What if people were camping and pooping everywhere?

Okay, we'd have to have rules about where you camp and how you poop.

What if too many people were breaking the rules?

Okay, we'd have to have more enforcement.

What if too many people got hurt way back there?

Okay, we'd have to have more patrols and more helicopter rescues.

What if things became just like they are in Banff National Park?

Whoa.

Let's see. What are things like in Banff National Park?

First, there are roads. Right: No roads in O Canada National Wilderness. Trails would be permitted, but only natural ones, and no signs to tell you which way to go. You'd have to use a map.

Second, there is commerce. Way too much commerce. Right: No commerce in O Canada National Wilderness. Well, maybe you could hire a guide … On second thought, no. This could easily get out of hand. I'm a guide, and I know what we're like: a bunch of territorial little experts who like to grab places for ourselves, even on Mount Everest. Right: Nobody would pay a fee to anybody in O Canada National Wilderness.

Fees! Ever counted the fees in Banff National Park? The government gets you at the gate, gets you again for your overnight permit, gets you to go in the hot springs, gets you for whatever it can. None of that in O Canada National Wilderness. To paraphrase Edward Abbey: "All citizens would have the right to get sunburned, blistered, bug-bitten and grizzly-mauled in their national wilderness, regardless of their credit ratings."

Besides, O Canada National Wilderness would be cheap to run, requiring only a minimal outlay of the citizens' taxes. It would be low-maintenance, and the citizens wouldn't have to buy trucks for the wardens. Or build patrol cabins. Or even pay much in the way of salaries, because there would be plenty of people (I'm sure of this — just look at the growth in volunteers in the national parks) who would offer to walk the place for nothing in exchange for supplies, decent gear and the right to be an Authority. Main cost: training these people not to be back-country amateurs.

Now that I think about it, I doubt that O Canada National Wilderness could ever become very much like Banff National Park. O Canada National Wilderness would start with the right philosophy: Don't do anything to make it easy for human beings to go there. In fact, if humans had already got in with their chainsaws and their hammers and nails, then we would start by undoing the damage. We'd blow up the bridges (Edward Abbey's dead, but he would have *loved* that) and we'd dismantle the outfitters' camps. We'd quit clearing the trails. Nature would take the hint and continue restoring the place without any further help from us.

This would effectively discourage the crowd that has turned Banff National Park into such a haven for ski-area operators, hoteliers, tramway tycoons, etc. Many of these scenery-peddlers proudly trace their ventures to some opportunist, way back when, who got a government permit to build something in the woods. Just something small, you know — like the cabin that became the town of Banff.

O Canada National Wilderness would not be a place for incipient industrial tourism. Yes, I think O Canada National Wilderness might actually work.

That's why it's such a dangerous idea.

MAUREEN SCOTT HARRIS

Being Homesick, Writing Home

1.

> The Greek physician Hippocrates noted, about 400 B.C.,
> that whenever people from one country were sent to
> another of markedly different terrain, "terrible
> perturbations" always followed. From this he concluded
> that people absorb topographical influences from the
> moment of birth and that separation from them could be
> perilous. These perturbations we now know as nostalgia
> (from the Greek *nostos*, to return, and *algos*, to suffer)
> and homesickness (from the German *Heimweh*).
> — Ronald Rees, *New and Naked Land:*
> *Making the Prairies Home*

It's June 1993 and here I am in the driver's seat at last. Not driving,
mind you. I've pulled over onto the shoulder of this gravelled farm
road in southern Manitoba, waited for the dust from my wheels to settle
and rolled down the window. I'm looking across an expanse of beige
gravel and green-brown stubble at a clump of empty, weather-peeled
farm buildings, among them a low-slung barn with a roof unlike what
I expect to see here in Manitoba. Its sides slope gently down and then
curve slightly upward like wings at the bottom of their stroke, echoing
the barn roofs of Quebec.

The buildings are a long distance away across the field, farther than
I want them to be and too far away for me to get the picture I want.
And there doesn't seem to be road access from here. The horizon line
is absolutely flat, the sky is absolutely blue with a single thin transpar-
ent cloud ruffle extending across it as far as I can see. No one will get
it, what I want them to see, in any picture I take from here. But I look
through the viewfinder anyway. I lean out the car window, grasping
my camera, too certain it's a no-go even to get out of the car.

2.

> ... desert dreams of prairie, prairie of forest, and forest of
> mountain. The lines of separate identity are blurred ...
> Borders on all sides are vague and transitory ...

Landscapes and bioregions intergrade, cannot be defined
without each other, and desire one another.
— Don Gayton, *The Wheatgrass Mechanism*

nostalgia, dislocation, desire, perception, landscape, absence, home

These words hang in my mind, forming a backdrop to my arrival on the
side of that road in southern Manitoba and to what I am writing about
here.

They have enticed and companioned me in internal and external
musing for several years now, as I move from thought to feeling, between memory and the present moment, among disparate places. I
type them in italics to convey the sensations they evoke in me when I
come across them still, be it in poems, history, theory, fiction, review.
Anywhere I find them they focus me, lying tremulous on the page,
beckoning. It's a kind of magic, a magnetic attraction, like falling in
love or being saved. If I knew how to do it, I would handle them like
strips of willow, soaking, twisting, bending, weaving them together
into a container, a basket I carry over my arm, holding what I believe,
what I want to say.

3.

disorientation, n. 1. Loss of one's sense of direction,
position, or relationship with one's surroundings. 2.
Intellectual or moral confusion. 3. *Psychology.* A
temporary or permanent state of confusion regarding
place, time, or personal identity.
— *The American Heritage Dictionary of the
English Language*, 3rd ed.

Begin here, driving through the fertile farmlands west of Toronto, where
I've lived for more than twenty-five years. Even from the expressway I
recognize the landscape. The sudden announcement of the escarp-
ment, shapes of woodlots and fields, farm buildings, fences, trees straggling towards the road, flowers blooming along the highway's edge —
are all familiars. Today, in late May, they give me particular pleasure.
I've been caught in the city too long.

But when I leave the expressway the names on the roadsides begin
to intrude. Breslau, Cheltenham, Heidelberg, Sheffield, Zurich, Ballinafad,
Lucknow, Rostock, Brussels trumpet at me as we slick by, large white
letters on a green ground sliding across the fields outside the window.
Where am I?

Suddenly I'm enormously cranky, reading all these foreign place names! I want to be surrounded by names which *don't* insist on elsewhere, names native to *this* place, arising from the countryside itself, presenting it directly, unfiltered by nostalgia or desire for some place else. The more I think about it, the more it seems to me we cannot even begin to live properly here until we learn the secret and powerful names which belong here.

4.

> **absence, n.** 1. The state of being away. 2. The time during which one is away. 3. Lack; want...
> — *The American Heritage Dictionary of the English Language*, 3rd ed.

What does it mean to be a human being in Canada or North America at the end of the twentieth century? Euro-Canadian female human being is who I am, fifty-two years old now, second-generation Canadian on my father's side (the side that counted) but uncounted generations of life in Canada on my mother's, and already it's splitting, this notion of myself, already I'm subject to (of?) more than one reading, even by myself. Through my father I've made it to the middle class, in some ways an educated, privileged elite. But these locations may be read as too particular, too limited, as if I had to start any novel by describing the desk at which I sit, the study that surrounds it, deferring a beginning that does more than circle itself, on guard, determinedly self-referential and definitely in charge of its small surface.

What I really want to know is where I am and if I belong here. I want to be *in place*. Where is home?

Looking up from my computer screen I see with surprise that the gabled roofs of the houses out back are coated with a thin layer of melting snow. It's spring. It wasn't snowing when I began this. I didn't see the snow begin to fall though I'm surrounded by windows on three sides. I'm mesmerized by the voices in my head, the white blips on the screen, this feeling that something's wanting.

5.

> When you've grown up in a place, much of what is there is interpreted forever by the myth-mind of a child. What you have is an intimacy that is mutual, always.
> ... Even decades later I still know things here the way I knew them when my own borders spread beyond the

flesh. I breathe the air the way I breathed the scent of
my mother's skin. I know the sounds. The seasons here
beat by like my own heart.

> — Diana Kappel-Smith, *Night Life: Nature from
> Dusk to Dawn*

Ecologist Paul Shepherd suggests that the human animal imprints on a
specific landscape in her earliest years, just as she does on her parents.
He believes that the interactions between child and the place(s) where
she plays serve as models for relationship which she will carry with her
throughout her life, much as the interactions among her parents, siblings, and herself form such models.

That being the case, I must wonder which landscape I've imprinted
on. Which one might have taught me my most basic sense of how to be
in the world? Is it prairie, where I remember playing, or westcoast sea
and forest, the landscape that surrounded me for the first year or so of
my life? I feel enormously at home on the west coast, comfortable, as if
life is simply easy there. But when I'm there I'm on holiday. It's prairie
I dream about. I'm conscious of missing the prairies, their weather and
spaciousness. And self-conscious about saying that too loudly here in
the glossy east. I'm secretive about my passion for flat horizons, monumental skies, the subtleties of ditches and fields in late fall and early
spring, a palette awash with the rich colours of dried weeds and grasses.

6.

> **landscape, n.** 1. An expanse of scenery that can be seen
> in a single view... 2. A picture depicting an expanse of
> scenery. 3. The branch of art dealing with the representa-
> tion of natural scenery. 4. The aspect of the land charac-
> teristic of a particular region ... 5. An extensive mental
> view; an interior prospect ...
>
> > — *The American Heritage Dictionary of the
> > English Language*, 3rd ed.

Forget the verb, with its notions of constructing, building, creating. The
noun is complex enough with its mingling of inner and outer, of literal
and metaphorical. What I meant by "landscape" when I began thinking
about it was the countryside around me, the natural world "out there."
I wanted to write down my feeling that we (late-twentieth-century
Canadians of whatever stock) don't see what's in front of us. We've
forgotten (if we ever knew) how to look at that world, its actual shapes,
trees, creatures, even as, at least here in southern Ontario, it is being

altered radically by our machines and our determination to mark and own it through the processes which masquerade under the name of "land development" — monster homes, suburbs, malls, franchises, and so on. But now I don't know whether I'm thinking about the things of the natural world or the ways I see and think. And the dictionary continues:

> **Word history:** It would seem that in the case of the word *landscape* we have an example of nature imitating art, insofar as sense development is concerned. *Landscape*, first recorded in 1598, was borrowed as a painters' term from the Dutch during the 16th century, when Dutch artists were on the verge of becoming masters of the landscape genre. The Dutch word *landschap* had earlier meant simply "region, tract of land," but had acquired the artistic sense, which it brought over into English, of "a picture depicting scenery on land." The fascinating thing is that 34 years pass after the first recorded use of *landscape* in English before the word is used of a view or vista of natural scenery. This delay suggests that people were first introduced to landscape in paintings and then saw landscape in real life.

Landscape comes into being as I step back to look at it, letting it spill away from me. When I'm within or on the land I don't experience it as prospect or view, at a distance; I'm in conversation with it, immersed, linked. "Landscape" is determined by notions from aesthetics, a knowledge of forms and light, elements I see cohering, as if in my mind or on a canvas. (Perhaps it's also about what I can grasp.) At least that's where it begins, and that beginning presupposes that, for the moment, I've left it, stepped out of it into a room perhaps, and turned back to glance through the window whose edges frame where I've just been. I alter my position in front of the window and I see different views of the landscape; one angle yields a more satisfying prospect than another to the eye that sorts planes and shapes, that savours colour and the movement of clouds or fields in the wind, the gusts of snow.

But perhaps the "landscape" I'm contemplating and want to write about is complex and inclusive, both nature and art: me at the window, the painted oak frame, my musings, the sumac-laden hillside I look across, and the stream I can't see but know runs along its base. So what I'm thinking about is not a matter only of geographical forms existing in relation to one another, but an intersection of multiple points, perhaps even a traffic circle. Add to the forms (which are themselves not permanent but changeable and changing) my own experience of the landscape, what I've noticed and named, what I've missed consciously but have registered subliminally, paintings and photographs I've seen, books I've read, as well as the lives and living systems taking place among/within the geographical forms. A landscape might be a gestalt then (but a gestalt continually shifting), of a place and my response to it, however shallow or deep that response may be. Plus the total of other responses to it, of which I may or may not be aware, the slight traces of another glance which remain in the air or in the imagination. Other presences.

7.

> Each of us harbors a homeland, a landscape we naturally
> comprehend. By understanding the dependability of
> place, we can anchor ourselves as trees.
> — Terry Tempest Williams, "In the Country of
> Grasses" in *An Unspoken Hunger*

If I step out from the frame of landscape into the land, I become a term in a relationship. Remembering the way the air hummed, its sweetness. Caragana, clover, dandelion, crabgrass, thistle. Oak, wood tick, bees. Sun beading my lip.

When I look through my camera viewfinder, those Manitoba farm buildings are so far away they are minuscule in relation to the expanse of field, road and sky. But I also see the car mirror in the foreground obscuring the road I'm following. Reflected in it is the stretch of road I've just driven along, flowing straight out of a white-blue sky to butt up against the mirror's frame. A mixed growth of trees on either side some distance back, dark green, cool, must enclose a house and yard, outbuildings, a road in. I'm looking behind me and ahead at once. The automatic camera I've got probably can't manage this double-view, but it's worth a lost shot to see. At least a blurred mirror will fill the foreground of the picture and maybe pull the buildings closer.

8.

> I would have wished that after my return people had
> asked me how it was out there. How I coped with the
> glistening blackness of the world ...
> — Reinhard Furrer, astronaut, quoted in Dennis
> Cooley, *This Only Home*

I've been here for a week already, living in the log cabin with my family. It's my second camp and I want to be here. I'm not afraid the way I was last summer when I came up on the bus from the city, my stomach in a knot. My father's been getting things organized. He's the camp director but he's not directing the girls' camps, and so just before the bus is to arrive he and my mother, brother and sister get into a car and drive away. I stand in the middle of a grassy set of tire tracks, waving and watching the car get smaller and smaller. I feel myself getting smaller like the car. Then the huge buses arrive and girls pile out, excited, screaming, laughing. That night I can't sleep. The cabin is flimsy, the floor rocks when people cross it, it smells musty and there are odd noises outside, noises I don't recognize. It's very dark inside and out, and the darkness rises up in my chest and I'm ashamed, knowing I'm going to cry.

I get through the night, with some help from Mickey, my counsellor, and have a good time for the rest of the camp. But in the middle of that first night I'm completely disoriented, surrounded by the unfamiliar, frightened and ashamed of being frightened. I don't want anybody to know about it. It's not a good story. For years afterward I think that's what being homesick means — that mixture of loneliness, fear, and shame.

9.

> **field, n.** ... **SYNONYMS:** ... *bailiwick, domain, province, realm, sphere, territory.* The central meaning shared by these nouns is "an area of activity, thought, study, or interest": *the field of comparative literature*; ...
> — *The American Heritage Dictionary of the English Language*, 3rd ed.

I've been reading books about landscape, particularly about the prairies, where I grew up. I've tried history and even some economics, settlement accounts, natural history. Squinting my eyes to make a clear picture of where I come from. One thing I've learned for sure is that the prairie isn't plain. It's a landscape literally hard to see, permeable to both desire and expectation. Again and again it has been described in terms which are more descriptive of the longings of the viewer than of the land itself.

Stand in the middle of a stretch of prairie and five of the six cardinal points open into space with an absence of definition or boundary. Really experience the landscape (space and light) opening about you and the sixth point, the one which lies beneath your feet supporting you, may for a moment seem to quiver and fall away beneath you.

Prairie is ambiguous, luminous, shifting.

Like language. Like the mind. Look how we take these terms whose basic meaning has to do with the way we parcel or divide land into bits which we own or control, and use them for those less concrete kinds of turf, the ideas and notions and obsessions and movements of our minds. As if the earth and the ways we carve it up mirror for us the space inside our heads and the motions of thought. How could we think about research, for instance, if we didn't also, in some way, know about ploughing and seeding and tending and harvesting? What is going on when we step from the field of daisies to the field of gynaecology, or from the province of Manitoba to that of politics? Can we really think clearly about one in the terms of the other? Is clear thinking the point? I wonder about control and what it means to "own" a thought. Or a piece of ground, for that matter.

10.

The first known sufferers [of homesickness] in modern times were seventeenth century Swiss mercenary soldiers in the pay of European potentates; they were overcome by lassitude and melancholia at sounds and smells that reminded them of Switzerland. Cowbells and the strains of the Swiss melody *"ranz-des-vaches"* are said to have disarmed Swiss soldiers as effectively as any enemy manoeuvre. Europeans first knew the ailment as the "terrible Swiss disease," but it struck at every nation once the Industrial Revolution and the opening of the new worlds began to scatter the old world population.

Throughout the eighteenth century *Heimweh* was treated as pathological, but today it is regarded no more seriously than a protracted cold.

— Ronald Rees, *New and Naked Land:*
Making the Prairies Home

I think stories of the discovery and settling of a new place, the movement of a family or a tribe, are something like stories of individual lives in their contours. They begin with the discovery (birth), continue chronologically through the exploration and mapping (growing up), and culminate in the establishment of a settlement and description of its subsequent history (adult life). Because of the concerted focus of such stories it often doesn't occur to us as listeners or readers that before, after and simultaneously, there are other stories going on.

Those stories of which we are at least partial subjects (our lives, our communities, our national histories) have enormous authority for us: they both contain and propel us. As long as they do so adequately, we are usually content to be so contained. But absence and discrepancy are feelings which can propel us towards new stories and new places both. Many people have come to Canada because their original stories and national histories offered them only limited presence or no presence at all. But they didn't come empty-handed. They came full of visions of what they wanted and images of the landscapes that had housed them.

As settlers and immigrants (or their children) we've often interposed these inherited dreams and mythologies between us and this landscape. I'm part of this problem, part of the dominant European-based culture of this country. How difficult it is now to see past that history of longing to what is rooted here. And what I learned as history in school I now read as stories full of absences and discrepancies.

A central myth in my culture is about being made homeless. Adam and Eve were expelled from the Garden of Eden and their children condemned to the wilderness for generations before coming home to the Promised Land. Lots of us came to this continent as to the Promised Land, certain of our right to occupy it. Many of us found a wilderness, a land we scarcely saw in our haste to transform and redeem it, desperate to construct versions of the landscapes we already knew. In that process we expelled the people who were already here, people almost as invisible to us as the land itself. Teaching them homesickness.

Believing that the land is here for our use, that its meaning is to be mined, harvested, hewed, shaped solely to suit our needs and wants, we move across it as if across the surface of a painting in which the middle ground is absent. What is wanting is any feeling of reciprocity; we rarely recognize that even as the land is subject to our manipulations, we are permeable to its influences. If we could achieve the middle ground of that recognition, we might learn both to know and love the land. Without it we are condemned to discrepancy, estrangement, a continual homesickness.

11.

dislocation, n. 1. The act or process of dislocating or the state of having been dislocated: *"the severe emotional dislocation experienced by millions of immigrants … who were forced to separate themselves forever from the … circle of people and places on which they had depended"*

(Doris Kearns Goodwin). 2. Displacement of a body part, especially the temporary displacement of a bone from its normal position ...

— *The American Heritage Dictionary of the English Language*, 3rd ed.

I'm twenty-one the first winter I spend in Toronto. Before this I've lived only in Winnipeg or Saskatoon, so far as my own memory goes. I'm living at home with my family, studying, trying to repair a ragged start at a college education. I'm working hard. Each day I take two buses and a streetcar downtown to the university campus. I have a part-time job in the library which keeps me there late several evenings. I don't know many people, and the ones who are my friends are all, like me, from some place else. Because I'm trying to do well and keep up in all my courses, I'm often tired. In February I feel I can't manage. I'll never read even the texts, let alone the secondary sources. I can't possibly write the papers required, not all of them, not well. I'll never feel comfortable here, where no one smiles on the street and people walk so quickly they seem to be running. I'll never make real friends, ones I can talk with. Sometimes when I walk along the street I feel my legs disconnecting from my body, space opening in front of me. One morning I round the corner by Varsity Stadium and know I'm going crazy. There's no other explanation for these sensations. It's cold and damp, I hunch down into my coat, my shoulders rounded. I'm surrounded by concrete, heavy as my failed life. And then sun breaks through the clouds and paints a pale yellow swatch up the side of the stadium. I look at it and think "I'm *not* crazy ... it's just that the sun never shines here!"

I didn't know homesickness means missing the way light falls, its colours, all kinds of familiar weather. Or that losing those things could dislocate me completely, making me feel my bones separating from each other.

12.

Perhaps a black-throated sparrow lands in a paloverde bush — the resiliency of the twig under the bird, that precise shade of yellowish green against the milk-blue sky, the fluttering whir of the arriving sparrow, are what I mean by "the landscape."... These are all elements of the land, and what makes a landscape comprehensible are the relationships between them. One learns a landscape finally not by knowing the name or identity of everything in it, but by perceiving the relationships in it

> — like that between the sparrow and the twig.
> > — Barry Lopez, "Landscape and Narrative" in
> > *Crossing Open Ground*

I've always said I don't know what I'm writing about until it's written, using sentences scrawled one after another as a kind of stalking tactic, trusting words to flush the creature from the undergrowth. The trouble is, until it flies clear out of the thicket into bright air, it's easy to get distracted by other parts of the landscape, that clump of poplars, for instance, or the crow passing overhead. Or to imagine I'm on the trail of something else altogether.

One day I look at the rivers I'm driving by here in Ontario and think absently, "The rivers at home don't look like this." *I've lived here for more than half my life now. Why isn't it home?*

Why has it been so difficult for me to say, even to myself, that I feel out of place? Why has it been so hard for me to say I want to write? The two questions are wound together somehow, I know it, so that thinking about landscape and how to be at home in it are ways of thinking about writing, and writing is a way of placing myself, of feeling, for a while at least, at home. Yet I'm profoundly suspicious of my own taste for a mixing of the actual and the metaphorical, fuzzing the boundaries between them or wanting them neatly aligned.

I've been trying to read and write my way home for a long time both secretly and openly, but I haven't walked the prairie in more than twenty years. Instead I've constructed a landscape in my head, from memory, from books, from my own fierce wish to be there. Or perhaps merely to be elsewhere. But it's not just a place in my head I'm after. How do I know if this place exists?

13.

> Esther had watched her parents depart, had turned and
> walked into the fields, dug her hands into the earth,
> examined the leaves of each crop. Later she ran her
> fingers over the bark of the orchard trees, strolled
> through the flickering woods. She was less staking out
> her territory than she was being claimed by something
> that was destined to be hers; the centre of the world, the
> ground on which she stood.
> > — Jane Urquhart, *Away*

It's July 1992. I'm standing beside the Red River in downtown Winnipeg. I look at the water. It's the dull brown I remember. I watch it slide by the bank as if it were heavy silk and then I see the mud, black, cracked into shapes. I'd forgotten that, forgotten the way the earth here dries and cracks at the surface, forgotten how it takes the imprint of a foot when wet. I want to cry, looking at this patch of cracked mud, and I don't even know why. I squint my eyes against tears and light both as I look across at the other bank, see the trees leaning over, their shapes. I was right, rivers on the prairies *don't* look like rivers in the east. All the plants by the water's edge are familiar. I can't name them, but I know they belong here.

I needed to come back here, to see this countryside. And I need to come back again. I want to find out if my internal and external landscapes can match at all. I want to be at home with them both.

14.

> The prairie horizon is the perfect metaphor for the
> furthest boundary, the ultimate reaches of earth-bound
> consciousness. On the prairie one twists around and
> around till the straight horizon line turns into its oppo-
> site, a circle, and the visual turns visionary.
> — George Melnyk, *Radical Regionalism*

When I get my pictures back a week or two later I can hardly believe my eyes. The image reflected in the car mirror is even clearer than are the field and buildings behind it. At one edge my forearm and clenched hand, my skin shiny enough to reflect the sunlight the way an apple does with its little window-glint dazzle. The curve of the car, dusty, behind my arm, and then the road leading past dark green trees into watery sky. Emblazoned beneath my arm in digital readout is '93 6 20. The camera, my face, aren't visible at all behind the heavy black frame of the mirror's mount, blurry where it joins the car.

What also isn't in the photograph is the smell of dust, the sunlight's grasp on my arm, the dry comforting heat spilling into the air-conditioned car when I roll down the window. Sensations whose familiarity threatens to disorient me as thoroughly as that line of trees afloat in the distance I'm driving towards, a landscape wavering as if these fields, this road, were cradled by a huge flat sea. Or is it the sky?

JOAN CRATE

The Invisible Landscape

Infants open eyes, ears, mouth to Mother, to her warm milk, enveloping flesh and soft voice; to the curious, poking fingers of siblings, to grandmother's worn lullabies, a father's rough hands. Beyond that 37 degree Celsius human circle exists the more variable family of sky and rock, summer grass, mosquito, ice and silence, the biting, breathing wind. How do we differentiate one from the other, these landscapes, earth-kin all of them?

My father is Yellowknife to me still, the outside come in. I watched him through the bedroom window as he blazed trails through snow — to the mines, to the trees, hunting, mysterious meetings about unions, native representation in the snow-white municipal government of Yellowknife.

His face is fogged by his own breath as he blocks the illegally bought caribou hanging in the front porch while the R.C.M.P. question him about his friend's dead duck, allegedly shot out of season. Hunger is a season, he mumbles.

Promises fall all around us like corpses. *Nothing can be trusted. Nothing is the same, his friend says later.*

The sun is a cataract thickening in the winter sky.

My father is smoke and talk in the living room with other men. Sometimes they smell like tobacco and wood smoke, sometimes like mineshafts. Some of the miners hold glasses of jiggling liquid darkness in their hands; their voices are filled with shadows. Lonely men, they've left their families behind in the south. They look at my sister and me from the corners of their eyes. We hover at the edge of their sight, learn the rabbit's avoidance.

Even when he stretches across his book-littered bed, groggy from the night shift, my father drifts through other rooms, other times. His hair, slick black, reflects the northern lights and the dusty light bulb hanging from the ceiling. He likes to think of himself as a practical man, a pragmatist, he tells us, but even before I am old enough to know what the word means, I don't believe him.

> Thick miner's fingers,
> the blackened nail my small
> hand caught and lingered
> with, and his dark head as always

in the (darkening) clouds. Before
I could fear the fall, before sick dread,
he threw me into the hot night sky
and I ached so quick and deep oh
for my cheek against the midnight sun,
for fire and blizzard speed,
for transcendence over wolves and bait,
a goodnight kiss, for angel prayer
and raven wings
                    to fly
in time
he caught me, brought me down to earth.

Decades later when he's grey and bearded, sitting in a wheelchair at a table flat as the prairie outside his door and pasting worlds together in collage, he cannot escape the geography of my early eyes. Half-memory, half-dream — that other world he will always live in.

He believes in the land beyond consciousness, open only to the lone traveller, and now, old and crumbling, he goes there more easily, more often, reproducing its topography with clippings and scissors. I watch him stride through snow on his young man's legs, axe in hand.

Plodding behind him, behind my sister, I am weary of always being the smallest, the last, bored with following. I step from his path, snow burning my eyes, nose, cheeks. Shamed, I have to cry out, Don't leave me! He turns, snow spraying from his heels.

Only the women — mother, grandmother — can escape mapping. They exist in all the kitchens in all the houses in all the towns and cities we ever lived. They are wood and oil-stove heat, food, soft breast brush as they bend to comfort. They master all territory, venture out with shopping bags, bring back food, clothing, visitors. Their bodies are the countries that nourish me. They know I will leave them and return, leave and return indefinitely. They anticipate crossed borders, new formations, babies at the breast, the continuity of blood and river delta — extensions that will reach forever outward from them, a hunger that will always seek the source of their love. They believe in reaching worlds in their children's footsteps. They will journey far, but they know patience. Feed, heal, fret over scraped knees and dinner: the future is measured in every heartbeat. Theirs is a practical place, a possible one, but impossible to see. For them, vision exists beyond the sense of sight. It is the necessity of meat in the mouth, danger and hunger.

Vancouver: On a brisk fall afternoon we took a bus through Stanley Park, and I was afraid of the squeaking vinyl seats, strangers, the torpedoing sense of time and the quiet fire in the trees outside the window — yellow, red. The world had frozen in explosion. I had never seen deciduous trees before, knew little about colour. I clutched my sister's bare arm, there next to me in air far too warm for October, her birthday month. I longed for the solace of dark winter sleep.

Nothing can be trusted. Nothing is the same, my father's friend had said. The world changes and we are sometimes left behind.

Lost between climates. In summer I get sick in the heat. The days are too short. Night is always hovering when it should have disappeared — a dark dream. Bit by bit my body forgets its seasons. My mother and sister take pills for headaches, shots for allergies. One day during a lightning storm, my sister turns blue. Terrified, my mother calls a cab which she cannot pay for. At the hospital, the electric lights flutter and die. Nurses with hypodermic needles attack like sharp-beaked birds. When my sister has turned back to the colour she should be, my grandmother and I leave. At home we light candles, eat tea biscuits and sing. I sound like a crow, but neither of us cares.

In this new, warm place my grandmother sprinkles brown sugar on onion slices and feeds me the syrup. *Good for you.* And fish oils in honey wrapped around a spoon. This is winter medicine, I tell her. *Shhh.* Time and place have both shifted.

Unlike Great Slave Lake, the coastal water is salty and devoid of bloodsuckers. Jellyfish hover instead — stinging full moons suspended in a liquid sky. I join them, learn to drift through this waterworld — like memory, like dream. I swim whenever possible, substitute swimming pools for the sea in winter, and submerge myself until my lips and fingertips turn purple. I have begun to like the new colours staining my life. This place is becoming home, the landscape of burnt trees, convoluted night, buildings, salt water, cars, and crowds of humid bodies.

Years and years later: I've had two children, left one husband. I've moved and moved and moved until I'm raw from brushing up against the rough edges of too many landscapes. Somewhere along the way, I've lost the concept of "home," don't get to know the neighbours well, never completely unpack. Instead I create worlds with words and then knock them down like saplings under bulldozer blades. I tell myself that re-creation is always possible.

My new lover tells me the story of his parents — runaways from arranged marriages on the other side of the globe, about the angry villagers, the unforgiving priests, his parents' eleven illegitimate children. I try to think of hot, dry mountains, erupting emotions, bury myself in his warmth. His story is full of ache; nevertheless I dig for golden-tongued romance. There aren't enough hours for my children, my job, my studies, for him, but I am starting to believe in the possibility of escape from the drought of poverty. Our hard work and fatigue begin to faintly glitter under the distant star of the future. One day, one day. My voice flickers in space. I hum out of tune. Somewhere in all that space I exist too.

I begin to discover new territories in myself, new possibilities. The earth tilts. Home, perhaps, is these places, a geography to invent together with this person and his memories of lost terrains of flesh and love. And he says he feels safe here in Canada, with me. I sleep in a hot country,

> trace borders with my tongue,
> settle in the soil creviced
> between your limbs.
> The land I love is foreign.
> I linger in orchards of figs,
> dates, carob. You pick each fruit
> for me, offer them with words
> I can't understand spoken
> in a familiar voice.
> *khudi, habibti*
> Beneath my lips your heart
> explodes, explodes, explodes.

Early afternoon I arrive at a writers' colony at Emma Lake in northern Saskatchewan and look around me. Thin evergreens growing out of basalt, clear lakes. Home, I think. A buried geography resurfaces: forgotten Yellowknife remembered. My beautiful construction, my fabrication. My yearning for that imaginary landscape is accommodated and embraced in this familiar, foreign place. I consider painting the kitchen when I return, wonder if fireweed has completely taken over the garden. I anticipate travelling back from this strangely familiar place to that other one. Home.

I have been home to four children, embraced their forming bones and appetites in my belly, crowned them with light of day and nourished them with my breasts, my work, faded them with my exhaustion and anger. Long after they have left, I embrace them still.

Children measure my reach and length,
the depth of sigh and bone.
They have lived in me and parts
they shed have never escaped my body.
I am implanted with soft moon
fingernails, crumpled snakeskin,
groping blind eyes, underwater wail:

Love me

Love me

(Leave me)

Their grandmother totters now, frail. Their grandfather is dead. And they are too old now to believe that I am beautiful, secure and smart, that I can always kiss it better. To their embarrassment, I reach out to touch their lovely youth.

Other days my body aches when I look out on brown autumn leaves, and in my throat I taste bitter winter. I know that I am locked in a rusting cage, suspended in another generation's landscape. Even so — even though many would say I can't — I sing.

BIRK SPROXTON

A Stickle of Smoke

1.

At ten years old, my usual morning practice was to read the sky. I leapt out of bed and hunched down to look out my tiny window. Scrunched and knotted and hating to touch the cold floor, I looked out. The world stared back and shouted at me. I was ten years old and the world was too much. I fell onto the floor.

(Look again.)

The tombstone rock planted itself hugely under the light pole. The street embraced the rock. Tracks skirted the lake in gentle curve. Watery grey shadows waved to the slanted morning light and the lake stretched a half mile across to the thousand-foot rocky outcrop of the far shore. Bedrock. (Look up.) Tiny houses sat there, and above them stood the brilliant red headframe of North Main Shaft and the black smokestacks of the smelter and zinc plants, pencil strokes against the blue sky streaked with morning gold.

A fiery sun drew the scene; the rocky earth displayed herself; the rock cradled the rolling lake. Fire and earth and water.

But there was no smoke.

The smelter smoke was gone.

2.

"That's not smelter smoke," Mr. Baldy said when people complained about the grit in their throats. "It's not smelter smoke, at all."

Mr. Baldy was a stickler for correct language. He stickled a lot. At school he made us do spelling every day. Print words once, and write them twice, in neat columns. He believed in factors of three. He required mistakes to be redone three times. Mistakes in the second round meant the exercise became nine times per word. You see what I mean.

He was a stickler and he wanted everyone to know that the Zinc Plant generated the foul smoke. Yes smoke ripped our throats, he admitted that, but the smelter smoke was innocent. He tugged on his vest for emphasis. "Zinc Plant smoke. That's what does it." Mr. B's stickles did not catch on. He could run on about sulphur and water and the smell and the sharp taste, and he could give us chemical explanations. But we paid little attention.

We sided with Early Wakeham. Whenever a westerly whipped smelter smoke down Main Street, Early, a bootlegger by trade, would perk up and smile and glad-hand everybody, even us kids.

"That's the smell of money, and good luck for you, too," Early said. "You can quench your thirst at my place any day and twice on Sunday. Finest homebrew this side of tomorrow. 'The Milk of Human Kindness,' I call it. Good for what ails you."

We knew better than to take Early's offer, but we liked to hear his stories. He made smelter smoke seem a friendly part of our town, despite the grit and bite, and since the smoke was inevitably there on those west-wind days, his approach surely was the proper one, certainly more comfortable than Mr. B's fussiness.

3.

You can see the smelter smoke from miles away, a marker in the sky, from whatever direction. At school we had learned about the mining and smelting processes, and we knew our town was special in being named after the hero of a novel. We knew these things in a schoolish way, a bookish learning that we more or less resisted, almost as much, perhaps, as we resisted memorizing for choral recitation the poem about Kew Gardens ("It isn't far from London / And you shall wander hand in hand / With love in summer's wonderland").

We knew the smoke on a more personal level. The plume of smoke forecast the weather. It signalled when in spring to pull on long-johns, when in summer to plan swimming or baseball, when to fall back into bed to daydream. Certainly the smoke had billowed and tattered and flapped in the wind, through whatever season, for all the days I could remember. The smoke made an everyday presence; smelter smoke lodged itself, whether fluff or stream, into our imaginative geography. We grew in it. The plant breathed smoke; and so long as the stacks snorted smoke into the sky, the town was alive and kicking. Smoke was part of our wonderland, and we walked with love, or at least thoughtlessness.

The day without smoke — in fact it probably was days, but it struck like a single blow — that day startled me into feelings I carry still, feelings that all the literature on acid rain cannot dislodge. The day provoked thought.

4.

Approach the town from the west and you will cross a landscape much more complex than what W.O. Mitchell called the least common denominator of land and sky. This world is the Pre-Cambrian Shield, and the land takes the shape of lake and muskeg swamp, spruce trees and rocky outcrops. And the sky holds headframes and smelter smoke. Here is what you might see.

As you drive along the Hanson Lake Road toward the twin communities of Creighton, Saskatchewan, and Flin Flon, Manitoba, the greenery begins to thin out. The outcroppings of rock become more and more visible. You can see the stack of the Hudson Bay Mining and Smelting Company about fifteen miles out of Creighton. By the time you reach the outskirts of Creighton, the forest has disappeared. What you see is a large pond, almost a lake, of grey sludge with a few thin and dying trees at its edge. Across the lake stands the smelter with its huge stack.

So goes the description in *Rain of Death: Acid Rain in Western Canada*, an accurate one in its way. The writers found something out of joint, something rotten in the province of Manitoba. That road was not there in my childhood, but when I travel it now I too notice how spindly the trees are and how much rock there is, and wonder why people think that trees can grow on rock (or money grow on trees).

Try another description, this time from a 1934 Winnipeg newspaper called *Voice of Labour*. The young woman who wrote them — she was nineteen or twenty — chose her words carefully. She signed her name, "Mabel Marlowe."

Dark and heavy is the smoke which pours from the chimney of the Hudson Bay Mining and Smelting Company; poisonous and deadly is the gas which fills the lungs of miners in the underground department, and which with the passing of years, turns them into dry, shrivelled lumps, or fills them up with ugly, yellow pus. For miles around the little town of Flin Flon the foliage on the trees yellows and dies as the fumes from the smelter kill all life.

Typing her words raises my hackles. Well, yes, the smoke does kill foliage, I argue, but surely not all life. The smoke meant my brothers and sisters and I had a roof. We had food. Surely these things cannot be dismissed. And so my hackles start in a quick wash of inexplicable feeling and the sudden dash of cold floor against naked flesh.

Rain of Death and *Voice of Labour* condemn the outpouring of smoke, and I hear the arguments. But whatever the arguments might be, I can no more change my view of smoke than I can change the colour of my eyes. (Smoke-coloured eyes.)

5.

For two summers, when I was nineteen and twenty, I worked for Hudson Bay Mining on the Open Pit crew. We repaired tracks in the main yards and around the plant. We slammed rails together, we dug out old ties with picks and shovels. We shovelled sand and rock and gravel and slag. We jumped on shovels to tamp the ties. (I used my shovel to shoot puck-sized rocks at power poles.) We leaned on our shovels and gazed at the sky. Foreman Dave warned us. "You guys Italians? You gonna lean like a tower all day? You stand like that," he said, "I give you shovels with rope handles." Behind his eyes I saw fire and brimsmoke.

6.

Monday morning we set off to the slag tunnel. We would tear out the old track and replace everything, rails and frogs and ties. We would be there all week, in the smelter itself.

The slag tunnel at that time ran under the huge converters which smelted the ore and poured molten copper into huge ingots on the copper wheel. Then the converter operator dumped the residue into pots on the slag train. Each car was a single pot, a short and stout bell-like vessel which could be tipped and emptied. The heavy trains had worn down the rails and crushed the ties. The frogs creaked with complaint each time the rails moved across them. (Frogs underlie the intersections of two lines of track. Great headless monsters with four splayed rails for legs and a solid iron cross-plate for belly and torso.)

The electric dinky humped the pots together and hauled the little train, two pots or three, from the slag tunnel out onto the slag pile. When tipped, like the teapot in the children's verse, the slag-pots fell sideways, and each set off a spectacular display. Smoke burst into black and white and shades of grey; the molten slag splashed and fingered down the slope in red and orange and pink, a sudden shower of yellows and golds. Think of slag as smelter smoke in molten guise, for they both carry the same smell and the smell strikes you first. Think of slag and smoke as money spent and money earned. Filthy lucre. (I could see the display from my tiny bedroom window if the night were dark or the clouds hung low.)

The dumped slag cooled and froze into amazing shapes, alternately sharp and glass-smooth and prickly. Over time, the slope itself formed a huge holding basin for the tailings excreted by the Zinc Plant. (These tailings make up the sludge-pond that the *Rain of Death* writers complain about.) The sludge-pond surges over the old lake bottom. In the late 1920s, engineers drained the lake to allow open-pit mining to begin.

From water (by way of smoke) to pay dirt (and slag). First things and last things.

We rebuilt the entire track. We dragged out the old rotten ties and replaced them with huge new squared-off timbers, the solid timber ties we used only under frogs. We pulled flannel masks over our noses and mouths, horseless bandits in hardhats, contemporary knights of labour. Tamp that tie, heave that rail.

In the slag tunnel, a dragon set up shop in my craw, made it red and inflamed and infected and rough-breathing sore. Foreman Dave heard my smoky exhalations and sent me with Crow Kohut to a fresh-air job about a mile away.

7.

Crow and I dodged along the tracks, past the Timekeeper's Shack and then along the Pit's edge. We kept a steady pace. The Mill and North Main Shaft stood hulking on the high side of the Pit. On the lake bottom, electric power poles punctuated the tracks and curved in a gentle arc toward South Main headframe.

"You've got two jobs," Crow said. He tiptoed along the rail. "You've got to shovel the sand, and you've got to keep out of the hole. You fall in, be nothing left." He stumbled onto the ties. "Tiny bits of Sproxton-burger, maybe. At the most. We won't even try to put you together. No king's horses and no king's men."

Crow showed me the Watchman's Shack — a bench graced three sides, the door at one end, a heater parked near the door. "Stay in here for lunch and breaks. Don't hang around outside. They can see you."

I looked through the frame window to the west. The Watchman's Shack lay between the tracks and the steel-mesh and barbed-wire fence. I looked to the eastern horizon, the town side of the Pit. The main line of track between South and North Main looked over the lake bottom. (Smelter smoke blew into the town.) Crow was right.

We went outside onto the tracks. They were covered with sand. "Don't even look at a shovel until you get this on."

He handed me a one-and-one-half-inch hemp rope and a huge leather belt about eight inches in diameter. He clamped the belt to the rope and gestured for me to hook the belt together. I looked for the other end of the rope. It was wrapped around a power pole. I was born again, a dynamo-child.

Or an anchor at sea bottom, a boat at dock, a toddler on a clothes-line. A plant growth, a tiny appendix wiggling in the smoke-free wind.

"Once you're all dolled up for the dance, you can start." He gave me a long-handled spade. "Square-mouth in the shed. You get bored, you change partners."

Crow gave me the word about the gash in the earth. I would shovel sand from the tracks and throw it into Forty-Four Stope. The slag tunnel's acrid smoke was far behind me, and the stack smoke rolled down Main Street. This earthy hole was new to me, a seductive blackness in contrast to the sunny openness of the open pit.

"That hole's 4,400 feet deep. It can explode. Scare you down the hole faster than a jack-rabbit."

I conjured up scenarios about underground explosions. I knew the sound of blasting and I could imagine underground blasts, a rock face tumbling into the cave and the air rushing out here, through this slash in the bedrock. My father was a foreman underground. He prowled around that very day. My brother too had worked underground; he climbed ladders with cases of dynamite strapped on his back. I thought myself well-qualified to imagine what happened down there.

"Got nothing to do with underground," said Crow. "The sand gets hung up on the way down, and then it works itself loose, and whoosh. Big blast up here. You're a university kid. Figure it out. And don't get too close."

Armed with the shovel, I shuffled back and forth down the tracks. As I went, my umbilical cord swept the rails clean, a hiss of consonants to the open vowel of the stope. I threw the sand from a distance. The earth would not swallow me, I would not splatter her with my scrawny carcass.

When he left, Crow said, "Don't fall."

8.

Strike a vein of clichés.

Miners are superstitious. They court lady luck, now here, now there. Into the underground caverns, stomping ground of the prince of blackness, miners lug their rumours and superstitions and desires. To harvest the fruits of the earth, they insinuate themselves into the beds of rock. They yearn to go from rocks to riches — quick-change artist. (Prospectors search for riches in rocky outcrops, and miners haul away the underground incrops.)

Miners descend into the bowels of the earth to make a pile, but all that glitters is not gold. Miners want smoke too; clear blue skies mean shutdowns and strikes. A knot in the gut and a sudden fall onto the cold floor. Miners desire the smoke even while they recognize the dirt.

My father urged me to study. "Go to school, so you don't have to work in the mines." I took off, rocks and smelter smoke packed in my baggage. I hacked and stickled at hockey, and then collected a string of degrees. I dirtied my hands in the bowels of libraries and archives. I mined them.

A friend said, "Sproxton, you must dream about rocks. You even have rocks in your name."

I said nothing. She knew I wanted to go underground.

9.

Sometimes I think Mr. B was done in by the poetry of the smoke. Surely the seductive call of the repeated *sm* sound alone was too much for him. "Smelter smoke," like *smack and smear* or *smooch and smush*, makes you kiss your lips together as you say the phrase.

Against this gentle pressing of lips, "Zinc Plant Smoke" has only the force of descriptive truth. The "smelter smoke" phrase has a rhythmic power to match its nice light caress. It makes an almost perfect dactyl — a long stressed syllable followed by two shorter unstressed syllables — and if you look up *dactyl,* you will discover it comes from a word that refers to the articulated finger joints. To say the phrase is to utter a caress. To stroke the oral cavity. The first sound engages teeth and lips, and the two other sounds roll off the tongue with the fluid intimacy of a kiss. "Smelter smoke."

(Try it in your mouth.)

10.

I rummaged around in old newspapers and found that Mabel Marlowe's nickname was "Mickey." She published her smelter smoke article in a newspaper called the *Voice of Labour* (Spring 1934). The voice of the *Voice*, Mickey was sensitive to lungs shrunk to "dry shrivelled lumps" or filled with "ugly, yellow pus."

She also spoke up about profits and about wage cuts and working conditions. And she spoke about the future. She saw how men and women would in the future gather together to celebrate May Day:

Although no one was selling ribbons, each toil-soaked jacket and cap bore a tiny emblem. One in the crowd had a few straggling ends of red string.

With their own hands they had pinned on the tiny banners. These men and women would no longer be slaves, but were ready to take their places in the long march of the ages. They had recognized their place under the banner which had one colour, one aim, one end in view — the freedom of the international proletariat — under the Red Flag.

Later that year Mabel Marlowe was sentenced to one year of hard labour. The law found her guilty of riot and intimidation and chucked her into the slammer.

I have slowly grown fond of her. She knew that the smoke caused real problems for real people. And she knew too that dead foliage was a symptom, not the problem. To her, the problem was a system that valued profits over people. She said nothing about the Zinc Plant.

I first read her words in the National Archives. Later I found her signature on a letter in the Provincial Archives of Manitoba. She had sent a demanding letter to the Premier and politely signed herself "M. Marlowe." That is as close as I have gotten to her, though I have searched for years.

I think I am in love with her, just as I love and hate the place that nurtured me. She, too, believed that smoke matters.

11.

Just before the outbreak of World War I, a group of prospectors hoofed through the bushes on the Saskatchewan-Manitoba border and came to a strange conical dip in the rock near a lake. An ice-cream-cone shape, let us say, without ice-cream. The men wrinkled their brows and pondered and chipped away, their picks made clicking noises, the quick tap of an outdoor cash register. They sang *waaaahoooo* and made deep throat noises. They toiled and bubbled. They had struck gold, a huge orebody, with the prospect of more under the lake, deep under the lake.

Earlier, the prospectors had found a dime novel in the bush called *The Sunless City*. The hero of the novel, named Josiah Flinabbatey Flonatin, a grocer by trade and descended from a long line of Bologna merchants, believed that the centre of the earth was inhabited. To test his theory, Flin Flon slapped together a one-man submarine and plunged to the bottom of the bottomless lake. He landed in a place where the sun didn't shine and the streets were paved with gold and women were in charge (they kept a king as figurehead). And Flin fell in love with a beautiful young princess and she fell in love with him, and he persuaded her to follow him back to the surface of the earth and, alas, she died (of course), and then the novel broke off, for the end-pages were missing. So the prospectors determined that Flin had exited the earth from that strange conical formation there on the edge of the lake. They called the lake Flin Flon.

12.

A new stack now reaches up 800 feet, 500 feet higher than the stack of my youth, and the emissions have shrunk to a mere tuft of smoke, a tiny breath against the hugeness of sky. Those Main Street gusts have diminished accordingly. But for me, smoke is everywhere.

For me, the smelter smoke plumes and drifts in the wind. For me, the smoke still billows and floats and gives depth to the sky, and when it zooms down Main Street, you smell, what? — a burning rock, a cinder, purple glass molten to a crisp, a whiff of ammonia flattened, or heightened, by sulphur.

For me, the smoke still plays canvas backdrop to the lighting display of the slag pour — now pink, now orange, now deep red. For me, the smoke wrenches ragged from the mouth of the stack in a grey November wind or delivers up soft white pillows to float across a midsummer sky.

The smoke speaks of fiery golden dragons and the full gritty taste of words in the mouth.

KAREN CONNELLY

Thoughts on Land and Language

Writing the land. What does this mean? At the moment, I am in Thai-
[...] month I will be in Canada. The
[...] is is not a list meant to make
[...] is exciting, yes, but it exhausts
[...] xpected territory. Through lan-
[...] rent cultures, what holds all of
[...] :r. Except that it is not so obvi-
[...] people forget the land, exclude
[...] arth and what happens to it as

[...] iscuss this phenomenon and its
[...] for the degradation of the land
[...] digenous people and peasants
[...] id) all over the world. Though I
[...] some of us believe the earth is
[...] seem numb to its power. As I sit
[...] hoose something for this anthol-
[...] work is tied to the land. Every
[...] poem abounds with animal meta-
[...] not only as a living force, but as
[...] those close to me. Though I am
[...] ous about it: I do not try to write
[...] d, nor do I write "odes" to nature.
[...] organic than that for me. (I laugh.
[...] mpost?)
[...] nt languages, different rhythms of
life, different landscapes. These new elements are deeply connected.
Different languages, for me, are a pleasure: one learns the whole world
over again — tree, hello, flower, cat, love — in a new tongue. Like
unexplored land, the wildness of language never ends; all you have to
do is cross a border and the world changes, everything is called something else, the language makes new demands upon you. Of course, the
physical realness of a place is as solid as that of any other place. The
tree, the flower, the cat remain touchable, even if they seem utterly
strange because of their new surroundings and their new names.

I have just started learning Burmese; what I am struck by is the way
the language "fits" everything there, how the words for particularly

Burmese things (clothes, puppets, certain animals, the ground sandal-
wood paste women wear on their faces) sound the way they look.
Every new language seems to echo, for me, the setting that surrounds
it, even though I know language is arbitrary, a human invention.

For a poet who loathed studying French grammar, it's a vindication
to understand that learning a language is ultimately about learning
rhythm; once you get the rhythm, the words slowly but very surely fall
into place. Every language is a kind of verbal dance. As soon as I write
that, I think of how Burmese fits the way the women and men walk
down the streets and gesture to each other, how any other language
would not properly accommodate those particular movements, and how
those movements are dictated by the land the people work on and
travel through.

I've chosen writing from four countries, three continents. Very different poems describing very different events. What remains constant,
however, and what sustains me wherever I am, is a conviction that the
earth we live on is sacred and deserves our love. If we have the patience to listen, the land speaks a language of its own which transcends
all our words.

Alexandra   (Canada)

She lay upstairs
inhaling the night,
asleep, her hair unbound on the pillows.
Mouth open slightly, her face
was grave and beautiful, engaged
in the fervent waltz of sleep.
Both arms flung open over the burgundy quilt.
She was dancing motionless like that
when I left her
and came down in the dark
to watch the moon, white,
rove over the whiter hills.
I thought of nothing but
her breasts,
my mouth,
how the tongue is the soft
moonbeam of the hard teeth.

I sat crying in front
of the big window, filled

with the inchoate emptiness
of moon-sky and snow.
I was feeling the surprise of it,
the absurdity, even,
and the absolute rightness
of such a landscape.
The way her ivory back was
like my own but smaller,
a smooth plain of
heat, strength, the long
hunger that leads eventually
to the mouth,
to the cunt.
I had never seen so much
clean white turned platinum,
rose-purple, blue in the dark.

I sat in the silent house.
For awhile, coyotes.
Once, her cough,
which made me still and hopeful
because it had the raw silk
of her voice in it.
I wanted her to call my name,
but she slept on
turning slowly in her dance,
tangled in tassels of dream
and breath, quiet

because I had loved her
well enough.

She has no idea
how awake I am,
after such long sleep:
it doesn't matter.
This is the way things
are now, these hills,
my life filled with
depths, roundnesses,
the deep basins of the land
she lives in,
the land she is

Voula (Greece)

> *... I was sitting under the streetlamp writing in my journal*
> *when Voula came along (Voula, who truly must never sleep)*
> *and, seeing that I was all thoughtful and sad-faced, said*
> *"Oh, Amalia. Just dream. When you're asleep. Dream. When*
> *you're awake. Dream."*
>
> — excerpt from a letter by Amalia Perkins

Little spot

is the meaning of my name,
but look at me, my life
is big as the sun, I am Voula,
I am famous.

"She is ugly," they'll tell you,
"a dirty-dog woman, a junkie
covered in sores
and a bitch besides,"

but look at my young lovers,
tarna-mou,
Sonia from Brazil,
Katerina from the north,
Sinead from Ireland with
all her silk and lace.

I am Voula
I am famous.

If you see me dance *rebetiko**
you too will love me,
you will watch and look away
with burning eyes.
Even Vaso's plates know
the disorder of love, they leap
off the tables and shatter
just to touch my feet.

With these scuffed boots
I sway hard and slow inside
the music, my arms in the air,

elbows crooked above my head:
I am balancing each star high
above the plane trees.

I close my eyes to dance like this.
You have to close your eyes
to see inside a woman,
and to see inside the gods.

The accordion and I
breathe the warm night wind.
The mandolin has my curves,
the same thin hardness and dirty
fingerprints all over her body.

Sweat shines like oil on my forehead.
I dance so slowly, a snake
without legs, without arms,
held up by the taut nerves
of music.

I have given my limbs to you.
I have given my eyes to you.
I am naked in my dance,
in this night
under the plane trees.

Na seis heilia kronia!
Na seis panda!

May you live a thousand years
May you live forever.

*Rebetiko is a hypnotic, passionate style of music and dance which
became popular in Greece in the 1930s and '40s. It was, and still is, the
music of the poor and of social outcasts, similar in many ways to gypsy
flamenco. Traditionally it is played and danced only by men.*

Women in the Heart (Thailand)

We thought they were mermaids,
the women in the heart of the bay,
rising black out of the water,
silhouettes holding fish against the sky
in the aspect of eagles.

There where the hills sweep down
in a green deluge to the sea,
and L'Isle de Cheval rears out
of the blue like a mount breaking
from heaven, not water.

Everything turned over, everything
a clue for some other mystery
but never the mystery of itself.
We wake and wash from our faces
the essence of not-knowing.

In seconds, the wind changes
the tide draws out, crashes in,
the coastline gives way
to another kingdom.

Suddenly the women in the heart
of the bay are fishermen
with green nets, not hair, draped
around their necks.
Suddenly they are close to you,
so close you feel their eyes
coming in like boats
to haunt your face.

They are there before you,
arms weighted with silver,
a treasure of fish.
And wordless, you love them,
these men tempered
by salt water and sky.
Their smiles burn white
beneath their sea-black eyes.

Despite Everything (Burma)

In the darkness above Mandalay
she is wondering
how to carry them properly.
The suitcase, the letters
from the exiles, the jagged
blades of history.

Down below, men with scars
on their ankles
are dreaming.
Down below, the people
eat silence
while their hearts
fill with thunder.

When she saw the thin women
carrying water
from the muddy holes
of Pagan, she learned
something about thirst.

One life
and the wide earth
bound, set in her gut
like a nugget of raw jade,
like a bullet.

She wants to say love
but the word is spoiled.
She wants to say fierce
but that isn't it.
Half a dozen languages but not
a word for what she knows now.

Maybe the beggars in Tachilek.
Maybe the bloated dog
in the river that divides two nations.
Maybe the children playing there
after the body floated by.
Remember how they stared up at her,

filthy children laughing
in the water, getting clean
despite everything.

FLESH and BONE

SKY DANCER Louise Bernice Halfe

Telling Tales/Telling Stories

I am sharing these words not in the attempt to clarify or convert, nor to brag about my spiritual practices. You need not have participated in my Native rituals to have had your own glimpses of those moments of Grace when the gifts of the Great Mystery illuminate the memory of your cells. This is my attempt to express my thoughts about when narratives of place and displacement marry or take leave of one another. I begin with the belief that when one is centred to one's Being, the divorce of these narratives is rare.

When a survivor enters therapy and pursues healing, becoming actualized, she revisits the place where the wounds were created. As a writer, I continue to be led to those places. My creative Spirit knows better than I, my umbilical cord is and will always be attached to the land. I go home each spring to the reserve for ceremony, to affirm the gifts I have received, home to that place where I celebrate the dichotomy between the deep scabs of historical wounds and the buckskin celebrations of our Native Peoples' inherent gifts. As I sit there alone in the womb of seeing, I perceive my companions — the dark of the Moon and the brightness of the Sun. I breathe in the musty smells of the Earth after purifying Rain. I chase away all my clutter, all my nonsense. Chasing that nonsense means stepping into dialogue with mySelf, acknowledging my demons and coming to terms with them. I cry, I acknowledge the anger of the self-inflicted sacrifice of fasting. Cry some more and when my wound is open, raw, exposed and bleeding, I still mySelf. That's when the Visions come. Then comes Communion and my Elders help me to decipher the meaning of my Visions.

But what was I going to say? Am I saying I've no need to go home physically? No need to write from where the wounds were inflicted in the first place? Daily I carry my weight of water-washed Stones to the Mountains, to the bush, to the prairie, these small pebbles of reMembering, and within these places I carry out the ritual of that smoking Memory, praying to the Grandmothers, celebrating the land that exists inside me. If place plays an important role in my writing, in the person that I am, in my psyche, then what is my responsibility to these Selves? To know I am attached to the land by an invisible umbilical cord is to be nurtured from my home place, this place of dichotomy. This home place, the land, its unpredictable weather turbulence, places its Centre in my existence. This home place goes deeper still through my Mother's Womb and my mother's Mother's Womb. It pulls me into history and allows me to be who I am. And so I attempt to share with you this story of how I came to writing. It's called "Comfortable in My Bones."

Comfortable in My Bones

In the Northern woods of Saskatchewan lies a creek; in the summer it's a slender, lazy snail. When the spring rain comes, it becomes a writhing snake creating turbulent waves, carrying everything before it. I walked the woods, following the creek, cradling paper leaves and talking stick, tobacco and sweetgrass in my hands. On many occasions I flew over logs in front of me, eager to gain my solitude, eager to unload the discoveries held close to my heart. My favourite spot overlooked the banks where I leaned against an old log I shared with ants. There, I contemplated something I had read, something I heard on CBC, something I dreamt, a conversation I had with my children or my husband. Sometimes these discoveries were not pretty. The landscapes of the earth and of my mind were both simple and complex. I bore feelings that needed song. I often suffered the rash of shame bursting through the thin layers of skin. Yet my Spirit demanded the spring of clear blood. My journeys became a ritual where I offered tobacco and smudged with sweetgrass. Whatever travelled into my thoughts, I immediately wrote, no matter how absurd or obscure. At times I did nothing but breathe, listen and sleep, comfortable in my bones. I saw no need to run. The land, the Spirit, doesn't betray you. I was learning to cry with the Spirit. I was safe to tear, to lick, to strip the stories from my bones and to offer them to the universe.

When I was a child, I was taught to lift a found bone from the earth and scrape my warts, then to return it the way it lay. Many times I watched my cousin grind bones for my Grandmother, medicines she added to her bundles. I was grinding my own bones. Through the leaves and pen, the elusive became concrete. My voice rose through my scribble. On many occasions I had watched my Grandfather's long-johns held by a string, flopping, waving, rolling on the edge of the culvert. We always knew when laundry day was. The foam the creek made provided the soap he didn't have. During our courting days, my husband and I would strip in the spring April heat, bask in the sun and plunge in the glacial Whiterabbit River on Kootenay Plains. The strength of water replenishes and destroys, the calling of the creek and my return are a single natural process.

The year rolled into two, three, four: my journals accumulated. The Great Mystery entered my dreams, and I heard its voice through its creation. Squirrels shared their chatter, the wind blew its soul into my ears, and the water spoke its very ancient tongue. These stirrings were not unfamiliar since I come from a place where all Creation and its gifts are naturally accepted. I went to the Elders and spoke to them about my dreams and revelations. I entered ritual once again to receive my spiritual name and to honour my journey.

I had a dream many years ago that I was repairing the cabin I grew up in with paper and books. I had entered this ceremony, the stirring in my marrow, a living prayer of building and healing, feeding my soul. I read a wide range of authors, including Joseph Campbell, Carl Jung, Mary Daly, Matthew Fox, Sheila Watson, Louise Erdrich, and numerous anthologies written by female and Native writers. My curiosity challenged, I covered topics around sexual morals, philosophy, religious and spiritual debates, symbols, myths and legends. I hoarded my solitude jealously and became angry when I wasn't fulfilling these needs. The map of oral storytelling had long been laid out for me. I often entertained my children with legends I grew up with or made up on my own through the images in classical music. Writing was a natural process. The stories inside me demanded face. They became my medicine, creating themselves in the form of poetry.

These egg-bones were the voice which I had been addressing. My bare feet had felt the drum of the earth and the heartbeat of my palms. I did not fight these stories, though many times I wanted to run. I became a wolf, sniffing and searching, pawing, nuzzling, examining every visible track I made or saw. I became the predator on the scent. I was the master, the slave, the beholder and beheld, the voice and the song. I was the dark, the light. Like the legend of Pahkahkos, my death-song grated, and when I honoured my history, Pahkahkos rattled her bones in the gourds of my memory. (Pahkahkos carries and reveals the skeletal shadow, and its insistent demand to face my demons grated my heart and my skull. It is these that are resurrected only to die again for such is the cycle of breathing and dying.) I will no longer be a binding sinew of stifling rules, but rather a sinew of wolf songs, clear as morning air.

BLANCHE HOWARD

Evening in Paris

There is a painting by the Ukrainian-Canadian artist William Kurelek of Inuit children lying on their stomachs on snow and peering into a long black fissure. The small bodies are stiff and respectful; they are not sprawled sideways nor are any of them attempting to straddle the crack; they are still, prone, wary, at right angles to the sawtooth edge.

The simple picture induces unease. The viewer wants to pull the children back from danger, to keep them from the blackness into which they might tumble, perhaps beyond recovery. I can imagine my brother and me stretched out alongside them, for ours in Saskatchewan was an arctic climate in winter. I would have edged away from the peril, while he — but I am not sure what he would have done. Even as a child he had a fascination with darkness; his was an imagination that from an early age toyed with forms of entrapment.

In sharp contrast to the winters, the summers of the "dirty thirties" were long, oppressive, grasshopper-ridden and hot with the bright, protected clarity that must have been the norm all those millions of years since the dinosaurs, before we started messing up. My brother and I, in the great hush before television, were outdoors from morning to night, exploring and testing ourselves — he with caution, me with abandonment, in accordance with our natures — throughout that dreamy stretch labelled "the innocent years."

Such presumptive innocence, I now think, may gleam more purely in the eyes of the nostalgia-beguiled beholder than it does in actual fact. Innocence is about much more than street smarts; innocence and its loss are at the very core of human tragedy and comedy. The facts we yearn to ferret out are both liberating and imprisoning. As our mother would say when the questioning got too close for comfort, "What you don't know won't hurt you."

Of course we *were* innocent in ways that are not offered to today's children. We were insulated compared to them, muffled in cotton batting against the unharnessed electronic universe — yet we knew something was up. Children can always tell. Even though the dimensions of our world were defined by the fairgrounds on the east, the highway on the west, the tracks and the distant bluffs of trees on the north and south, inside those boundaries we may have had a better crack at losing at least one kind of innocence than children in the middle of large cities today, because *we weren't watched*. We were turned loose in the mornings of the great daylight and encouraged to stay out of our mothers' hair until hunger and sleep gathered us in.

Small prairie towns were hotbeds of childish shenanigans, or at least ours was. Barefoot boys and girls of four and five were easily hidden by the low bushes, and in tiny clearings we explored our orifices and appendages with mutual giggling curiosity, well aware that such explorations were forbidden; aware that our parents knew something and did something they weren't talking about; curious, as all children are, to find out what it is. I remember, when we were very little, trying to figure out where my brother's tiny penis could possibly be inserted to cause such loaded silences, but I never understood it; as for him, he hated being the subject of experiment.

Certainly we gave our versions of original sin more than passing thought, but no more than we gave to the building of tree houses, the late dusk challenge of "hide and seek," the tantalizing reward of a Sunday trip to the lake.

Not that we didn't have our adult child abusers: they weren't sprung unheralded into modern times. In the tiny village where we lived before moving to the relative metropolis of Lloydminster, my closest friend was the daughter of the station agent (a job of some prestige, bringing with it a red-shingled two-storey house by the tracks), and one evening when I was about five and the children were playing a wild game of tag in the little woods of aspen poplars and saskatoon bushes near the station, Mr. B played right along with us, just like one of the kids.

They were coming after me! Suddenly Mr. B swooped me up in his arms and ran through the woods to a small clearing, me giggling and excited from the wild run and the close escape. As he set me down he said, "Let's play pretend married. I'll be the Daddy, you be the Mommy." He smoothed the leaf-strewn patch of ground beneath us. "We'll lie down here, and I'll show you what Mommy and Daddy do," he whispered.

Oh, children have a built-in radar! It was as though alarm bells went off in my head, as though every sense stood at attention, as though I had met and was now in mortal danger.

This is what surprises me now, that I knew peril when I met it, even then, even though it appeared in such affable guise. To this day I can feel the coolness of the darkening evening, the springiness of the mouldering leaf-bed, its smell of damp decay. I can look up still, in my memory, at the leering giant — a slim, shadowy, pale man in braces and a hat, whose breath smelled, not unpleasantly, of booze — and who was reaching and trembling with his enticing hands.

Are children pre-wired against sexual predation? Or is it the function of fairytales, with their wicked giants, their ogres, the gap-toothed, leer-

ing witches, to implant a necessary message that there are some inhabitants of this strange new world who will do us irrevocable harm?

I broke free and ran. I tore through the spindly, closely-spaced as-
pens on my sturdy brown legs as though the monsters of nighttime
terror were breathing down my neck. Branches reached out to pluck at
Mr. B, at his clothes, his grasping arms, while I slid through below
branch level. I out-manoeuvred him, and I didn't pause for breath until
I got back to the others.

I was imprinted, during that wild run, with a caution that has stalked
me throughout my life and that will never leave me now. Looking back
I see that it started then, for even at five I knew enough to never again
let myself be in a situation where I was alone with Mr. B. Nor, in the
years since, with his fellow travellers.

After we moved to Lloydminster I forgot, or perhaps mislaid, those
early memories. School and new friends filled my head, and summer
freedom became a novelty that sustained and delighted my brother and
me through the heat of July. But it was then as it is now: as surely as
July melted into August, novelty melted into boredom. "There's nothing to do," we would whine, and our mother would pause in the midst
of canning fruit in a kitchen as hot as the seventh circle of Hell and
wipe her glistening brow. If we didn't get out of her sight, she would
murmur ominously, there might not be money enough for …

But we would be gone before the words could become form, for we
already knew that words, once uttered, may harden and set like cement. Of course we knew what she meant. Posters everywhere, in the
drugstore windows, flapping in the breeze on telephone poles, nailed
to weather-beaten board fences, proclaimed the Big Event, August 15,
16 and 17, the jubilant three days when the fair would hit town. That
was the way people said it, as though the fair came at us like a tornado
and smashed the whole place sideways with its tinsel and lights, its
raucous barkers, its tinny music, the practically bare-naked ladies, the
shooting galleries, the noise, the dust.

My brother and I lay tingling and wakeful the night before, and
when in the morning my father dug deeply into his pockets and found,
among the nails and staples and candy wrappers (he loved sweets, and
children loved him), two whole dollars for each of us, we ran to the
fairgrounds so fast that my heart pounded in my chest and I had to
slow down, and my brother got there first.

The area was — except for a weather-beaten grandstand and wooden
stage — a barren tract of ground, a breeder of whirlwinds, a home for

wandering tumbleweed and purple Russian thistle, usually deserted, but now magically transforming itself — for they were still setting up, we were so early — into a metropolis of Ferris wheels, Tilt-a-Whirls, an Octopus, candy floss and hot dogs and Crown and Anchor and (gasp) prizes! Cuddly teddy bears, fake-fur rabbits, beautifully packaged "toiletry sets," and even — oh, how my brother's eyes flashed — a .22, a beautiful, shiny, wooden-handled rifle. In those days .22s were revered by boys and tolerated by men; they were great for gophers and for practising — before the manhood-confirming acquisition of a shotgun — on the swarms of wild ducks that stirred the dark surfaces of prairie sloughs.

"I'm going to win that," my brother said.

He was ten and I was thirteen. The organizers of the grandstand show had recruited the local high-school girls as their chorus line, and by the time I had seen my brother firmly ensconced in front of the little shooting gallery where he was going to win the .22, several of my classmates were already being fitted with their "outfits": tight "electric blue" satin briefs and matching bras. I remember that my bra was loose, the slight swellings that passed for breasts insufficient to fill the wired curves, and below the elasticized satin of the briefs my thin white thighs would not meet unless I bent my legs slightly at the knee. We were given cursory training, which none of us believed we needed.

There were two grandstand shows a day. I stood there before the uncritical farmers and townspeople and their families, knees slightly bent, occasionally straightening the balancing leg when a frayed line of us kicked more or less on cue. Afterwards my mother said, "For heaven's sake stand up straight. You look like a stork with your knees bent like that." My father just snorted.

What did parents know, then or now? In our hearts we were the Goldwyn Girls, the Ziegfeld Follies and R.K.O. Radio Chorus all rolled into one, high-stepping and pirouetting in our shiny satin on a magical stage under glittering silver spangles and a décor of bluest crêpe paper, riveting the eyes of the talent scout from Hollywood who would surely have found his way to our little northern town.

We were — at least as far as I was concerned — handsomely paid. We were each given a pass for all the rides, and I spent hours swinging in a chair on the Ferris wheel, rewarded with an occasional stop at the very top, surveying below me the plains of waving golden wheat which I thought must be like the ocean, and out of which rose skyscraping red elevators, Alberta Wheat Pool, Saskatchewan Co-op (Lloydminster is on the border of the two provinces), Federal Grain, where my father worked, and one other whose name has been buried in the sloughed-off cells of dead neurons. And then I would look inwards from the sea to the island of the fairgrounds and watch the mad gyrations of the Octopus, and laugh at some of my bolder classmates clutching one another in the Tilt-a-Whirl; and usually I saw almost directly below me my brother, standing in front of the shooting gallery where the .22 was displayed, hoarding the dwindling change from his precious two dollars, determined, in spite of the greasy barker who kept urging him to get lost, to win.

I was supposed to keep an eye on him, but the responsibility didn't weigh too heavily with me. He was always in the one place, counting his money, weighing his chances. He was a cautious boy; and yet, gazing down on him, the euphoria of the Ferris wheel was momentarily stilled by something I thought I saw, something at the corner of my eye that I couldn't quite catch, a stealthy shape, a darkness that seemed to settle around him, even then, even there in the harsh August sun whose glare could penetrate and backlight the deepest shadows.

I shrugged it off. What could happen to him? In those days the things that could happen to boys were never mentioned; certainly girls knew nothing of them. We knew almost nothing of what could happen to girls for that matter — and yet, I suppose I did know. How many years had passed since our childish explorations? At some level sex is known early, and then forgotten.

As time went on, all the kids came to "know" about Mr. B — or at least they knew something, a personal experience, a bit of hearsay, some wildly inflated, titillating tale, unlikely amalgams of invention and partial truths. We giggled and exchanged gossip, how he had driven his other daughter (not my friend) and a companion to a lonely road and persuaded the companion to "do it," although we were still unsure of what "it" consisted of.

I don't know where the truth lay. I know now that Mr. B drank and that his wife covered for him. She was a stout German woman who could throw the heavy switches on the CPR tracks, and she learned to send telegrams in Morse code in a language that would remain forever clumsy on her tongue. The adults in the town treated him with ill-concealed contempt, but they tolerated him; they knew nothing of the Mr. Hyde hidden beneath the bumbling, good-willed exterior. Years later, when I finally told my mother, she was horrified. "But why didn't someone tell?" she gasped.

I don't know the answer to that. All I know is that we, the children, all knew about him, and that not one of us ever told an adult. His daughter who was my friend was a self-possessed child who never hinted that she knew anything of her father's predilection; we exchanged

Christmas cards until she died, young, at forty, in a far-away country, in Africa. I never heard what happened to Mr. B. For all I know he sank into a boozy old age and died, mourned, I suppose, by those who thought they knew him.

At some point on the second day of the fair I did seek out my brother. He had used up nearly all his money, but just as I came up to the little shooting gallery he scored a direct hit and won.

With the ill-disguised, hard-bitten cynicism that characterized the swarthy men who worked the circus, the operator flung a box at him. "Here ya are, kid. Now get lost, will ya?"

It wasn't the rifle. I don't know whether my brother hadn't scored the points that were needed or whether the operator cheated him in not awarding him the prize that was the gallery's chief attraction; all I know is that he tossed a beautiful blue box at my brother, and the look on his face would have prevented most men from protesting, much less a ten-year-old boy and a thirteen-year-old girl.

"Evening in Paris" the box was labelled. The cover was the colour of the late evening of a perfect day. Silhouetted against the darkening blue was the Eiffel Tower, and in front of it were the figures of a woman and a man. The woman was wearing a long, flowing dress "cut on the bias," something my mother was attempting to do with the dress she was making for the Thanksgiving dance at the church hall. The shiny satin was draped over the perfect hips of the woman as she leaned against the man's tuxedo-clad shoulder.

My brother stared at the box for a long moment, while I held my breath. He didn't handle frustration well, even then. Once, when I had tried to comfort his measles-stricken anger with my most precious possession, he had sent the china egg-cup hurtling across the room, smashing it to smithereens against the wall. Alternatively, he looked as though he might cry, an indignity not tolerated in days when frontier life demolished men for less.

"Take it," he said suddenly, shoving the box at me. He hurled his few remaining pennies in the dust, spun around, and stomped out of the fairgrounds without a backward glance. He didn't return; he sat for uncounted hours in his narrow little bedroom, staring at a wall.

I spent those hours with the box and its contents, trying to unravel the mystery that must be concealed in it. To begin with, there was the sophisticated world of Paris and the Eiffel Tower. I knew little of the French. They spoke a foreign language that we were taught in school because some people in Canada spoke it. I knew they were a lewd lot, because I'd heard of "French safes," which had something in common with "French kisses," "doing it" and Mr. B. It never occurred to me that women who wore dresses cut on the bias and men who wore black jackets and funny ties could have anything in common with Mr. B's besotted fumblings.

The interior of the box contained *parfum, eau de cologne*, talcum dusting powder, and *huile pour bains*. The latter, after laborious translation, I added to the round tub set in the kitchen on Saturday night, in which we bathed. I doled out the oil a few drops at a time over the space of a year. After the bath I patted powder over my skinny body with a voluptuous white puff that had been concealed in the shiny round powderbox, dabbed myself with the *eau de cologne*, saved the *parfum*, whose secret was surely concealed in the blue box with its blue inset bottles, and waited for revelation.

At the end of three days my brother got over his sulk. Years later, when he was nineteen, I gave him a .22 for his birthday — such gifts were acceptable in those days. By then he may not have cared, although he expressed pleasure.

He died last winter, alone, in a shabby room in Calgary. They didn't find him for several days. The floor was littered with bottles whose contents had become his path through the frustrations of life. Some of the bottles were not meant for drinking — cooking sherry, shoe polish, cleaning fluid. I'm told that in earlier times there would have been bottles of perfume, of Evening in Paris, perhaps.

They don't make Evening in Paris any more. Perfumes are more realistic now. We don't have the same illusions. Even little children know what tongue-kisses are, and they know the meaning of "condom," if not of "French safe." They know the man will shed his tuxedo and the woman will discard the dress that is cut on the bias. They know, too, where the man and woman are headed and most of what they will do.

"Obsession," the perfume currently touted as being the most seductive, strips away any remaining shred of illusion that may have been left to console us. Its advertisements feature an androgynous pre-teen whom I once would have thought, in the days of Mr. B, must surely be female. Now I sometimes wonder if Mr. B's predation had extended to boys, but I doubt it. In the gossipy world of children we would have known, and I suspect I am searching for reasons where none may exist.

Obsession's predecessor sported an even more chilling label, but it too has been superseded. Possibly it was too straightforward even for these casually cynical times. It was a name that stripped away not only our illusions, but our hope; it was the only one whose favour my brother courted. It was called, simply, "Poison."

Among the Inuit children who peered into the crevice, no doubt there was one who, like my brother, was at one with the darkness. My brother searched it out as a child in his small darkened room; as an adult he found his own, more lethal source. When he fell, none of us could reach him.

THERESA KISHKAN

Undressing the Mountains

I had not remembered the mountains to be so visible. Driving to the Pacific rim, five days before Easter, I am shocked at the way they have been clearcut, shorn of their trees. This has been in the news, of course, and I've written letters to various politicians about forests I am familiar with at the age of thirty-nine — the Caren, the Carmanah which I knew in my days of canoeing the Nitinat triangle and hiking the West Coast Trail, the last of the spotted owl habitat around Lillooet Lake. But these mountains, high and austere above Kennedy Lake and Taylor River, are not what I think of when I hear of the Clayoquot protests. And yet this stretch of Vancouver Island was once a place I came to as though to the arms of a family.

Who was I then, the woman who drove a small red truck through Sutton Pass in November, desperate to stand among the shore pines and bog laurel? Or who walked the long beaches in 1973, naked but for delicate shells laced to her throat and ankles with seaweed? Now I am arriving with my husband, our three children, many suitcases, our parents following in separate cars with similar luggage. We have reserved a duplex cabin one row removed from the beach, complete with bedding and cooking facilities. My husband's mother will be in the upstairs unit and my parents in a campsite next door. We have booked an afternoon whale-watching charter on the *Chinook Key* and we've planned a number of hikes and expeditions.

Among the first things I notice are the signs warning visitors of the risks: "It is unlawful to feed wildlife" on both a sign and brochure; and "Wildlife and Natural Areas can be hazardous" in both English and French. The brochure elaborates on the dangers of wildlife, showing a rearing bear, teeth bared, and an agressive Coast blacktail deer striking out with its hooves. I remember seeing the deer passing along the roadsides at dusk, feeding on wild roses and the new growth of huckleberry, and their calm faces as we slowed to watch them. And once I imagined them looking at me while I slept at Schooner Cove, wondering who this unfamiliar mammal was with its odd smell and salty hair. Waking, I found their heart-shaped prints in the sand.

The glimpse of ocean as we make our way north toward Tofino reminds me of how I drove in a kind of frenzy twenty years ago, hungry for the grey sand and the curve of Florencia Bay. I'd bring some bread, a block of cheese, apples, maybe a bottle of Irish whisky to drink as the sun eased its way over the horizon towards Asia, sometimes a tent, sometimes a friend, always a book to read in a sheltered cove of driftwood, my body impressed on the warm sand. Or I'd walk in mist or rain, coming back to my small tent to sleep with the booming surf drowning all other sounds. Once a bear made its way along the high-tide line, grazing on huckleberries, pausing now and then to sniff into the wind. And once, I remember, I stood in the waves at low tide, watching the spume of whales as they passed in November to calve off the beaches of Baja California. Always eagles in the high amabilis firs and cedars, and ravens floating down with a throaty chuckle.

This time we unpack our truck at Ocean Village Resort and lug in the cooler, bulging suitcases, a bag of swimsuits and towels for the indoor pool and hot tub, and first-aid kits containing all our medications. The children shed shoes and run down to the water. I make coffee and lie back with my book in a Cape Cod chair, wishing I'd brought sunglasses. Our parents sit at the picnic table and talk about elderly neighbours with their eccentric habits, how much the campsite next door charges, what it charged five years ago, and three, their arthritis, a friend's brain tumour, the price of bacon at Mr. Grocer. My husband cheerfully moves between the groups, agreeing or disputing so nicely that no one can tell the difference, while I am sullen and quiet, remembering how it used to be.

In so many ways, nothing has changed, although in Tofino every second place advertises whale-watching trips and the shops are full of sweatshirts with the familiar grey whale tail arching over, in purple and teal green and raspberry pink. At Wickaninnish Beach, we see no one for hours and my children run in the breakers, finding sand dollars, crab shells, goose barnacles, and a headless sea lion carcass rotting in the sun. I show them eagles and a long tangle of bull kelp strewn with barnacles. Our parents sit on logs, happy in sunlight to watch their grandchildren write messages in the sand: *Have a nice journey!!* (to be read by migrating whales); and their names, to claim the day. Later there's coffee in the Wickaninnish Centre and a picnic lunch set out on some bleached logs, a few Steller's jays waiting for crusts. I want to walk the beach until the sand ends (where? I wonder). Maybe at the point of land curving to Vargas Island, but there's the whale-watching trip we planned a few weeks earlier, so we load up in the truck again and drive to Tofino where we are given red all-weather flotation suits and told to walk down the hill to the boat. "Look for the *Chinook Key.* Your skipper for this trip will be Carl." Carl takes us to see a nesting pair of eagles on a small island in the harbour and then we head out to sea to find whales. The sea is not choppy, but there are big swells and one of my children hangs over the side to vomit in the waves. My mother is sick. The whales do not appear as I dreamed they would, huge and near, but we see spray and a bit of back and a few shows of tails rising just out of the water. There are smooth lengths of water that we are told indicate whales beneath the surface. I ask if they travel in family groups and the skipper tells me yes, but that there are also groups of two males with one female and he has seen them mating, one male supporting the female while the other copulates with her in the green water. I turn my head to hide tears.

Out on the water I can see the mountains, clear against the eastern sky. Some of them are bare and scarred in the late March light. Such vistas startle me, accustomed to the sight of mountains draped with low cloud or else treed to the summits. At Sutton Pass when we drove through a day or two earlier, an entire mountain side was denuded, and there was so much waste, trees stripped of their branches and left. A creekbed running down the mountain was full of logs, no fringe of trees left on its banks to shelter young fish, give shade to amphibians, protect the banks from falling in on themselves. In the letters I get back from the silver-tongued politicians I write to, I am told things are different now, rules are enforced, wildlife respected, habitat protected. And yet these mountains stand in the elements, unprotected and vulnerable. And they go on for miles in their shame.

The skipper takes a long way back to Tofino, around Vargas and Stubbs Islands, hoping, I guess, for something dramatic to show us. Trees crowd close to rocky shores — cedars, hemlocks, Sitka spruce — and are draped with moss. A pair of loons swims close to the shore in one little bay and a small rocky island is dark with cormorants. "I bet that's called Cormorant Rock," I say to the skipper. "Well, Shag Rock, actually. They're always there," he replies. I had hoped to see the vast bodies of grey whales rising out of the water, but instead there are birds, trees and the naked mountains, one of them ringed at the peak with high white cloud.

In the evening, after a walk along MacKenzie Beach as far as we can go until we're stopped by the tide, my husband and I take our children to the swimming pool. We soak in the hot tub, telling ourselves that we'll sleep like babes tonight. Children shriek and splash in the blue pool and when it's time to leave, I find myself shy in the changeroom, trying to cover my body as I struggle out of my bathing suit and into my T-shirt and leggings. Two other women are changing, too, helping their children; they think nothing of standing naked to dry off a child. Twenty years ago I walked on the beach wearing nothing but my necklace of shells, thinking only of the beauty of the waves. This night I am ashamed of my loose skin and heavy breasts and hold a green towel with pink palm trees under my arms as I pull on my underpants. When I see the two women later, out on the grass with the sweet stars above, I look away, embarrassed.

On our way home, we stop at Ucluelet so our parents can shop for trinkets, drink coffee in a converted ship, and we drive out to the Coast Guard Station at Amphitrite Point. Each of us has a souvenir — shells, a little flag with a killer whale, a memory of cormorants muttering on a stony island. Our suitcases are stacked in the back of the truck, our cameras and binoculars accounted for. Then we take the Port Alberni Highway east, towards home, thinking how much everything has changed and yet remained recognizable enough for nostalgia. While we drive past the first huge clearcut, crisscrossed with wasted timber, stumps charred, and the streambeds littered, I look up high to see waterfalls, silver chains shimmering down the necks of the mountains. Who would have dreamed twenty years ago that the girl who bedded down under stars, who made her fire in a ring of stones and tied back her hair with seaweed, would return as a mother, heavy-fleshed and wrinkled? And yet she never noticed the mountains as I do now, sharing something of their great burden of shame and sadness, wishing for low cloud, at least, to give them privacy.

THOMAS WHARTON

The Country of Illusion

> The promise of mountains. The promise of glaciers. But
> those promises are without pastoral implication. They
> announce a fugitive concern. By hiding one insists that
> one is part of the landscape.
> — Robert Kroetsch, "Lonesome Writer Diptych"
> in *A Likely Story*

History

In 1924 an American named Lewis Freeman took a movie camera with
him to the Columbia Icefields. He was there to make a documentary
about the region for the National Geographic Society. In his book about
the expedition, *On the Roof of the Rockies*, he mentions the difficulty of
conveying the awesome spectacle of mountain scenery within the narrow frame of a camera. A tremendous storm, in one instance, ended up
looking quite tame and domesticated on film. Freeman soon realized
he would have to help nature out a bit to get the effects he wanted.
And so he used dynamite to set off a "natural" ice avalanche, and threw
the carcass of a mountain goat off a precipice in order to create a
dramatic "leap of death."

One of his biggest disappointments was the Athabasca glacier. He
had seen it before in the photographs of Byron Harmon, when its terminus was "a towering wall." But by 1924, melting and recession had
left the glacier with "the flattened snout of a shovel-nosed shark …
devoid of pictorial possibilities."

Photograph

The object that I would like you to take note of, on the front of this
postcard, is a large boulder, an erratic. It's really somewhat difficult to
see, camouflaged as it is by the stippled grey mud flat where it sits,
equally stippled and grey, and overshadowed, in accordance with the
conventions of postcards, by the peaks and the glacier that fill the top
half of the frame and are the real subject of the photograph.

Journal

May 17, Athabasca Glacier: I park the car, button up my coat and step out into snow falling on snow.

A white world, blue-shadowed, hushed. Above, a smear of more luminous whiteness where the sun might be. The low whine of wind off the barely visible glacier, its upper reaches lost in a haze of snow and ice fog. The season is officially spring, yet here that fact is still a month and a valley away.

We, on the other hand, have arrived too soon. Cars and busloads of us, all making an early pilgrimage to the ice. I pass an older couple sipping coffee on the steps of their motorhome. A young man with a baby in a carrier on his back. I take my place in the slow, meandering procession, across the footbridge and up the rising path to the terminus. With a nod and smile for those who pass me on their way back down, their faces flushed and wind-bitten, their eyes glistening with tears. Faces that register both weather and dissatisfaction. I struggle over the icy gravel of the path, lowering my head against the wind, raising it every now and again to keep my bearings. Reading the dates on the few stone recession markers that are not blanketed in snow. *1967. 1979. 1984.* And ignoring, like everyone else, the posted signs that advise me to stay off the ice.

Eventually gravel disappears under snow and I realize I have climbed from the terminal moraine onto the glacier itself.

Ahead of me is a group of Japanese tourists, five men in business suits and dress shoes, scrambling, slipping and laughing their way upward. I pass a family — a boy skipping on ahead, a smaller child riding piggyback on dad, mom bringing up the rear and calling above the wind: *I think we should turn back.* A young couple huddled together on an outcrop of rock, sharing sips from a juice box. I squint into the falling snow and see the hazy shapes of the foolhardy few who have hiked far out onto the ice. One of the Japanese businessmen pans a video camera across blank whiteness.

What are we doing here? What will the businessman see when he takes that tape home and plays it back for his family?

Some uncertain distance ahead I can make out a stretch of the glacier's slope which the wind has almost cleared of snow. The pale blue of ice suggests itself there, and it is to that possibility of revelation that most of us are heading, intrigued, determined, but perhaps, bitten by the unrelenting wind and numbed by a shrouded, featureless world, already disillusioned.

Moving through the flurrying stillness of falling snow, I wonder about the desire to turn the world of substance into words. About the unforeseeable events that create that desire or at least make one aware of its dormant presence. I remember a moment, years ago, when instead of a slow and chosen ascent like this one, I made a swift and unforeseen descent.

> This is the field the Canadian writer walks onto, with no stick to prod for snow pockets, no gauge for the solidity of the earth. The open field of snow, the page, the white space of the Canadian voice, whatever that is.
> — Aritha van Herk, "A Frozen Tongue/Crevasse" in *A Frozen Tongue*

Memory

One Saturday in late winter, two of my high-school friends invited me to go ice-scrambling with them in Maligne Canyon. Or I may have talked them into letting me come along. I'm no longer certain on that particular point, but there is no doubt that among many ignorances, I could claim a complete absence of experience in ice-scrambling. My friends were not professional climbers, but they had explored the canyon in winter before. They knew enough to bring rope, as well as ice axes and crampons for themselves, and they were also thoughtful enough to suggest that I take along a stick.

We headed upstream along the frozen floor of the canyon, but soon found our way blocked by a towering icefall and so had to turn around and be content with exploring the lower reaches. Despite my lack of appropriate gear, I managed to keep up with my friends and consequently felt pleased with myself, conveniently forgetting that we had so far avoided any of the canyon's real difficulties. Then we reached a narrow spot where the gentle slope of snow and ice we were inching down dropped at a suddenly precipitous angle and out of sight around a curve in the canyon walls. Confronted by the unknown, we stopped. There might be an icefall or, on a warm day like this, a pool of open water just around the bend. My friends decided to go on ahead and explore, leaving me to wait either for their return or for a signal that it was safe to join them.

I resented being left behind. The three of us had worked as a team up to this point, I thought, and I felt I'd earned the right to share in the adventure of discovery. I crouched, leaning on my stick, and listened impatiently as the voices of my friends gradually receded. Finally I called out, "Is it safe to come down?"

I thought I heard a muffled *yeah*, although my friends later denied they'd replied to, or even heard, my shouted question. I stood up. I set aside the stick because at the entrance to the curve, the canyon walls were narrow enough that with arms outspread I could brace myself against them. Somehow I imagined this would be enough to keep me from falling, and so I stepped eagerly forward.

I like to think now that it was during those next few frozen seconds, as I lost my footing, crashed down and slid around the curve, that I entered the country of illusion. There was the brief image of my friends turning in shock as I shot toward them. A gloved hand reaching out to grab me and only giving me a clout on the nose as I swept helplessly past. And then the slope ended and I soared off the edge into the unknown.

Some years later, I wrote a short story about that lesson in the unforgiving character of mountain landscape. I tried to capture in words the moment before I went over the edge, and what happened afterwards, because I could not remember the fall itself. As it turned out, beyond the edge of the ice slope was a mere ten- or twelve-foot drop to a lower and more level section of the canyon. In the story, I described how I landed and sat there, stunned, as my mind tried to catch up with what had happened to the rest of me. My only injuries were a bruised backside and a bloody nose from my friend's attempt to catch hold of me. The story ended with something that happened after the fall: I looked up and saw the contrail of a jet cross the narrow strip of blue sky between the dark canyon walls. I suppose, with an epiphany like that, I had decided this mishap could be read as the myth of Icarus.

I was never happy with that story. And now, wondering about the events that brought me to writing, I see that it was the instant before the fall that really mattered. That was the scene that I would replay over and over again in memory. Entertaining other possibilities of its ending. Wondering how I could have been so uncharacteristically reckless. Somehow I had been tricked, or more likely I had tricked myself, and the rest was left up to the capricious recalcitrance of ice. At that moment, sliding toward the edge, watching the unknowable future rush ineluctably toward me, I knew that there was no way out of this story, however it might end. At that moment, perhaps, began my obsession with narrative. And with landscape.

Journal

May 30, Mt. Edith Cavell. Today the sun is fierce in a cloudless sky. Climbing the path alongside the wall of the lateral moraine, I hear the trickle and clunk of meltwater gently nudging the stones.

I move in and out of the range of sounds: an endless, intermittent conversation going on among the elements. And I wonder what I think I'm doing here, an interloper who cannot understand the language.

A distant crash. I turn too late and glimpse only the tumbling fragments of the serac that has just detached itself from the foot of Angel Glacier.

As I descend toward the meltwater tarn at the base of Cavell, the tiny dark specks I had glimpsed from high up on the path have become massive boulders. I climb a huge table rock near the shore of the tarn, sip steaming tea from a thermos and take out my notebook. Cloud shadows ghost across the valley floor.

As I write, I remember why I've come here, again.

Crack and rumble of an avalanche. I search Cavell's face. There. Smaller than the sound led me to imagine. Powdery spume over a lip of rock. Dull succuss of thunder. Distance collapses in vertigo: it seems for a moment as if the avalanche might pour across the tarn and engulf me. I look and look until I am exhausted.

June 16, Sunwapta Lake near Athabasca Glacier:

Rock. Clay. Water. Flap of a page in the wind.

The difficulty: how to write about this landscape? How to write beyond the familiar words that obscure the world in a white-out of cliché? Rugged grandeur. Brooding majesty. Monarchs. Mountains as heads of an outmoded body politic.

Sometimes a mountain is too familiar to look at. Sometimes an entire mountain is too insignificant for words.

Better to pick up one of the morainal fragments of rock at my feet. To describe the cool, pitted, secretive age of it in my palm. An immensity of time and pressure within its light heft. The play of surface: streaks and filaments of copper, nacre, ebony. Delicate striations, scratches. Tiny craters. Satellite of the mountain.

Reading the surface of the rock, I know that I am reading a fragment of a larger story. I set the rock down in a different place from where I picked it up and turn a page in my notebook.

Story

> Indeed, to tell a story is to leave most of it untold. You
> mine it, you take ore from the mountain. You carry the
> compass around it. You dig down — and when you have
> finished, the story remains, something beyond your touch,
> resistant to your siege; unfathomable, like the heart of the
> mountain. You have the feeling that you have not reached
> the story itself, but have merely assaulted the surrounding
> solitude.
>
> — Howard O'Hagan, *Tay John*

How to write this landscape? Howard O'Hagan's novel, *Tay John*, is set
in the Jasper area, but strangely enough I never heard it mentioned
when I lived there. Perhaps, in its violence and darkness, it is not an
evocation of place that would endear itself to those who live there.
Whatever the reason, it was only after several years, and many other
books, that I finally discovered this novel set in a landscape that I had
known, or thought I knew.

O'Hagan's narrator, Jack Denham, draws together hints, rumours
and recollections of the enigmatic blond Indian known as Tay John.
But the various fragments of story, as Denham himself recognizes, do
not nestle together comfortably or even convincingly. We are not allowed to forget that, while Tay John may be in some sense a symbol of
the mountain wilderness and of the clash of cultures that has taken
place there, he is also a figure composed of different kinds of narrative:
myth, legend, hearsay, tall tale, police reports and "evidence — without a finding." This patchwork novel, that begins with Tay John's role
as a mythic messiah, gradually recedes farther and farther away from
him through a series of narrators within narrators, none of whom seems
absolutely certain of the facts. The narrator continually cautions us to
"remember that I speak to you in the country of illusion."

That phrase, country of illusion, stuck with me after I'd read the
book. I like to think that it is not only an apt metaphor for the mountain
landscape, but also for the language with which one must attempt to
describe it. Jack Denham admits that he has not actually "reached the
story itself," but rather, in his ordering of the fragments of Tay John's
life, he may only have "assaulted the surrounding solitude." At the
centre of his tale is a figure who remains always on the edge: of language,
of human community, of the new frontier society that is replacing an

ancient way of life. And during a snowfall at the end of the novel, Tay John disappears, literally, into ground. He becomes the landscape, and in his enigmatic disappearance he enacts the slipping away of solid earth from underneath the feet of those who, like the developer Alf Dobble, forget that their very presence remakes a world they would insist on seeing, or packaging, as pure wilderness.

O'Hagan's novel suggests that writing alters and obscures even as it reveals. In our attempt to render a landscape in words, we may be tripped up not only by the landscape itself, shifting and evading the names we give it, but also by the capricious recalcitrance of language itself. Not because writing the land is a mapping of uncharted territory, but because, as O'Hagan and later writers of the west have made us aware, it has been mapped many times already. And as these maps layer over one another, some small detail or larger feature always remains hidden. Or escapes, slides off the edge. And so another map must be drawn up. Our understanding of what is really "out there" can never be complete.

When I first attempted to write a novel, I found myself chained to chronology, linearity and the careful separation of character and the natural world. I forgot or refused to see what *Tay John* had already shown me: a novel in a circular, mythic, patchwork shape. What poet and novelist Michael Ondaatje has called a darting about, an outrider's movement, in which the natural world and human fears and desires cannot be set to opposite sides of a neat boundary. Finally landscape and memory instructed me. I reread what I had written in the journals I kept of my glacier scrambling and saw that landscape and memory had offered me only a jumbled moraine of fragments, incomplete stories, erratics. So I gathered them, set them side by side, unable to see how they could be pieced together. And somehow tricked myself into writing a novel.

Now I write in the hope of such possibly accidental connivance between my intentions and the slippery character of language. The desire to trick myself into that other country of illusion, where the ending of the story, the meaning of the story, is always about to arrive. A writing that has no idea what lies around the curve in the rock and is hopeful enough, foolhardy enough, to believe it can stand on its own two feet.

SUSAN ANDREWS GRACE

Heart Break

I'd believed in her since I was a little girl playing in Saskatchewan clover and green grass, making daisy chains of camomile flowers in the land of rape and honey. Now we say canola and honey, but I think rape is still apt, the rape of the soil still with us. Fair warning.

She, I believed, would lead me to safe pastures. Green valleys, vulva clefts on the prairie parkland furred with mauve and grey bush and dotted with flocks of sheep, white ovals on the green. In winter she led me along the snowy lanes around our house, the town not organized the way towns are now, her crystals beckoning me to a halo of light illuminating faint memory I was not supposed to have according to my mother who was embarrassed when I spoke of it. The snow in our northern town was foreign to my people. I somehow knew this, and knew it was my privilege to experience it and all the abundance this continent had to offer me and my parents, brothers and sisters.

Sometimes she came embodied, sometimes not. She kept me from throwing myself down the stairs in walking night terrors. Her hand was firm like my mother's, broad, squarish fingers, womanly as they smoothed my hair away from my face, the thin bangs making a little wind as they returned to my forehead, cooling my face, her other hand on my back warm, lifting my heart, my body coming along back to the bed and peaceful sleep.

Summer and she was at the lake. Brown of sunburnt grass, purple blue of berries, soft as warm air moving across my skin. Her hand on that spot of my back between the shoulder blades behind my heart, lifting it, filling me with sunlight.

She came sometimes in traditional Cree dress. To our house. Looking for blanket materials. Sitting silently in the kitchen, waiting, unsmiling. Perhaps uncomfortably hot.

When I was five our family moved to a city. The city lost her and killed my beloved dog. I went to school. There, terror waited for me all day long, not just sometimes in sleep.

I lost all but the faintest memory of her. I learned about the Virgin Mary, who seemed more believable than Jesus who apparently had died for me. It seemed so crazy that he died for me when I surely never asked that he be killed. Someone was lying or they had me confused with someone else. My friend Sharon maybe, whose parents bought her anything she wanted. I learned in a Catholic school that the spirit never dies. I savoured that and tucked it away, decided she'd been lost, not killed.

Life without her wasn't the same. I missed riding in the back seat through an August evening, alfalfa smell blowing through the open window, her scent mixing with earth's rich perfumes.

She started to come back when my life was at its most extreme. I was lost in a huge, ugly city, living with a man, in name my husband, who gave his heart and soul to alcohol, his eyes and hands to other women. She'd be there, a moment of clarity and peace, in the narrow hallway of our apartment, its ribbon oak floor creaking two floors above the angry street, and I could sleep at last.

I didn't recognize her. When I was twenty-five years old, in Toronto, despairing at having lost so much hope and wishing for a good life, she appeared in the dining room of our apartment on Sudan Street, but I didn't know who she was. She had a kind but tough face. Grey hair. She stood at an old bird's-eye maple table, the kind used in nineteenth-century kitchens. A low ceiling. There was nothing on the table. Behind her was a fireplace with an oak mantel. On the mantel was a delft blue vase with pussy willows in it. She wore indigo. She had a deep joy. I could see that. She seemed to be asking me to come into the room. I seemed to be at its edge.

I was afraid. Afraid I'd lost my grip on reality. Which was true, I had. I just didn't understand what a good thing that was. And so I lost her again.

It wasn't until quite a few years later, when I'd had three babies and had to acquire the maturity to try and raise them in a manner acceptable to myself and had made the decision to write, that I realized that she was the connection between the desire to write and what she had taught me in my childhood, the essence of my beginning. She knew what I was to write and that she would help me with the obstacles in my path: terrifying inadequacies, horror of beginning, not knowing anything, necessity of doing what must be done to begin. And the lovely long green avenue back to her was in the magic of creative process: manipulation of textile with a needle and thread, threading words through the eye of poetry's needle.

When I finally was on the way to my real life, she began to appear regularly and I knew her and all her works. I didn't need the scare tactics of embodiment or strange, low-ceilinged cottages in order to believe. She surely and steadily led me to right pastures even when I mistakenly prayed to a male god.

It was she who compelled me to make a paisley bag for myself. A swirly, blue-green-of-the-sea paisley bag with a grey grosgrain ribbon closure. I'd bought the cloth on a sunny Tuesday in May on my way home in a hurry and made myself even later by ducking into the Army and Navy's basement yard goods department, just to look, a bit of pleasure. And there they were: two pieces in the same paisley pattern, but one more blue and the other more green. I paid for them and ran home with a little guilt and deep satisfaction. I used them both for the bag, a subtle mixture. I didn't measure. It was the kind of bag to hold a notebook, books, groceries, extra clothes, or all those at once.

The bag was part of a vision she set before me of a woman on a ferryboat. The woman wore a sea green coat. And she had the bag with her. She was peacefully and with some joy in her heart, going.

She looked a bit like me. A bit like my sisters. She seemed of this century. And not.

I'd made her bag in an effort to follow her and the vision, to find what I knew I would find if only I did what I was meant to do with that cloth. The bag turned out to be very useful, handy because of its generous, unmeasured proportions. After using the bag for some time and every once in a while losing myself looking into its swirling weave, the first Ferry Woman poems began to come sure and easy onto the page. Pure. And for the first time I had a name for she who had existed in that place just beyond me.

Then there was a nagging insistence that she and I had Norman souls. I went to university libraries in Saskatoon, Vancouver and Québec City, driven to substantiate her insistence on our Norman connection. And found it: the leader of the Norman invasion of Ireland in 1169 was Raymond le Gros, from whom the Grace family descended.

Next she turned my attention to the route the Normans, my ancestors, took to Ireland, where they consequently became more Irish than the Irish and were ousted centuries later for that very reason. It became imperative that I take the ferry from Wales to Ireland, from the Pembrokeshire coast to Wexford.

I dreamt of going to Ireland but knew it would be impossible. Then a lucky grant relieved me of having to take regular employment and freed me to work on the poems. I did. But the money was spent, every cent, for subsistence. The notion of a real ferryboat journey receded. Then, in the winter, a freelance job came up. The pay would be exactly what was needed to do the trip cheaply. I decided we didn't absolutely need the money, and I would make the trip. I was beginning by this time to feel morally obligated to do so. May was the only month I could go to Ireland.

My friend Jeanette said she would go with me. She was exhausted and hadn't had a holiday in years Her mother had just died a long and slow death. Her mother's family had come from Ireland at the same time as my family had — the famine of 1847. Her mother had always wanted to go.

Now Jeanette would go, was eager to go and to arrange everything. I warned her what it would be like to travel with a writer, and she still wanted to go. Even after I told her how we were to enter Ireland from Wales, not the usual way to enter the country and potentially very inconvenient.

We landed in London's Heathrow Airport on May 2, 1992. Jeanette's first tube trip. I'd been to London twenty years before, a sooty miracle. This time London's underground trains seemed clean and orderly. A bit of a disappointment. However, the rest of London was as I remembered, sooty and dirty and nonchalant about civic tidiness but cast with a heavy mist from the sea and history.

On the tube, a romantic impulse to go to Russell Square hit me. Jeanette, used to me and my intuition, humoured me. In fifteen minutes we found a hotel we could afford.

Jeanette sensibly got into bed.

I walked. Spring. Lilacs. A bank holiday. People out eating chips, sandwiches, sitting in the grass in the Square.

I was in Virginia Woolf's neighbourhood. I'd read all her books and biographies when I first began to write seriously. At the lake with my small children, I had marvelled at the difference between our lives. Hers a literary one, mine a very simple life of keeping the wilderness in my children at bay. Hers was complex and important, although it seems she didn't have any idea of how important. Her pain probably didn't allow her that.

I felt grateful for her life, her writing keeping me afloat those years, a beacon floating ahead, bobbing, eventually drowned. She walked out into the water, stones in her pockets. I walked up and down every street, imagining. And more than once being reminded by the architecture, narrow streets and poor food that London is a cruel and unfair world unto itself.

In London the people were emotionally crisp, visibly disgusted with my inability to handle the phone which gobbled coins and cut me off for no apparent reason. Jeanette was feeling ill and stayed in our dismal room.

When I tried to find out about this ferry of my visions, I cursed my romantic notion to enter Ireland as the Normans had. As is the case with most visions, it wasn't very practical. The ferry from Pembroke Dock left only at two a.m. on some Tuesdays and Fridays. In London, they didn't care if or when the boats in Wales left for Ireland. I finally found out about one leaving Fishguard Harbour, still on the Pembrokeshire coastline. Doubting my sanity, seeing myself caught in a deranged pursuit of the dream of a dream, I bought the very expensive tickets at Paddington Station.

But the pleasantness of Paddington Station and its restaurant, where we had breakfast before leaving London, reassured me. I think it made Jeanette feel a little better about following a woman following a ghost.

As we left London, I felt the promise of the journey rising up to meet me. The city seemed to have been grinding us in its metal industrial jaw. After paying homage to Virginia Woolf, I wanted to get out. I'd felt stopped and frustrated and felt I was rapidly losing faith in my purpose. The one thing that working on the Ferry Woman poems had given me was a sure and steady feeling of purpose. It was something recognized retroactively as a goal from much earlier in my life. It seemed a way to contribute, give back to the world which had so generously given me life, parents, a healthful, peaceful, prosperous childhood in which to grow. If the world, my world that is, was willing to accept it. It was a new kind of writing for me. I had been accused of being a "ladylike" poet. A well-established poet declared one of my poems "fucking pastoral," dropping it disdainfully, as if it smelled. And now I was writing a pushy, profane and sacrilegious thing, the form of which I was inventing as I went along. This, like Ireland, was new territory for me. When I first began writing it I was worried about being hit by a bus or some other freak accident which would kill me before I got it all down on paper. It was urgent.

And now, leaving England, mile by green and yellow mile, the urgency, excitement and purpose were returning. The fields were mostly green, but every once in a while there'd be a yellow one. Rape or canola it seemed to me, but no, I'd think, that's just because I live in Saskatchewan that I think it's canola; it must be mustard. Later I learned that canola had indeed invaded England and Ireland's agriculture.

I looked forward to Norman architecture, not sure if I would recognize it when it was right before my eyes.

What I'd learned in Canadian libraries was that my ancestors had left Wales on the Pembrokeshire coast and had entered Ireland May 1, 1169, at Bannow Bay and were the first generation of Normans in Ireland, to be distinguished from the Anglo-Normans who came later. Bannow Bay is approximately where the modern Rosslare Harbour is now.

We crossed the roughest part of the Irish Sea in perfect calm after a train breakdown in Wales and a bus ride the rest of the way. Nine centuries after he did, we crossed the same sea that Raymond le Gros, my ancestor, patriarch of the Graces, had. In May, just as he had. Everything went smoothly even when it wasn't going as planned. Story clattered along on its wheels. History. Hidden stories peopled with ghosts who haunted my dreams.

Jeanette seemed to have been cured of her Londonitis at the Paddington Station restaurant. In Ireland she was in high spirits, her jet lag caught up to her. After a lovely evening in a nineteenth-century bed and breakfast, and after a Guinness, a salad sandwich (which was pallid letttuce and cucumber between slices of white bread) in a village pub, a hot shower, a good sleep and a bracing Irish breakfast, we left in our little blue rented car, bravely driving on the left side of the road, impressed with the high quality of everything Irish.

Suddenly over a hill, a ruin. Jeanette took the line of least resistance, veered left, and there we were at Jerpoint Abbey in all its roofless glory. I was pretty sure it was Norman architecture. We entered through the Interpretive Centre. I went to the graveyard first, hoping to recognize some Norman names on the headstones. None. The shock only North Americans can experience. The names had centuries ago been worn off by rain and wind. They bore only moss.

An interpretive plaque in the chapel described a wall painting that was barely there. Family shields it said. And one my family name, Grace. I was stunned. Jeanette had gone back to the Interpretive Centre and asked the young woman there if she knew of the family Grace. Yes, she did. She said that many of the headstones in the east graveyard were Graces and that the last Abbot had been a Grace. She told me about a book on the family's history in the Kilkenny Library. So my goal of finding one Norman family to trace, any one, was achieved, and it was my own, and this in our first two days on Irish soil, entering as the Normans had.

Since landing on Wexford soil I had been experiencing a strange mixture of surprise and recognition, but most of all a feeling of home that I had not anticipated. My ideas of Ireland, as a child, had been of a rather bad place. I am not sure why I got this idea, but it was there, and it was connected in my mind with being a Catholic and the ghetto negativity of parochial schools in provinces where a Catholic education is a private education. All that guilt for the sacrifices our parents made, added to the fact that Jesus had died for me.

My research in Canada had begun to make Ireland seem noble and romantic. And incredibly and indelibly sad. I began to feel an expanding debt to those great-grandparents on both sides of my family who had endured and survived the famine and the treacherous trip to Canada and all that they and the Irish before them had endured just for being Irish.

So when I arrived I was ill-prepared for the irritation I felt at the solidly built modern buildings, bungalows, the port of entry my father or uncle could have built at Lake Blackstrap or in the village of Muenster. I didn't come halfway across the world to see something I could have seen in Saskatchewan.

One thing I'd never been able to understand about my family was our uncivilized ability to be late, a lot. I found in my twenty-three days in Ireland an abundance of people like my mother, who could be an hour late for dinner and hardly notice it herself.

I saw people who looked like people in my family. Over and over I saw my cousin Desmond. In an Irish Tourist Board office I saw my Aunt Margy when she was thirty-five and I was ten. In the stairwell of the Natural History Museum in Dublin I saw my brother Tommy when he was nine years old and I was fourteen. The shock of recognition was so strong I stopped climbing the stairs and stared. His gene pool must have included someone who looked just like me, because he was about to say something, standing, staring back at me, when he realized I wasn't who he thought I was and continued his madcap hurry down the stairs, just like Tommy used to do.

And everywhere there were children who looked like my own, making me more lonesome for them. I longed to touch and kiss their faces, which haunted me everywhere.

The countryside in Wexford was beautiful and I felt totally at home. I saw landscape that I knew and recognized, even though I was surprised at how like southern France it appeared, with palm trees growing everywhere. It was a knowing much like the one my son, when he was four-and-a-half years old, used to describe; he just knew how green energies cured headaches. He just knew.

My friend Ven Begamudre told me about the idea of a pilgrimage, described it fully, in a conversation I had with him after I'd returned. It was only then that I realized I had made one.

From the history book in Kilkenny I discovered the place in Tipperary, near Nenagh, called Puchane, which my great-grandparents, the Normans, had left to come to Canada. They were the branch of the family who had left Wexford and lived at Castle Carnaigh. An illustration of the place in 1820 showed a ruin. Just remnants of a few walls and the keep in somewhat better state.

We went to Nenagh, a very sad-looking town, depressingly like Humboldt, Saskatchewan, on a windy day. Landlocked, wind blowing dirt in our eyes. The blackened poorhouse I'd read about in Canada still standing on the edge of the town. The ache that kept me from reading the Irish history books straight through gripped me. I wanted to leave Nenagh quickly. Jeanette was surprised. We stopped at a tweed shop Jeanette wanted to see. The proprietor seemed interested in a gab. I was getting used to resemblances and only felt a little irritated that she looked a bit like my Grandma in the precise way her chin and jaw moved to pronounce words exactly as they should be, if you please. She was surprised I hadn't been to Ireland before. She asked the inevitable: was I looking for my roots? I said not really but I was sort of interested in finding Castle Carnaigh, if it wasn't too far. It turned out that it was near where she lived, on her road. She drew a map and indeed, after one false stop and one terrified walk through a pasture of mean-looking horses, we found the stone stiles, walked up the most beautiful lane I had ever in all my life seen, and we were at the iron gates the tweed lady had described. It was the avenue she described. She'd told us to just climb the iron gate. As shocked to see us as we were to see him, the farmer, who had been having himself a snooze in his tractor, came to talk to us. I asked was this Castle Carnaigh? Yes, it was, he said. We could see the ruin, but first he'd disconnect the electric fence.

So I entered the ancestral home I had no idea still existed. I no longer felt the home feeling Wexford had given me, but the half-mile-long, beech-tree-and-ivy-on-either-side avenue to the castle ruin was beautiful beyond description. The keep was huge. The walls had fallen some more since 1820, but otherwise everything was as it ought to be. I found the stone well I'd known in my imagination existed. I collected little stones from the rubble and plants which I pressed in my sketch book. And one stone from the mortarless wall along the avenue now sits on my desk.

For the last weeks before we left, and the whole time I was in Ireland, I had dreams which left me, in the morning, feeling bereft. Dreams in which I reached out but fell short, somehow separated from someone, someplace I loved more than my life. I would remember only a fragment, sometimes nothing at all, or I would know who was in the dream and the fact of separation but no other detail. The mist of sadness would last until noon sometimes and all day long other times.

We left Tipperary for the wild shores of Dingle, feelings of home completely gone. Now I was truly in a foreign country, where I would come to shaky terms, in my dreams at any rate, with ghosts related or not. I'd found the nature of a Norman heart and the land it loved. I finished writing the poems which explained she who had been with me since before time, since before any May on the open sea.

PETER CHRISTENSEN with ROBERT J. ROSEN

Canyon Shadows: "Stones"

Exploring the Architecture of the Spirit of Place, Being and Time

Introduction

A Review of *Canyon Shadows: "Stones"* by Kathie Joblin, *Parry Sound North Star*, July 29, 1992

> ...Following an old railway bed, we strolled through the woods, accompanied by our guides and hosts, John Macfie and Midge Strickland, who set the tone for the morning by suggesting that we consider the theme of "man's impact on the environment." As we climbed over rocks and tiptoed around mud puddles left in the path by the recent rains, John and Midge explained some of the history of the area, described the process of the regrowth of the forest following the logging of the white pines 100 years ago, and identified many wildflowers and plants.
>
> A 15-minute walk brought us to the place where the event would occur. Mr. Rosen states in his program notes that *Canyon Shadows* has no beginning and no end, and indeed, this proved to be true. As we paused in our walk, Mr. Christensen, who was walking with us, began to speak the words of his poem, "Stones." We left the main path and walked down toward the water, and as we walked, singing began, like an echo on either side of us. A tuba played deep notes that could easily be confused with the groan of large oaks or pines swaying in the wind.
>
> The sounds of the gentle waves lapping on the rocky shore mingled with the echoing voices, the tuba, and a periodic drumming on a gong as we chose places to sit on the rocks. There was no conductor, and the only visible evidence that a musical event would occur here was a log drum sitting on the rocks with a sheet of music in front of it, and a second music stand fifty feet away on another rock. The curved, rocky bay in which we sat was a natural amphitheatre, and the sounds seemed to be coming from all around us. They had a haunting quality, almost as if the

trees and rocks and water were speaking to us through the voices and instruments we were hearing.

As we sat looking out over the bay, the singers gradually emerged: Michelle Todd as the Stone Spirit and Catherine Lewis as the Echo Spirit. Their two soprano voices soared on the breeze, sometimes together, sometimes in canon. They did not sing to us (the audience) in the conventional manner, as if on a stage; rather, they seemed to move from place to place on the rocks, and to face each other, or the water, or the trees, as if they were flowing with the poetry they were singing.

While this was happening, and the two instruments were periodically speaking, the Stone Shadow emerged. Bathed from head to toe in white body paint, Jay Hirabayashi crept and evolved and unfolded in an exceedingly slow rhythm from the forest, across the rocks and down to the water's edge. Against the backdrop of the lapping waves, his eerily white form sculpted visual images of what a spirit of stone might do if it could move. He displayed a masterful control of movement, holding difficult positions for long periods and evolving into new ones so slowly that he gave the uncanny feeling of not moving at all; yet he was constantly changing positions.

As he edged nearer and nearer to the water, I found myself wondering, "Will he go in / fall in / get wet?" As I watched in fascination, he moved down the gradually sloping surface of the rock into the water, going ever further, ever deeper, until he was submerged up to his chin. Then, just as slowly and gracefully, he swam across the bay in front of us, and disappeared.

I realized that the music around me was becoming less continuous now, and finally, it ceased. But I and the other listeners sat, spellbound, for several minutes in complete silence as the waves continued to lap on the rocks and the leaves of the trees continued to rustle in the breeze. I got up slowly and walked down to the water's edge, where the Stone Shadow had gone into the water, and there, on the rock under the water, were traces of white footprints. I thought again about man's impact on the environment, and then felt a surge of gratitude towards these artists who had given expression to the earth's speaking to us.

Stones

Stones, sometimes I feel
I could breathe the stones.
Inside this folding earth
this grotto, silent place,
water
stone
forest
forever.

You are the furnace
the sun awaits your sensations.
What you do to the stones
you do to yourself.

The whirlwind comes
that you may know yourself,
windfalls
windfalls
through a nation of pines
trembling, they whisper secrets.

Now the stones I am.
Now the forest I am.
Now the water I am,
with a path to follow
the wind.

Canyon Shadows: "Stones" is a synchronous gathering of creative energy to interpret our environment in a participatory way. It is soft ritual, taking the shape of music, poetry, dance and declaration. Robert and I make no demands on you for belief in anything; rather we humbly ask that you agree to spend an hour listening to your surroundings, to your self and to the performers. We hope to encourage you to feel the material and spiritual interconnection of all things. If *Canyon Shadows: "Stones"* opens just one flower in your brain, then we will have done our work well.

I sing in a house of stones
wind has shaped
water has shaped

In this house of rocks
I am the enemy.
In beauty we are finished.
Do you see the rock,
Is it your heart,
is it your head?

If the rocks have no spirit
then you are the rocks.
If the water has no life
then you are the water.
If the wind has no heart
then you are the wind.

Stones for your feet.
Stones for your feet.
Rock and steel
rocksteel.

Robert Rosen: My language is music. That is why I need Peter in this project — for his words. He and I follow similar lines of thinking. Our discussions on trails to glaciers or around the dying embers of fires last for hours.

We can talk politics while we are in buildings, but to talk about art we need to be outside. He thinks with words, I think with sounds. In his poetry, the ideas cut straight to my soul. We spend a lot of time discussing choice of words.

We decided to disregard our desire for artifact in this project. Process and evolution are at the centre and the observer will only see and hear momentary glimpses of our converging artistic pathways.

I am a composer with a passion for vertical structures and angular rhythms. Probably deeply rooted in my past — years of high-class rock music. I'm simply moving from "rock" to "stone."

In the late '70s I was dreaming of the day when I could have an orchestra under my control, all in the little black box of technology. Now I have it — an orchestra, a jazz band and many other things — in a couple of little boxes. I can produce a complete compact disc master with the technology sitting in my basement studio. Right now, though, I am much more interested in being outside and working with real musicians in real environments.

⌒

Canyon Shadows: "Stones" is contemporary consciousness recognition. It is not so much a product as an idea or a way of thinking. Performances of it are gatherings evolving from the structures inherent in the interactive synchronousness of the irreducible whole Self or universe.

These pieces are intended to suggest a path toward recognition of universal interconnection. This is a work about love. Each performance is an event which questions the dualistic implications of a world interpreted and controlled through cause and effect. If you are watching Newton's world, you may be watching old reruns. The worldview that results from humans believing they are not part of nature and using that distance to abuse the cosmic ecology and each other is on the brink of extinction.

But when and how did western civilization separate the body from the soul, humankind from nature? In 325, at the First Council of Nicaea convened by Constantine the Great, the 225 or so Church Fathers gathered together and affirmed the view that the Son of Man and Son of God were the same and had equality and divinity in the Trinity. This declaration suggests that nature (the universe) and humans are all imbued with equality of spirit. Later, at the Council of Chalcedon held in Rome in 453, the Christian church again declared that Jesus Christ, the Son, had two distinct and perfect natures within one perfect being and that through Jesus Christ, humankind was "divinized" and, as Archbishop Joseph Raya of the Byzantine Church teaches in his contemporary book, *Abundance of Love*, "was robed with a divine character … and *the matter of the universe became a 'divine milieu'*" (my italics). In other words, all of nature was imbued with the life and breath of a loving god. This divine milieu is the indivisible stuff of which our universe is made. At that point, nature and humankind were still bound together by form.

During the Renaissance, with the rise of humanism, artists began to depict the human figure standing alone and self-reliant. Later, at the time of the Reformation, the idea of original sin grew in popularity, along with the concept that God lived only in heaven. By the dawn of the industrial revolution, the belief that God dwelt only in heaven — although for a while within the body of the man Jesus Christ — implied that animals, plants and terra (and even other races) were coyly arranged by an abstract god to challenge the human ability to conquer, exploit and structure. God did not live within the self or among the trees or within the animals, but was innocent, omnipotent and distant in heaven, much like the earlier Greek gods who visited occasional vexations upon humans but were ultimately separate. These "God-in-heaven folks" rationalized their struggle for dominion over the earth on behalf of their abstract steals from the concrete.

We are presently experiencing the fall-out from the legacy of this thinking in the form of environmental crisis. The separation of nature and god, with humankind as god's special envoy, has led western thought into a labyrinth of theological and secular fallacies. I believe we should regain our sense of unity with nature. Perhaps if we chose to believe that the earth, trees, thunder, land and its inhabitants had a spirit and sense of being similar to our own, and if we regarded these things as family, then we, not God, would have to take responsibility for our actions. *Canyon Shadows: "Stones"* is an effort to *affect*, through performance, our ecology (to change the way we change).

> Inside this folding earth
> this grotto
> silent place,
> given love
> makes lost sensibility.
>
> Waterstoneearthwind
> forest in memory
> forgive.
>
> In this earth paradise
> trusting in clean and loving purpose
> we are each other.
> Unify our bonds
> broken from the earth,
> fallen from grace
> fallen original sin stones,
> seeing ourselves as having
> dominion over the animals.
> Our arrogance
> alibi for the desolation of precinct,
> our food sources.

Collier's Dictionary defines environment as: 1. Whatever encompasses. 2. The aggregate of all external and internal conditions affecting the existence, growth and welfare of organisms. 3. One's surroundings or external circumstances collectively. 4. The act of environing, or the state of being environed.

Modern physics holds that matter changes the way it changes as a direct result of its being observed. Early Christian, Eastern and Primal religions hold that the spirit affects all matter, that our individual choices change the way things change. The wholeness of humankind and its unity with the universe is a transcendental precept recognized and confirmed by modern science and by many religions.

Konrad Lorenz, in his book *On Aggression*, quotes Albert Einstein: "The most beautiful and most profound is the sensation of the mystical. It is the sower of all true science … to know that what is impenetrable to us really exists, manifesting itself as the highest wisdom and the most radiant beauty which our dull faculties can comprehend only in primitive form — this knowledge, this feeling is at the centre of true religiousness."

Robert and I acknowledge the canyon, the lake, the forest path and all of nature as mystical. Energy flows through it at all times. We feel tension created or relieved as we walk against the flow of air and water into a mountain canyon's narrowing embrace, or follow a path to the edge of the Atlantic sea or wind our way down a wooded trail toward Georgian Bay. We are transformed by nature's awesome structures, by its transitory energy, by wind, rock, forest and water. The change it works is subtle and constant. A walk in the forest changes us. Frank Waters of New Mexico writes in *Mountain Dialogues*: "with every breath there is a change of thought."

Robert and I believe it is possible to work at realizing a sense of mysticism within ourselves and our audience. Change is the link between the observer and the observed. In our performances we work at creating openness to change through enhancing sensory experience. The transformations we are speaking about here are subtle: they are changes of heart. Our events strive to foster a feeling of unity and a perception of the encompassing universe beyond our senses; we are inclined to discover forgotten feelings of belonging to a greater circle.

By taking an early-morning walk to listen to the self, the performers and the environment, we are tuning our sensory perception so that we may become aware of an integrated duration rather than a mere passage of time. We synchronize with the environment, realize we are fully part of it as it is part of us.

For our purposes, an integrated duration might be visualized as a shallow pond of liquid containing interacting molecules, whereas passage of time is a straight line, chronological, progressive and causative. If we liken our event to pebbles being dropped on this liquid platter of time, place and being (integrated duration), then we might see that the ripples and boundaries of the pond affect and shape the surface tension of the whole period.

Canyon Shadows: "Stones" is an integrated duration, a platter of thinking, if you will, that accepts experience. If a jogger takes his usual morning run and encounters our performance, as happened at St. John's, we say nothing to him. If he chooses to run through the performance area, he is part of the performance. Performances of *Canyon Shadows: "Stones"* cannot be interrupted, because we choose to accept the elements of the integrated duration without judgment. Jay Hirabayashi's Butoh dance is different at each location. We are different. The soundscape is different. That is the whole point. We are not interested in reproducing performances. This does not mean that we just stand back and let things happen. We do work very hard at the circumstances that might create the opportunity of a meaningful, transformative performance.

Many times during the development of *Canyon Shadows: "Stones,"* Robert and I went through transformations. For instance, we spent considerable time discussing the possibility of audience participation and how to situate the audience. We considered that rather than having our audiences suspend their disbelief while having their senses deprived, sitting in crowded uncomfortable chairs all pointed in the same direction in a temperature-controlled black room, we wanted to give them some control of their experience. We decided to move the performances outside and immediately sense freedom.

With this change of mind we also dropped the notion of creating a controlled and repeatable reaction in our audience. As we began to leave the idea of product behind and focussed on process, we moved forward quickly. This divorce from product raised the question of what Robert and I wanted from the audience. The answer surprised us both: nothing, except for them to attend. We realized that real self-discovery is more likely wholly subjective, not intellectual. At that moment we fully sensed that we were part of a mystery. A paradigm shift had taken place. Our project values had changed. It was more logical, yet more mysterious. Ironically, the further we moved from the idea of controlling our audience, the less stressful the project became.

Robert: R. Murray Schafer's notion of the "hi-fi soundscape" is emphasized as I read my notes from my soundwalks into Grotto Canyon, soundwalks taken to prepare for the first performance.

At the entrance to the canyon I hear a factory in Exshaw two kilometres away and the sound of the Trans-Canada Highway. On the near side of the Bow River the train runs through the heart of the valley. My "sound" walks into the canyon. I notate the changes in my listening patterns, both particular local sounds and global ambient sounds.

They read like a performance score. As I read my notes, I can hear every sound or sound combination in sequence. For me it is the same experience as sitting in silence with an orchestral score.

My notebook has scribbles of solo voice ideas, contrapuntal inter-weaving and ensemble writing; but none of them have stability. I sit in the canyon in the middle of a mountain winter. The canyon floor is a sheet of wet ice, changing every minute.

I am surprised by the number of chickadees flying about or sitting in the trees. I write their intricate song and movement rhythm-patterns, sketch a percussionist with mallets tied to her knees and double headed mallets in her hands. A dance. I feel a dance. Or is it just the chill setting into my bones?

My flute is very cold. I blow one note and listen. I blow two notes and listen. Then I improvise a phrase. Suddenly I realize I have crossed a line. I have just polluted this space with too many notes. At that moment I decide that in my work I do not want to pollute this environ-ment with artistic waste and cultural by-products. What does this mean?

When I reach home I file away the first draft of the voice parts and start again.

Be at ease in grotto canyon,
enter the stone garden,
water has made a place for you.
The sun awaits. Your sensations,
your body, the small furnace.

You have the knowledge
haveyouwill
haveyouwill …

It is human nature to want to believe in something and to express and formalize those beliefs. I am reminded of a sign I read beside a stone jaguar at the New Museum of Anthropology in Mexico City:

Man is creative, he created God in his image. He creates
art, religions, war and politics to give life meaning and to
answer that nagging question he is born with, what is the
meaning of life and what is its purpose?

Humankind's purpose and task is to create. We create cities, pollution, war, machines, sports, art, commerce, industry and more people. We may as well decide not to eat as make up our minds not to create. Without the opportunity for creativity it seems that we become individually and collectively neurotic. Through creativity we are fulfilled. Our inner nature is uncomfortable with stasis, for we are always changing, as is the universe. It is our ego that wants security.

It is interesting that people are now trying to create virtual reality machines that would imitate what some religions have known for centuries and western science has recently proven: the observer affects the observed. The desire to create a machine to mimic our real relationship with nature is itself a statement about how far removed some are from nature.

> The whirlwind comes
> that you may know yourself,
> windfalls
> windfalls
> through a nation of pines
> trembling, they whisper secrets.

At the dawn of consciousness humankind lost its innocence of nature and gradually discovered ego, death and beauty. Over one million years ago the ancient tools of our ancestor *Homo erectus* exhibited a form far beyond utility. The dead were buried in a fetal position with the jawbone of a bear in hand. Favourite animals, objects, plants and, sometimes, other people were buried with the dead, presumably to aid them in their journey through the mysterium.

As the human animal became conscious, it experienced a great fear of the unknown and consequent need to explain the mysterium. Humankind created a creative God/gods in its own image, then created religion as a vehicle for the actions of myth and ritual that would relieve its fears of the unknown.

Whether or not one agrees with the suggested theology of these statements, it is a part of human nature to use ritual, myth and ceremony interacting to alleviate fears and relieve anxiety. *Canyon Shadows: "Stones"* is, as I have said, soft ritual. It is a search for a feeling of connection to the universe. It also tests the possibility of the artist as shaman, spiritualizing a place and time through transformative performances.

Joseph Campbell writes in *Mythologies of the Primitive Hunters and Gatherers* that "it has always been the business of the great seers (known to India as 'rishis,' in biblical terms as 'prophets,' to primitive folk as 'shamans,' and in our own days 'poets' and 'artists') to perform the work of the first and second functions of mythology by recognizing through the veil of nature, as viewed in the science of their times, the radiance, terrible yet gentle, of the dark, unspeakable light beyond, and through their words and images to reveal the sense of the vast silence that is the ground of all of us and of all beings."

Robert and I, as artists, choose to attend to the myriad relationships that bind all of us to each other and to the world. All societies need such people to create and interpret ceremony. What is a poetry reading but the trying out of a new liturgy? Is soundscape art just something to listen to and distract us for a moment or does it contain the action of myth and ritual? Artist as shaman? Why not?

Robert: In my preliminary design for *Canyon Shadows: "Stones"* I identify three phases. First, the performance in the environment itself; second, a video document of the performance; and third, a hypermedia installation.

The video and audio footage from the premiere of *Canyon Shadows: "Stones"* sits in an unedited state. I feel it still holds possibilities but I need to rethink the reason. Maybe video is too closely tied to the idea of artifact. A video cannot recreate the event for the viewer. It can be something else, but I haven't decided what.

I do not have a reproducible version of the score.

I threw out the hypermedia idea. I work around technology and have a good perspective on the virtual reality work being done at Banff. What Peter and I are working toward is incompatible with the implications of technological control.

I was present when Hu Hohn showed John Cage the possibility of casting the I Ching using a personal computer. There was a gleam in Cage's eye, but to him the computer was no more important than the piano or the air conditioner. It was the act of doing and observing that fascinated him.

The act of casting the I Ching is more important than the result because it is the casting that determines the synchronicity of the moment.

> *It is only crying about myself that comes in song.*
> — Nootka saying

Now the stones I am.
Now the forest I am.

Now the earth I am.
With a path to follow
I am the water.
Shaaaaaaaaaaa.
I sing
this house of stone
windshaped
watershaped.

In this house of rocks,
I, am my enemy ...

Stones for your feet.
Stones for your feet.
Rock and steel.

Speak the place.
Scream the stones,
scream canyon cracks,
scream all is created
in you the stones.

As it was in the beginning
is now and ever shall be.
World without end.
Ahhhhhhhhhhhhhh
m e n.
Open stones
accept our love of water
Speak, Stones.

Individually and collectively, many people are trying to understand our changing cultural roles and our archetypal desires for the action of ritual and myth. Some are rediscovering the hunter self by exploring the origins of our apparently "nasty" patriarchal structures. The poet Robert Bly uses myth and ritual for the purpose of self-realization: a good idea, although I doubt that looking for his "wild man" of old Europe in the psyche west of Lake Winnipeg or the Mississippi would prove fruitful.

I believe I am of this land and belong here. I have no cultural background beyond the boat my father crossed the Atlantic on in 1928. He was a refugee. He was very young, had very little cultural baggage and only one small suitcase. He came to the west, lived in the bush and made a farm. He said, "I came here to be a Canadian." I was made, shaped and fed by this land. I am of this place. I recognize and identify spiritually with it. I am strongly tied to my culture. I am Canadian. I will make peace with the land.

> I call this feeling
> of need want lust desire
> possession praise prayer tangle
> I call this biology.

> Stoneman
> water woman
> shape the earth wind
> by need or desire
> shaaaaaaaaaaaa
> met a mor phosis
> met a mor phose
> mi cro cosm
> ma cro cosm
> firestoneswindwater.

We have struggled to categorize this piece we are building, this poemsongtonepoemcontemporarynewmusicperformanceoutdoor-operasoundscapesoliloquy. We have tried to categorize it and failed.

Robert: I was frustrated by the administration of the first performance, the eternal search for funding. I signed my name on all correspondence as composer / producer / director. We envy the free enterprise system of the American entertainment industry; so much money flowing in so many directions. American artists envy our public funding. What makes it all bearable is working with the right people. I have a sense where they are by how they act in the outdoor performance environment.

During the tour down to St. John's, Newfoundland, and Parry Sound, Ontario, I find myself less frustrated. There is no money in it, never is, probably never will be. Jay Hirabayashi has taught me that it does not matter. You do it because you are compelled. Robert and I considered it illogical and arrogant to suppose that we as artistic "scientists" could create spontaneous moments within others, when they would laugh, realize or feel something together. Only the participants and elements of the circumstances of a certain time and place can create such a moment. Yes, it is possible to effect a desired emotion; all animals can be trained, including humans. But these methods are for those who seek power; we want to surrender control.

But really, how does one create a spontaneous moment? This apparent contradiction, like many problems, was solved by gathering more information. By broadening the scope of the performance to include the events leading up to it, as well as its total environment including the audience and performers, we were able to create a greater possibility of the audience, performers, producers and environment being synchronous in the wholeness of a particular performance moment, whole performance or memory of a whole performance.

It became a fundamental underpinning of our project and our lives to accept the place, participants, actors, singers, musicians, the spring snowstorm, the jet passing, the discussion that we had five years ago hiking to Stanley Glacier, the text — in fact, everything — as directly contributing elements of a performance. We acknowledged our participation in an integrated duration rather than along a chronologically identifiable section of history. We realized that *Canyon Shadows: "Stones"* could neither be started nor finished, but it could have its moments. *Nature, unlike history, does not seek closure.*

> Stones for your feet.
> Stones for your feet.
> Rock and steel
> rocksteel.
>
> Stones are problems,
> round ragged moods ...
>
> Mindstone
> hard cold
> heart stone
> stone heart.

Robert: In early May 1990 we perform twice in Grotto Canyon, Mother's Day weekend, a spring snowstorm. Some people have driven 200 kilometres to be here. Our mountain-climber volunteers lower Jay, the dancer, slowly down a cliff face past the audience's point of view. It takes forever, a climber's worst nightmare, falling slowly and never hitting the ground.

In the freezing temperatures, Jay strips his gear off and begins to move his half-naked body, belly to the ground, toward the icy stream; he is sweating.

St. John's two years later, in July, it is only two degrees above freezing, the wind is howling off the icebergs nesting in the Atlantic just off shore. As we prepare for the performance, people ask me what my contingency plans are for performances that need to be cancelled because of rain or snow. I tell them we will perform anyway. My only fear is the wind, but after five performances in three different locales, I have now learned to work within the wind. We have no need to cancel a performance if we are prepared.

Our rehearsals are being blown off the rock by cold Atlantic winds. It has been like this for three weeks. On the morning of our performance the sky clears and it is still. The sun shines, an iceberg drifts in close to our performance site. As our first performance begins, observers see whales breaching in the inlet to St. John's harbour; as our second ends, the fog and storms roll in again. I think it was Louis Pasteur who said "Chance favours the prepared mind."

Although we feel that our work explores a new approach to creativity, we are at the same time working out of a very traditional Canadian theme: landscape. I believe that in the case of a good landscape artist, the landscape creates the painting using the artist as an instrument for expression. But the instrument must be in tune in order for the landscape to speak clearly. Our part is to have the will to be in tune, the patience to listen, to be open to experience.

The contemporary British Columbia painter Roger Aldworth works in this way. He is trained, yet untrained. While painting, he is in a trance as he creates his magic expressionist canvases. He never paints from photographs or indoors or from other pictures. He puts himself in the environment, lets the day have its way. Roger's art is interactive rather than reproductive. Similarly, jazz pianist Cecil Taylor plays the room.

Our approach is traditional, yet in some way pre-dates tradition. It seeks to allow the audience members an essential role in relation to the performance work, to make the audience members ever more aware of their sensations and our mutual responsibility to form, by which I mean our willingness to come together to create "soft ritual" or celebrate ourselves as part of nature.

Robert: When people in the music business hear about this work their first reaction is usually, "Oh, just like R. Murray Schafer's work." I acknowledge the relationship because Schafer has been a great mentor to me and a supporter of my work. But while we both work in the same genre, there are considerable differences in our individual harmonic languages, uses of pitch and rhythm, and notions of randomness.

The stone fears us,
it envies our movement
icewinterwindwater.

I break like a stone.
Ice of your winter tongue,
in your beauty I am afraid,
stones break.

A stone tumbles into the canyon
I heard it
flipping from ledge to ledge
rattling.
Is it an animal, a man?
Windwaterwork.
It means something,
it did not fall all by itself.

We climb,
flex bone and spirit.
We climb for fashion.

Our egos tender
bear us up walls,
to fall is nothing.

Rock bone sinew bend.
Rock bone sinew bend.
Rock and steel
rocksteel.

Robert: The *Toronto Star* review trumpets "Robert Rosen claims *Canyon Shadows* is a search for spirituality!"

I think the reviewer liked the performance. More importantly, *Canyon Shadows: "Stones"* — and something from it — stayed with him. Spirituality is about internal transformations affecting perceptions of the world around us. My role is to use sound to encourage this process.

A review appears in the *Parry Sound North Star* by Kathie Joblin. She writes about her personal transformation through the experience of the performance and closes the article by thanking the artists. Wow! She does not recount the performance's details but eloquently tells how each aspect affected her. It is the best review an artist could ever hope to receive.

Dualism: Any theory which holds that there is, either in the universe at large or in some significant part of it, an ultimate and irreducible distinction of nature between two different kinds of things.

If we "sing" the stones to search for what is common in them and in humankind, we can then sense ourselves as made of the same elements and subject to the same forces.

> Winter bone wind.
> Winter bone wind.
> Muscle mind matters most,
> I stone.
>
> The heart trembles.
> Stones are never the same.

The image of transformation as a joining of the material and spiritual self through ritual which recognizes that stones and humankind are both integral and valued parts of the irreducible whole, allows us to travel in and respect the relationship between cosmos and reason. We need the stones as much as they need us. This is the environmental message. Like the transmutation of wine and bread into flesh and blood during the Christian ritual of communion, we must now understand that the universe is the outcome of transmutation, and we are it. Our western psychology must continue to progress into the spiritual if we are to survive. The moral law within is not separate from the outer world, but integral to our survival as a universe. *Think of the universe as an idea.*

By harmonizing with the process of transformation we may be able to navigate our psyche through the present turbulence. Frank Waters writes in his *Mountain Dialogues*: "to avert a cataclysmic rupture between the spiritual and material, between our hearts and minds, we must re-establish our relationship with all the forms of living nature."

Modern physics now takes for granted the interconnection of all things in the universe, takes as truth Heisenberg's theory that the observer affects the observed, that total objectivity is not possible. Some wise soul has observed that in the future, those looking back at our physics, mathematics and policy structures will see them as cultural phenomena.

And we are of the world and in the world. The self and the greater Self are not separate entities. Dualism was a convenient worldview that let modern humankind rationalize irresponsible use of the land. The self and the physical world are not separate, but are aspects of the same whole universe; and we and all things in it reflect that sameness. There is only the Self.

> Water rocks forest.
> Rock womb
> stone womb
> bone and flesh womb.
> Stones measure time
> by your wearing down.
> Stones. My breath as wind
> wearing the life down.
> Stones.
> We join forces
> bones breaking stones blood rain is not
> east.

Sources

The Way of the Animal Powers, Vol. 1. Campbell, Joseph. (Perennial Library, Harper & Row, 1988)

On Aggression. Lorenz, Konrad. (Harcourt, Brace and World, 1966)

Abundance of Love: The Incarnation and Byzantine Tradition. Raya, Archbishop Joseph. (Educational Services, Diocese of Newton, 1989)

Mountain Dialogues. Waters, Frank. (Sage/Swallow Press Books, 1981)

Notes on the Contributors

MURRAY BANTING is an engineering technologist and businessman. Between the ages of six and twelve he ran a trapline in the northern Manitoba bush. He lives in Bragg Creek with his wife Debbie, who is his partner in Ice River Suppliers.

WADE BELL's work has appeared in some thirty literary magazines and anthologies in Canada, the U.S. and Japan. A collection of stories, *The North Saskatchewan River Book* (Coach House), was published in 1977 and his novella, *The House of the Americans*, was published in *Descant Magazine* in 1994. He attended Carleton University, lived in Spain for five years and now lives in Calgary.

ROSE BIBBY and her husband Garth grow mostly grass and cattle on Rosebriar Ranch near Westlock, Alberta. With their three daughters grown, Rose has turned to poetry, publishing and live performances. Calling herself the "Hayshaker's Wife," she garners much material from the personality and vocabulary of her husband, the "Old Hayshaker." Rose and Garth have performed at cowboy poetry gatherings and concert halls in Canada and the U.S. Books and audiocassettes by the Bibbys are available from The Hayshakers, Box 1502, Westlock, AB, Canada, T0G 2L0.

DORIS BIRCHAM says she has been partnered with the wind and rolling grasslands forever. When she and her husband Ralph bought their ranch on Bear Creek in the Cypress Hills thirty-five years ago, all their possessions (except fifteen cows) fit into a half-ton truck. Now their two grown children have chosen ranching as a career, and Doris recites and entertains at clubs, poetry gatherings, schools and festivals. She is poetry co-ordinator for Maple Creek's Annual Cowboy Poetry Gathering and Western Art Show. Her self-published books include *Calving and the Afterbirth*, *Teamwork* and *Pastures, Ponies and Pals* (cowboy poetry and songs for children, co-authored with Anne Slade). Her work has also been anthologized in *Maverick Western Verse*, *Graining the Mare*, *Heading Out*, *Riding the Northern Range* and *Northern Range*. Doris' books may be obtained by writing to Box 237, Piapot, SK, S0N 1Y0.

GEORGE BOWERING was born and brought up in the Interior of British Columbia, mostly in the South Okanagan Valley. When he was a kid, the highways were narrow and had no stripes down the middle, and the asparagus grew wild alongside the road. One of his recent books of poems is *Elegie di Kerrisdale* (Empìria, 1996). His most recent book of prose is *Bowering's B.C.* (Penguin, 1996).

DI BRANDT is the author of four books of poetry and two books of non-fiction. Her first book, *questions i asked my mother* (Turnstone, 1987), broke the public silence of Mennonite women in Canada and created a scandal in her community. Her latest poetry collection, *Jerusalem, beloved* (Turnstone, 1995), received the Canadian Author's Association Poetry Award and was shortlisted for the Governor General's Award, the Pat Lowther Award and the McNally Robinson Award for Manitoba Book of the Year. Her work has been translated into German, Spanish and Catalan. She teaches creative writing at the University of Windsor.

SHARON BUTALA is the author of two collections of short stories, a trilogy of novels and two books of non-fiction, *The Perfection of the Morning* (HarperCollins,

1994), which was nominated for the Governor General's Award, and *Coyote's Morning Cry* (HarperCollins, 1995). She ranches with her husband Peter in the Cypress Hills area of southwestern Saskatchewan. The Writing the Land Conference which she and Terry Jordan coordinated in the summer of 1994 was one of the inspirations for this anthology.

DAVID CARPENTER writes and teaches in Saskatoon. His second collection of essays, *Courting Saskatchewan* (Douglas & McIntryre), a book about seasonal rituals, was published in 1996. He claims that he sleeps nightly and fishes daily and paddles his boat with a ukulele.

PETER CHRISTENSEN has lived in the remote areas of western Canada for the last twenty-five years. He worked as a guide for twelve years. He presently lives near Radium Hot Springs in the Upper Columbia and makes his living as a consultant, writer and park ranger. Thistledown Press of Saskatchewan published his poetry collections *Hailstorm*, *Rig Talk* and *To Die Ascending*, and Hawk Press of New Mexico published *Sierra Sacrament* and *I Came Upon a Bear*.

KAREN CONNELLY was the youngest person ever to win the Governor General's Award, which she won for her first non-fiction book, *Touch the Dragon: A Thai Journal* (Turnstone, 1992). She has also published three books of poetry with Turnstone Press, *The Small Words in My Body*, *This Brighter Prison* and *Disorder of Love*, and a second travel narrative *One Room in a Castle* (Turnstone, 1995).

JOAN CRATE is the author of the novel *Breathing Water* (NeWest, 1989) and a book of poems, *Pale as Real Ladies: Poems for Pauline Johnson* (Brick, 1989). She has also written a vampire novel. She lives with her family in Red Deer, Alberta, and teaches at Red Deer College.

LORNA CROZIER was born in Swift Current, Saskatchewan. She has published nine books of poetry. *Inventing the Hawk* (McClelland and Stewart, 1992) received the Governor General's Award for Poetry in 1992, the Pat Lowther Award for the best book of poetry by a Canadian woman and the Canadian Author's Association Award for Poetry. *Everything Arrives at the Light* (McClelland and Stewart, 1995) received the Pat Lowther Award and a selection of poems from that book was awarded the National Magazine Gold Medal for Poetry. Her latest book is *A Saving Grace: The Collected Poems of Mrs. Bentley* (McClelland and Stewart, 1996). Lorna teaches at the University of Victoria.

SLIM DAVIS was born in 1908. He was raised in Carmangay, Alberta, and attended school as far as the third grade. When he was ten years old, he went to work for Brewsters, packing horses in the mountains. He has worked with horses all his life and learned to ride before he could walk. He began writing poetry as soon as he grasped the concept of putting words on paper — or on the chalkboards that were then used by schoolchildren. He has self-published two collections of his poetry, *Rhymes of the West Country* and *Poems of Alberta Long Ago*. Every one of his poems tells a story of what it was really like to roam the west country. Slim lives in Red Deer, Alberta. His books can be ordered by calling (403) 346-7256.

CHARLENE DIEHL-JONES' work conjures the flat land of southwestern Manitoba near Boissevain from southern Ontario where she now lives. When she isn't writing or tending her overgrown garden, she teaches Canadian literature at St. Jerome's College at the University of Waterloo.

CHARLES A. FINN is a poet and essayist. He lives with his partner Dea and cat 42 in Argenta, British Columbia, a community of about 200 at the north end of Kootenay Lake. His work has been published in *Explorer Magazine, Pegasus Review, The Conservative Review* and the 1996 *Anthology of New England Writing*. Before moving to B.C., Charles spent three years teaching English as a second language in Hiroshima, Japan.

BEN GADD has lived in or near the Rockies all his life. Educated as a geologist, he is now a freelance interpretive guide in Jasper National Park, a job he describes as "rent-a-naturalist." He also directs the non-profit Jasper Institute, which offers natural history courses to park visitors, and sits on the board of directors of the Alberta Wilderness Association. The author of *Handbook of the Canadian Rockies* (Corax, 1995) and four other books, Ben is a recognized authority on the region. Lately he has been working with protected areas, designing nature trails, producing interpretive signage and advising park administrators. When not otherwise occupied, Ben hikes, climbs and cross-country skis in the mountains he loves best.

MYRNA GARANIS says that she writes from Saskatchewan even while living for the past thirty years in south Edmonton. Her hometown is Floral, Saskatchewan. Her work has been anthologized in *200% Cracked Wheat, Tracing One Warm Line, Coffeehouse Poetry Anthology* and CBC Radio's *Alberta Anthology*.

DON GAYTON was born in the U.S.A. in 1946. He has an M.Sc. in Plant Ecology from the University of Saskatchewan and is currently employed as a range ecologist with the British Columbia Ministry of Forests in Nelson, B.C. His first book, *The Wheatgrass Mechanism: Science and Imagination in the Western Canadian Landscape* (Fifth House, 1992), won the Saskatchewan Writers' Guild Non-fiction Award. His latest book is *Landscapes of the Interior: Re-Explorations of Nature and the Human Spirit* (New Society Publishers, 1997).

SUSAN ANDREWS GRACE is a poet, novelist, textile artist and publisher. Her most recent collection of poetry is *Water is the First World* (Coteau, 1991), and her novel/long poem *Ferry Woman's History of the World* is forthcoming in 1998. As a visual artist, Susan works in textiles, usually in three dimensions. She was the co-designer and co-ordinator, with Judith Fretz, of a community project producing a Peace Quilt, which received a Peace Messenger Award from the United Nations in 1987 and is now installed at the Canadian Permanent Mission to the U.N. in New York. Susan is also the publisher of Hag Papers, an imprint of Underwhich Editions, which has produced six titles in limited-edition chapbooks.

JIM GREEN was born in High River and grew up in the shadow of the Rocky Mountains at Pincher Creek, Alberta. As a boy he wandered the hills and valleys of southwestern Alberta, learned to hunt, fish and trap and he acquired a lifelong passion for fried brook trout and warm huckleberry pie. The author of two books of poetry, *North Book* (Polestar, 1986) and *Beyond Here* (Thistledown, 1983), Jim is a writer, storyteller, poet, broadcaster and entertainer. He is presently writing the history of Waterton Park, finishing a collection of early cattle country stories and editing his own compilation of western poems.

SUSAN HALEY completed a Ph.D. in philosophy at the University of Alberta. After her degree, she owned and was general manager of a charter airline, Ursus Aviation, in Fort Norman, Northwest Territories. In 1989 she was the mayor of Fort Norman. She also wrote the background report for the Fort Norman town plan. When her partner retired from flying, they sold the airline and moved to her family home of Black River, Nova Scotia. She has published three novels: *A Nest of Singing Birds* (NeWest, 1984), *Getting Married in Buffalo Jump* (Macmillan, 1986) and *How to Start a Charter Airline* (Macmillan, 1994). The first two were made into CBC-TV movies.

SKY DANCER LOUISE BERNICE HALFE grew up in a log cabin on the Saddle Lake First Nations Reserve in northern Alberta before she was removed and placed at Blue Quills Residential School outside St. Paul, Alberta, for a total of six years. In later years she moved to Kootenay Plains near David Thompson Resort where she lived in a tipi and tent with both her parents and her lover (who, a year later, became her husband). She and her husband lived in their tipi in the mountains off and on for several years. After her husband's university training, they lived in Meadow Lake, Saskatchewan, for six years where again they lived off the land, six miles out of town. This was where her career bloomed and scattered its seeds through the winds. The couple has since moved to Saskatoon. They have raised a son and a daughter.

MAUREEN SCOTT HARRIS was born in Prince Rupert, British Columbia, in 1943 and raised in Winnipeg. She has lived in Toronto for the past twenty-five years. As a librarian she worked for many years in various libraries at the University of Toronto. Her current projects include a poetry manuscript, a poetry sequence called "The Drowned Boy Poems," and several essays. She also works part-time at Writers & Co., a literary bookstore in Toronto.

ELIZABETH HAYNES has published poetry and fiction in *Absinthe, Capilano Review, Other Voices, Prairie Fire, Room of One's Own* and in several anthologies. She was co-winner of the 1995 Western Magazine Award for fiction. She works as a speech-language pathologist in Calgary and edits fiction for *Dandelion* magazine.

ROBERT HILLES was born in Kenora, Ontario on November 13, 1951, and grew up in the bush ten miles out of town. This part of the Canadian Shield is seldom found in Canadian literature. Much of Hilles' writing tries to come to terms with that harsh but beautiful landscape. Various aspects of bush life can be found in his books of fiction. His book of poetry, *Cantos from a Small Room* (Wolsak and Wynn, 1993), won the 1994 Governor General's Award for Poetry. His first non-fiction book, *Kissing the Smoke* (Black Moss, 1996), tells of the lives of the people of Longbow Lake near Kenora who hunted, fished, logged and farmed the rocky terrain.

BLANCHE HOWARD's latest novel, *A Celibate Season,* was co-authored by Carol Shields, and another of her novels was awarded the Canadian Booksellers' Association Prize. Her short stories appear frequently in literary magazines and one of her plays was produced in Vancouver. The schooling of her early years in the harsh prairie climate east of Edmonton was interspersed with occasional school terms in Calgary. She has since sought milder climes and lives in Vancouver.

HAZEL JARDINE has lived most of her life on the prairies, and the last twenty years in Fort Qu'Appelle, Saskatchewan. A mother of five, she began taking writing courses when her children left home. This opened up a new career in freelance writing and broadcasting. Hazel has written over 350 short humourous sketches for newspapers and magazines in Canada and the U.S. When her husband built their retirement home high on a hill overlooking the lake and surrounded by trees, it included a small writing shack. From here Hazel writes, prepares sermons for her lay ministry work and spearheads global justice actions.

THERESA KISHKAN was born in 1955 on Vancouver Island and has lived on both coasts of Canada as well as for extended periods in Greece, Utah and the west of Ireland. She is married to the poet John Pass, and they live on the Sechelt Peninsula. Theresa has published several collections of poetry and has written two novels, *Inishbream* (forthcoming from Barbarian Press) and the most recent, *Sisters of Grass*. A collection of her essays, *Red Laredo Boots* (1996), was published by New Star Books as part of its Transmontanus series. Theresa says, "I like what Gary Snyder has to say about the lessons we take from the wilderness: 'The wild requires that we learn the terrain, nod to all the plants and animals and birds, ford the streams and cross the ridges, and tell a good story when we get back home.' Living where I live, on an acreage of second-growth temperate rain forest, I find myself thinking that I am ideally placed to be a writer. Living up to the place, its weather, temperatures, rainfall, its very genius, will be the best work I can hope to do."

MYRNA KOSTASH says that it is an enduring notion among Albertans that we are more powerfully connected with the Americans immediately south of us — who are continuous with us culturally — than with fellow Canadians to the east and west of us with whom we are merely politically connected. She writes: "As a passionate Canadian nationalist, I have always resisted this particular mythocartography and insisted on my common cause with Canadians with whom I construct a shared political value rather than with Americans who happen, like (some) Albertans, to wear cowboy boots and herd cattle on the Great Plain. In the summer of 1993 I decided to put the argument to the test by driving around Montana. Just how disconnected would I feel, I challenged myself. In the end, the surprise was that, while I did feel powerful contiguities (some of them positively paleontological!), I understood I am not from there — not from Montana, not from the Great Plain, not even from southern Alberta. I am a Canadian from the parkland, from the southernmost edge of the vast bush that lies north. But that's another story." Kostash's books include *All of Baba's Children* (NeWest, 1977) and *Bloodlines: A Journey into Eastern Europe* (Douglas & McIntyre, 1993)

LEA LITTLEWOLFE grew up on a mixed farm on a river north of Edmonton. She went to university in Edmonton, taught for nine years in white Alberta schools, and then left to teach on a reserve in Saskatchewan. She is Abenaki-Odawa-Cree-German-Irish-Scots. Her poetry has appeared in *Grain*, *Western People* and *NeWest Review*.

SID MARTY lives with his wife Myrna in the montane foothills of southwestern Alberta, north of the town of Lundbreck. His books have won numerous awards and *Men for the Mountains* (McClelland and Stewart, 1978) has remained continuously in print. He has published two books of poetry and his most recent work of non-fiction, *Leaning on the Wind: Under the Spell of the Great Chinook* (HarperCollins, 1995), was nominated for the Governor General's Award. He publishes regularly in

Canadian Geographic and has a column in the *Pincher Creek Echo*. He is also a singer-songwriter and performs his work in Alberta, Montana and England.

JOHN PASS lives on eight-and-a-half acres of forest, garden and orchard in a self-built house near Sakinaw Lake on British Columbia's Sunshine Coast with his wife, Theresa Kishkan, and their three children. His most recent collection of poetry is *Radical Innocence* (Harbour, 1994). *The Hour's Acropolis* (Harbour, 1991) was shortlisted for the Dorothy Livesay Prize. He won the CIVA Canadian Poetry Prize in 1988 and placed second in the League of Canadian Poets National Poetry Contest in 1994.

HILARY PEACH has come to view driving the back roads in a pickup truck with a big dog, drinking beer and searching for a sexy little trout stream to curl up with as a political act. One of her favourite role models is a hard-hearted waitress with painted-on eyebrows at a truck stop in a little town called Woss. Hilary often performs her poetry together with poet Alice Tepexcuintle. Hilary currently lives, studies welding and performs in Vancouver.

ELIZABETH PHILIPS is a poet and journalist living in Saskatoon, Saskatchewan. Raised in Gimli, Manitoba, she grew up in thrall to the rhythms of Lake Winnipeg. She has lived in Saskatoon for fifteen years. She is a former poetry editor and former editor-in-chief of the literary magazine *Grain*, and she has published two poetry collections, *Time in a Green Country* (Coteau, 1990) and *Beyond My Keeping* (Coteau, 1995), which won the Saskatchewan Book Award for Poetry. Her poems have appeared in *Event*, *The Malahat Review*, *Prairie Fire*, *Grain*, *Prism*, and *ARC*; her non-fiction articles have also been published in numerous magazines and journals.

SHARRON PROULX-TURNER is a sixteenth-generation Métis of Mohawk, Huron, Algonquin, Ojibwa, French and Irish ancestry, and a member of the Métis Nation of Alberta. She was born on a potato/corn farm in a small Irish-Canadian community in the Ottawa Valley, which is where her parents met after her mother was fostered out into her husband's family. As a girl growing up on an army base, the river valleys of the Ottawa and the Petawawa shaped her perceptions. Sharron says that, "The land is sacred and next to my kids, over the last forty-some years the land has been my most intimate and valued friend. Water and wind and wet and soil and voices in the air. I have a powerful connection with birds, particularly crows and ravens." She has completed both a B.A. and an M.A. in English. She is a two-spirit, a mother, an activist, a teacher and a writer.

BARBARA SCHOTT's work as a fashion stylist in the import trade frequently takes her around the world. But rather than diluting her sense of place, the travelling only intensifies a powerful yearning for this country and this land. She says, "Even when I am at home, I long for where I am, as if I'd misplaced myself. To write is to never be at home. I would argue that the land is writing me." Her publications include a chapbook, *The Waterlily Pickers*, and poems in *Border Crossings*, *Canadian Literature*, *Tickle Ace*, *Prairie Fire*, *Room of One's Own*, *Contemporary Verse 2* and *Absinthe*.

GREGORY SCOFIELD's first book, *The Gathering* (Polestar, 1993), won the Dorothy Livesay Poetry Award. He was awarded the Canadian Authors Association Award for the most promising young writer for his second book, *Native Canadiana* (Polestar, 1996). His third book, *Love Medicine and One Song* (Polestar, 1997), celebrates relationships with the land, with our bodies and with the bodies of our lovers.

THERESA SHEA is an Edmonton poet whose work has appeared in a number of literary magazines including *Queen's Quarterly, Antigonish Review, Matrix, Other Voices* and *Contemporary Verse 2*. She is currently completing a manuscript of train poems, and she is a member of the editorial collective of *Other Voices*.

ANNE SLADE ranches with her husband and sons in the east block of the Saskatchewan Cypress Hills. Her poetry, prose, articles and songs about rural life have been published in numerous magazines, chapbooks and other publications and have been performed at cowboy poetry gatherings, on radio and on television. She co-authored (with Doris Bircham) a book of poetry for children called *Pastures, Ponies and Pals* (self-published, 1993). A chapbook of her poetry, *Denim, Felt and Leather*, was published by Shea Publishing in 1995. She enjoys both writing and performing. Like other writers from her area, Anne believes that her creativity is enhanced by the mystery of the ever-changing prairie landscape. Shea Publishing can be reached at Box 242, Tompkins, SK, Canada, S0N 2S0.

ARTHUR SLADE is from the Cypress Hills near Tompkins, Saskatchewan. His fiction deals with everything from prairie life to imaginary worlds of science fiction and fantasy. His short stories have been broadcast on CBC and published in magazines across North America. He is currently at work on three comic book titles and has recently published a young adult novel entitled *Draugr* (Orca, 1997).

BIRK SPROXTON was born and raised in Flin Flon, Manitoba, and lives now in Red Deer where he teaches creative writing and English at Red Deer College. He has published a long poem, *Headframe* (Turnstone, 1985) and a book of short fiction, *The Hockey Fan Came Riding* (Turnstone, 1990), and has edited a collection of essays, *Trace: Prairie Writers on Writing* (Turnstone, 1986). His latest novel is entitled *The Red-Headed Woman with the Black Black Heart* (Turnstone, 1997).

FRED STENSON is a Calgary-based writer originally from the foothills of southwestern Alberta, where for two generations his family ran cattle and farmed. He has published eight books including the novel *Last One Home* (NeWest, 1988) and the short fiction collections *Working Without a Laugh Track* (Coteau, 1990) and *Teeth* (Coteau, 1994). He has just completed a novel about the fur trade. He has also written more than a hundred films and videos and has edited two collections of Alberta writing, *Alberta Bound* and *The Road Home* (Reidmore, 1992).

MARGARET SWEATMAN's first novel was *Fox* (Turnstone, 1991). She adapted *Fox* for the stage and it was produced at Prairie Theatre Exchange in Winnipeg in 1994. She has also published three chapbooks, *Private Property, Kore in Hell* and *Broken Songs*, and a second novel, *Sam and Angie*. She is presently working on a novel which takes place in St. Norbert, Manitoba, on the land on which she herself lives (which was submerged during the 1997 Red River Flood). The area was the scene of Louis Riel's 1869-70 resistance to Canadian annexation.

GUY VANDERHAEGHE has written the novels *My Present Age* (McClelland and Stewart, 1991), *Homesick* (McClelland and Stewart, 1993) and *The Englishman's*

Boy (McLelland and Stewart, 1996); three short story collections; and the plays *I Had a Job I Liked. Once* and *Dancock's Dance.* He has lived all but two of his forty-six years in Saskatchewan. Mostly he writes about parkland rather than prairie, but "Blue Horse In A Blizzard" is an exception.

FRED WAH says, "All of my early books track the topos of the Kootenays (Selkirk and Purcell ranges), trees, earth, gravel, scree that I grew up in and came back to — still do. Then the ramparts slipped into memory and the dust, wind, grass of prairie origins, family, migration until all the thingnesses of living in a west hyphened by mountains iterates a presence, in writing, simply as document of some soulness, some place, and sometimes word."

JOHN WEIER was born in Winnipeg in 1949 and grew up on a peach farm near Niagara-on-the-Lake, Ontario. In 1975 he began work as Winnipeg's resident luthier, making banjos, violas and violins. John has also worked in the Canadian book publishing industry and as a musician with the Duck Mountain Bluegrass Band. He has two children and lives in Winnipeg with his wife Susan. He is the author of three collections of poetry, a cross-genre work and a children's picture book. His collection of stories, *Friends Coming Back as Animals,* was published by Moonstone Press in 1996.

RICK WENMAN has worked in animal care since 1979, specializing in endangered and exotic animals such as the Przewalski's horse, Grevy's zebra and the whooping crane. He lives and works on a ranch just south of Calgary, so he is able to enjoy both country life and urban accessibility. He says that he sees landscape as more than geography. "It encompasses not only the land but the people, animals, plants and weather that exist in a particular environment. The voice of the storyteller constantly evolves and changes with its environment." His stories have been published in *Secrets from the Orange Couch, Filling Station* and *Mattoid,* and broadcast on CBC Radio's *Alberta Anthology.*

THOMAS WHARTON was born in Grande Prairie, Alberta, and also lived in Jasper for several years, an experience that inscribed itself deep in his imagination and resurfaced years later, to his surprise, when he first attempted to write a novel. At present he lives in Calgary with his wife, Sharon, and children, Mary and Conor. He is working on his doctoral dissertation, a creative project entitled "Imaginary Novels." His parents both lived on farms and he loves the outdoors, but he says he is for the most part a creation of the urban environment. His first novel, *Icefields* (NeWest, 1995), arose partly out of a frustration with certain conventions of nature writing. Instead of trying to capture the essence of a place, he wanted to look at the ways in which history, culture and imagination are always present in our understanding of landscape and "wilderness."

RUDY WIEBE is the award-winning author of *The Temptations of Big Bear* (McClelland and Stewart, 1991), *A Discovery of Strangers* (Knopf, 1994) and *Playing Dead: A Contemplation Concerning the Arctic* (NeWest, 1989).

Further Exploring

Due to the wealth of the material available and the limitations of space, I cannot offer more than a preliminary sketch of nature writing in Canada and the U.S., and lists of names of writers who are working in the field. One index of the current resurgence of interest in the environment, nature writing and sense of place is the number of recent and upcoming conferences on these subjects. Book sales are also powerful indicators of the popularity of literature about the western landscape. To give just a few examples, the bestseller status and major award nominations accorded to Sharon Butala's *The Perfection of the Morning* and Sid Marty's *Leaning on the Wind: Under the Spell of the Great Chinook* signify a hunger for creative nonfiction about sense of place. Robert Kroetsch's *Alberta*, first published in 1968, was recently reissued with a new introduction. Rudy Wiebe's novel *The Temptations of Big Bear* is being made into a movie. Thomas Wharton's award-winning novel *Icefields* remained on the bestseller list for weeks. W.O. Mitchell's *Who Has Seen the Wind* is a well-loved Canadian classic.

In addition to the fifty contributors to *Fresh Tracks*, some of the other western Canadian writers who are engaged in writing about this landscape include Manitoba writers Sandra Birdsell, Patrick Friesen, Armin Wiebe, Lois Braun, Carol Shields, Jake MacDonald and Méira Cook; Saskatchewan writers Thelma Poirier, Gary Hyland, Maggie Siggins, Terry Jordan, Tim Lilburn and Bill Robertson; Alberta writers Thomas King, Roberta Rees, Aritha Van Herk, Marilyn Halvorsen, Gloria Sawai, Merna Summers, Marilyn Dumont, Lorne Daniel, David Poulsen, Monty Reid, Bert Almon, Douglas Barbour, Christine Wiesenthal, Kristjana Gunnars, Hiromi Goto, Tim Bowling, Scot Morison, Andrew Wreggitt, Ian Tyson, Charlie Russell and screenwriter and filmmaker Francis Damberger; British Columbia writers Diana Hartog, Sharon Thesen, Paulette Jiles, Mary Burns, Robert Bringhurst, David Suzuki, Jay Ruzesky, Tom Wayman, Daphne Marlatt, Patrick Lane, Jeannette Armstrong, Kevin Paul and Terry Glavin. There are many, many others, including dozens of cowboy poets both male and female from all four provinces.

American nature writers are also enjoying a renaissance. Barry Lopez, Pattiann Rogers, Annie Dillard, Terry Tempest Williams, William Kittredge, Richard Manning, Mary Clearman Blew, James Welch, Cormac McCarthy, Barbara Kingsolver, Gretel Ehrlich, C.L. Rawlins, Gloria Anzaldúa, David Abram, Ivan Doig, Rick Bass, Gary Snyder, Gary Paul Nabhan, Wendell Berry, Leslie Marmon Silko, Kathleen Norris, Edward Abbey, Joy Harjo, and N. Scott Momaday are just a few of the Americans who are tracking concerns, topics and genres similar to those of their western Canadian counterparts.

Recently, a number of important critical books and anthologies on western life, land and culture have emerged. Prominent reader-response theorist

Jane Tompkins has published *West of Everything: The Inner Life of Westerns*. Former ranch kid turned academic Blake Allmendinger published *The Cowboy: Representations of Labor in an American Work Culture*, a study of cattle branding and symbolic wounds, livestock castration and square dancing, rustlers and cowboy detectives, and orphanhood and orality on the range. Another former ranch kid Teresa Jordan produced a book of interviews called *Cowgirls: Women of the American West* and the anthology *The Stories that Shape Us: Contemporary Women Write About the West*. Gail Gilchrist and Canadian Candace Savage have published *The Cowgirl Companion* and *Cowgirls* respectively. Ranchwoman, poet and environmental activist Thelma Poirier has just published the latest in Red Deer College Press' "Roundup" series, an anthology entitled *Cowgirls: 100 Years of Writing the Range*.

For those who are interested in ecocriticism — the study of the relationship between literature and the environment — an anthology called *The Ecocriticism Reader: Landmarks in Literary Ecology*, edited by Cheryll Glotfelty and Harold Fromm, is an excellent point of departure. The best parallel anthology to *Fresh Tracks* and a wonderful read is a collection of essays and poems edited by Deborah Clow and Donald Snow called *Northern Lights: A Selection of New Writing from the American West*. For U.S. anthologies to use as undergraduate teaching texts in conjunction with *Fresh Tracks*, four of the best are *A Forest of Voices: Reading and Writing the Environment*, edited by Chris Anderson and Lex Runciman; *Being in the World: An Environmental Reader for Writers*, edited by Scott H. Slovic and Terrell Dixon; *Writing Nature: An Ecological Reader for Writers*, edited by Carolyn Ross; and *Reading the Environment*, edited by Melissa Walker.

Allmendinger, Blake. *The Cowboy: Representations of Labor in an American Work Culture*. New York and Oxford: Oxford, 1992.

Banting, Pamela. *Body Inc.: A Theory of Translation Poetics*. Winnipeg: Turnstone, 1995.

Bell, Wade. *The North Saskatchewan River Book*. Toronto: Coach House, 1976.

Bibby, Rose. *Family, Friends and Fun*; *Hayshakers "LIVE" 1 & 2*; *Haywire and Happiness*. Audiocassettes.

—. *Rosie's Rhyme and Reason*. Westlock, AB: self-published, 1993.

Bircham, Doris. *Calving and the Afterbirth*. Piapot, SK: self-published, 1992.

—. *Teamwork*. Piapot, SK: self-published, 1995.

Bowering, George. *Bowering's B.C.* Toronto: Penguin, 1996.

—. *Caprice*. Toronto: Penguin, 1987.

—. *Shoot!* Toronto: Key Porter, 1994.

Bowling, Tim. *Low Water Slack*. Gibsons, BC: Nightwood Editions, 1995.

Brandt, Di. *Dancing Naked: Narrative Strategies for Writing Across Centuries*. Stratford, ON: Mercury, 1996.

—. *Jerusalem, beloved*. Winnipeg: Turnstone, 1995.

—. *mother, not mother*. Stratford, ON: Mercury, 1992.

Butala, Sharon. *Coyote's Morning Cry: Meditations and Dreams from a Life in Nature*. Toronto: HarperCollins, 1995.

—. *The Perfection of the Morning*. Toronto: HarperCollins, 1994.

Carpenter, David. *Courting Saskatchewan*. Vancouver: Greystone Books/Douglas & McIntyre, 1996.

—. *Writing Home*. Saskatoon: Fifth House, 1994.

Christensen, Lisa. *A Hiker's Guild to Art of the Canadian Rockies*. Calgary: Glenbow Museum, 1996.

Clow, Deborah and Donald Snow, eds. *Northern Lights: A Selection of New Writing from the American West*. New York: Vintage-Random, 1994.

Connelly, Karen. *One Room in a Castle*. Winnipeg: Turnstone, 1995.

—. *Touch the Dragon: A Thai Journal*. Winnipeg: Turnstone, 1992.

Cooley, Dennis. *The Vernacular Muse: The Eye and Ear in Contemporary Literature*. Winnipeg: Turnstone, 1987.

Crate, Joan. *Breathing Water*. Edmonton: NeWest, 1989.

—. *Pale as Real Ladies: Poems for Pauline Johnson*. London, ON: Brick Books, 1989.

Crozier, Lorna. *Angels of Flesh, Angels of Silence*. Toronto: McClelland and Stewart, 1988.

—. *The Garden Going On Without Us*. Toronto: McClelland and Stewart, 1985.

—. *A Saving Grace: The Collected Poems of Mrs. Bentley*. Toronto: McClelland and Stewart, 1996.

Cruikshank, Julie in collaboration with Angela Sidney, Kitty Smith, and Annie Ned. *Life Lived Like a Story*. Vancouver: University of British Columbia Press in collaboration with University of Nebraska, 1990.

Dickson, Lovat. *Wilderness Man: The Strange Story of Grey Owl*. Toronto: Macmillan, 1989.

Dofflemyer, John C., ed. *Maverick Western Verse*. Layton, Utah: Gibbs Smith, 1994.

Duncan, James and David Ley, eds. *Place/Culture/Representation*. London and New York: Routledge, 1993.

Fairley, Bruce. *The Canadian Mountaineering Anthology*. Foreword by Sid Marty. Edmonton: Lone Pine Publishing, 1994.

Gadd, Ben. *Handbook of the Canadian Rockies*. 2nd ed. Wildlife drawings by Matthew Wheeler. Jasper, AB: Corax, 1995.

— and Chris Yorath. *Of Rocks, Mountains and Jasper: A Visitor's Guide to the Geology of Jasper National Park*. Toronto and Oxford: Geological Survey of Canada and Dundurn Press, 1995.

Gayton, Don. *Landscapes of the Interior: Re-Explorations of Nature and the Human Spirit*. Gabriola Island, BC: New Society Publishers, 1996.

—. *The Wheatgrass Mechanism: Science and Imagination in the Western Canadian Landscape*. Saskatoon: Fifth House, 1992.

Glotfelty, Cheryll and Harold Fromm, eds. *The Ecocriticism Reader: Landmarks in Literary Ecology*. Athens and London: University of Georgia, 1996.

Grace, Susan Andrews. *Water Is The First World*. Regina: Coteau, 1991.

Green, Jim. *Beyond Here*. Saskatoon: Thistledown, 1983.

—. *North Book*. 1975, 1976. Vancouver: Polestar, 1986.

Grey Owl. *The Men of the Last Frontier*. 1931. Toronto: Stoddart, 1992.

—. *Tales of an Empty Cabin*. 1936. Toronto: Stoddart, 1992.

Grove, Frederick Philip. *Settlers of the Marsh*. 1925. Toronto: McClelland and Stewart, 1989.

Halfe, Louise. *Bear Bones and Feathers*. Regina: Coteau Books, 1994.

Haley, Susan. *A Nest of Singing Birds*. Edmonton: NeWest, 1984.

—. *Getting Married in Buffalo Jump*. Toronto: Macmillan Canada and E.P. Dutton, 1986.

—. *How to Start a Charter Airline*. Toronto: Macmillan Canada, 1994.

Harris, Maureen. *A Possible Landscape*. London: Brick Books, 1993.

Hilles, Robert. *Kissing the Smoke*. Windsor: Black Moss, 1996.

—. *Raising of Voices*. Windsor: Black Moss, 1993.

Jordan, Terry. *It's a Hard Cow*. Saskatoon: Thistledown, 1993.

King, Thomas. *Green Grass, Running Water*. Toronto: HarperCollins, 1993.

—. *Medicine River*. Toronto: Penguin, 1989.

—. *One Good Story, That One*. Toronto: HarperPerennial-HarperCollins, 1993.

Kishkan, Theresa. *Red Laredo Boots*. Vancouver: Transmontanus-New Star, 1996.

Kostash, Myrna. *All of Baba's Children*. 1977. Edmonton: NeWest, 1992.

—. *Bloodlines: A Journey Into Eastern Europe*. Vancouver: Douglas & McIntyre, 1993.

Kroetsch, Robert. *A Likely Story: The Writing Life*. Red Deer: Red Deer College, 1995.

—. *Alberta*. 1968. 2nd ed. Afterword Rudy Wiebe. Photo essay Harry Savage. Edmonton: NeWest, 1993.

—. *Completed Field Notes: The Long Poems of Robert Kroetsch*. Toronto: McClelland and Stewart, 1989.

—. *The Crow Journals*. Edmonton: NeWest, 1980.

Leedahl, Shelley. *Sky Kickers*. Saskatoon: Thistledown, 1994.

Lilburn, Tim. *Moosewood Sandhills*. Toronto: McClelland and Stewart, 1994.

Livingston, John A. *Rogue Primate: An Exploration of Human Domestication*. Toronto: Key Porter Books, 1994.

Marty, Sid. *Leaning on the Wind: Under the Spell of the Great Chinook*. Toronto: HarperCollins, 1995.

—. *Men for the Mountains*. Toronto: McClelland and Stewart, 1978.

McKay, Don. *Birding, or Desire*. 1983. Toronto: McClelland and Stewart, 1993.

—. *Night Field*. Toronto: McClelland and Stewart, 1991.

McQuarrie, John. *Cowboyin': A Legend Lives On*. Self-published. Distributed by Macmillan Canada, 1995.

McQuarrie, John and Kim Taylor, photography. Text by Sherm Ewing and Joyce McElroy. *Great Centennial Cattle Drive, Western Stock Growers' Association 1896-1996*. Self-published by John McQuarrie. Distributed by Raincoast Books, 1996.

Mitchell, W.O. *Who Has Seen the Wind?* 1947. Toronto: Macmillan, 1971.

Mowat, Farley. *Sea of Slaughter*. Toronto: McClelland and Stewart, 1984.

O'Neill, John. *Love in Alaska*. Lantzville, BC: Oolichan, 1994.

Ostenso, Martha. *Wild Geese*. 1925. Toronto: McClelland and Stewart, 1961.

Philips, Elizabeth. *Beyond My Keeping*. Regina: Coteau, 1995.

—. *Time in a Green Country*. Regina: Coteau, 1990.

Poirier, Thelma. *Grasslands: The Private Hearings*. Intro. Grant MacEwan. Regina: Coteau, 1990.

Poulsen, David. *Don't Fence Me In: A Romance of the New West*. Red Deer: Red Deer College, 1993.

Rees, Roberta. *Beneath the Faceless Mountain*. Red Deer: Red Deer College, 1994.

Reid, Monty. *Crawlspace: New and Selected Poems*. Toronto: House of Anansi, 1993.

Robinson, Harry. *Nature Power: In the Spirit of an Okanagan Storyteller*. Compiled and edited Wendy Wickwire. Vancouver and Toronto: Douglas & McIntyre, 1992.

Ross, Sinclair. *As For Me and My House*. 1941, 1957. Toronto: McClelland and Stewart, 1989.

Rowe, Stan. *Home Place: Essays on Ecology*. Edmonton: NeWest/Canadian Parks and Wilderness Society, 1990.

Ruffo, Armand Garnet. *Grey Owl: The Mystery of Archie Belaney*. Regina: Coteau, 1996.

Russell, Andy. *Adventures with Wild Animals*. Illustrations Harry Savage. 1977. Toronto: McClelland and Stewart, 1991.

—. *The Canadian Cowboy: Stories of Cows, Cowboys and Cayuses*. Toronto: McClelland and Stewart, 1993.

Russell, Charles. *Spirit Bear: Encounters with the White Bear of the Western Rainforest*. Foreword Andy Russell. Toronto: Key Porter Books, 1994.

Ryden, Kent. *Mapping the Invisible Landscape: Folklore, Writing, and the Sense of Place*. Foreword Wayne Franklin. Iowa City: University of Iowa, 1993.

Savage, Candace. *The Nature of Wolves: An Intimate Portrait*. Vancouver and Toronto: Douglas & McIntyre, 1996.

—. *Wild Cats: Lynx, Bobcats, Mountain Lions*. Vancouver and Toronto: Douglas & McIntyre, 1996.

Scofield, Gregory. *The Gathering: Stones for the Medicine Wheel*. Vancouver: Polestar, 1993.

—. *Native Canadiana: Songs from the Urban Rez*. Vancouver: Polestar, 1996.

Slade, Anne. *Denim, Felt and Leather*. Tompkins, SK: Shea Publishing, 1995.

— and Doris Bircham. *Pastures, Ponies and Pals*. Tompkins, SK: self-published, 1993.

Sproxton, Birk. *Headframe*. Winnipeg: Turnstone, 1985.

—. *The Red-Headed Woman with the Black Black Heart*. Winnipeg: Turnstone, 1997.

—, ed. *Trace: Prairie Writers on Writing*. Winnipeg: Turnstone, 1986.

St. Pierre, Paul. *Smith and Other Events*. Vancouver: Douglas and McIntyre, 1985.

Stegner, Wallace. *Where the Bluebird Sings to the Lemonade Springs: Living and Writing in the West*. Toronto: Penguin, 1992.

—. *Wolf Willow: A History, a Story and a Memory of the Last Prairie Frontier*. 1955. Toronto: Macmillan, 1962.

Stenson, Fred. *Great Centennial Cattle Drive: Western Stock Growers Association 1896-1996*. Narrated by Sid Marty. Calgary: White Iron Productions, 1996.

—, ed. *The Road Home: New Stories from Alberta Writers*. Edmonton: Reidmore Books, 1992.

—. *Working Without a Laugh Track*. Regina: Coteau, 1990.

Stone, Ted, ed. *Riding the Northern Range: Poems from the Last Best-West*. Red Deer: Red Deer College, 1993.

—, ed. *A Roundup of Cowboy Humour*. Red Deer: Red Deer College, 1995.

Suknaski, Andrew. *Wood Mountain Poems*. Toronto: Macmillan, 1976.

Sweatman, Margaret. *Fox*. Winnipeg: Turnstone, 1991.

Tefs, Wayne, Geoffrey Ursell and Aritha van Herk, ed. *Due West: Thirty Great Stories from Alberta, Saskatchewan and Manitoba*. Edmonton, Regina and Winnipeg: NeWest, Coteau Books and Turnstone, 1996.

Tepexcuintle, Alice. *Welcome to Wild Iguana Country: Four Western Tales*. Vancouver: Zapazoli, 1995.

Tompkins, Jane. *West of Everything: The Inner Life of Westerns*. New York: Oxford, 1992.

Vanderhaege, Guy. *The Englishman's Boy*. Toronto: McClelland and Stewart, 1996.

—. *Homesick*. 1989. Toronto: McClelland and Stewart, 1993.

—. *Things As They Are?* Toronto: McClelland and Stewart, 1992.

van Herk, Aritha, ed. *Alberta Rebound: Thirty More Stories by Alberta Writers*. Edmonton: NeWest, 1990.

Van Tighem, Kevin. *Coming West: A Natural History of Home*. Canmore, AB: Altitude Publishing, 1997.

Vogelaar, Susan, ed. *Bards of the Saddle: The 10th Anniversary Anthology of the Alberta Cowboy Poetry Association*. Surrey, BC: Hancock House, 1997.

Wah, Fred. *Among*. Toronto: Coach House, 1972.

—. *Diamond Grill*. Edmonton: NeWest, 1996.

—. *So Far*. Vancouver: Talonbooks, 1991.

—. *Waiting for Saskatchewan*. Winnipeg: Turnstone, 1985.

Watson, Sheila. *The Double Hook*. 1959. Toronto: McClelland and Stewart, 1969.

Weier, John. *Friends Coming Back as Animals*. London, ON: Moonstone, 1996.

—. *Ride the Blue Roan*. Winnipeg: Turnstone, 1988.

Wharton, Thomas. *Icefields*. Edmonton: NeWest, 1995.

Whyte, Jon. *Homage, Henry Kelsey*. Drawings by Dennis Burton. Winnipeg: Turnstone, 1981.

Wiebe, Rudy. *A Discovery of Strangers*. Toronto: Knopf, 1994.

—. *Playing Dead: A Contemplation Concerning the Arctic*. Edmonton: NeWest, 1989.

—. *The Temptations of Big Bear*. 1973. Toronto: McClelland and Stewart, 1991.

Wilson, Ethel. *Swamp Angel*. 1954. Toronto: McClelland and Stewart, 1990.

York, Annie, Richard Daly and Chris Arnett. *They Write Their Dreams on the Rock Forever: Rock Writings in the Stein River Valley of British Columbia*. Vancouver: Talonbooks, 1993.

Permissions

All contributions to this anthology are published with the permission of their authors.

"The End of the Hunt" by David Carpenter was previously published in *Courting Saskatchewan* (Greystone Books/Douglas & McIntyre, 1996). Reprinted by permission of the publisher.

"Canyon" by Don Gayton was previously published in *Landscapes of the Interior* (New Society Publishers, 1997). Reprinted by permission of the publisher.

"Charlie Butterfly" by Rick Wenman was previously broadcast on CBC's *Alberta Anthology.*

"Medicine Line Crossings" by Myrna Kostash was previously published in very different form in *Border Crossings.*

"The Farmhouse Poems" by Barbara Schott won second prize in *ARC Magazine*'s poetry contest and was previously published in that magazine.

John Pass' poems were previously published in *The Capilano Review.*

"lamentations: prairie winter" by Charlene Diehl-Jones was previously published in *lamentations* (Trout Lily Press, 1997). Reprinted by permission of the publisher.

Gregory Scofield's poems were previously published in *Love Medicine and One Song* (Polestar Book Publishers, 1997). Reprinted by permission of the publisher.

Pamela Banting's poems were previously broadcast on CBC's *Alberta Anthology.*

Lea Littlewolfe's poems were previously published in *NeWest Review.*

"Blue Horse In A Blizzard" by Guy Vanderhaeghe was previously published in *The Englishman's Boy* (McClelland and Stewart, 1996). Reprinted by permission of the publisher.

"A Career in Farming" by Robert Hilles was previously published in *Kissing the Smoke* (Black Moss, 1996). Reprinted by permission of the publisher.

Lorna Crozier's poems were previously published in *A Saving Grace: The Collected Poems of Mrs. Bentley* (McClelland and Stewart, 1996). Reprinted by permission of the publisher.

"This land that I love, this wide wide prairie" by Di Brandt was previously published in *Borderlines #45* and *the text 8.*

"Undressing the Mountains" by Theresa Kishkan was previously published in the *Vancouver Sun* and in *Red Laredo Boots* (New Star, 1996). Reprinted by permission of the publisher.

"Heart Break" by Susan Andrews Grace was previously published in *Prairie Fire.*

PAMELA BANTING was born and raised in the
northern Manitoba bush in the village of Birch
River. She has taught at the Universities of
Western Ontario, Alberta and Calgary. She
presently lives in Calgary. She has published
poetry, fiction, non-fiction, literary criticism and
literary theory. The first chapter of her novel
Godiva Rides Again won third prize in the
Prairie Fire Magazine Short Fiction Contest in
1995 and was also published in *Due West: Thirty
Great Stories from Alberta, Saskatchewan and
Manitoba* (joint publication of NeWest, Coteau
and Turnstone, 1996). Her most recent book is
Body Inc.: A Theory of Translation Poetics
(Turnstone, 1995).

Fiction

Head Cook at Weddings and Funerals by Vi Plotnikoff
These simple and authentic stories reveal the heart of a young woman, and the Doukhobor community.
0-919591-75-2 • $14.95 CAN/$12.95 USA

Our Game: An All-Star Collection of Hockey Fiction by Doug Beardsley, ed.
Thirty stories — from writers such as Roch Carrier, Morley Callaghan, Roy MacGregor, Audrey Thomas and others — that capture the essence of hockey.
896095-32-1 • $18.95 CAN/$16.95 USA

West by Northwest: British Columbia Short Stories by David Stouck & Myler Wilkinson, eds.
A brilliant collection of short fiction that celebrates the unique landscape and literary culture of BC. Includes works by Bill Reid, Ethel Wilson, Wayson Choy, George Bowering, Evelyn Lau, Shani Mootoo and others.
896095-41-0 • $18.95 CAN/$16.95 USA

Poetry

Inward to the Bones: Georgia O'Keeffe's Journey with Emily Carr by Kate Braid
Compelling poems about the relationship between place and art, the struggle to be an artist, and friendship between two famous and creative women.
1-896095-40-2 • $16.95 CAN/$14.95 USA

Love Medicine and One Song by Gregory Scofield
"[Scofield's] lyricism is stunning; gets within the skin. Be careful. These songs are so beautiful they are dangerous." — Joy Harjo
1-896095-27-5 • $16.95 CAN/$13.95 USA

Thru the Smoky End Boards by Kevin Brooks and Sean Brooks, eds.
This collection of sports poetry features the work of Margaret Atwood, George Bowering, Al Purdy, Bronwen Wallace, Michael Ondaatje and others.
1-896095-15-1 • $16.95 CAN/$14.95 USA

Time Capsule by Pat Lowther
Time Capsule consists of excerpts from a manuscript Lowther had prepared for publication at the time of her death, as well as poems selected from her earlier books. An important collection by a strong and passionate poet.
1-896095-25-9 • $24.95 CAN/$19.95 USA

Whylah Falls by George Elliott Clarke
Clarke writes from the heart of Nova Scotia's Black community. Winner of the Archibald Lampman Award for poetry.
0-919591-57-4 • $14.95 CAN/$12.95 USA

Polestar titles are available from your local bookseller.
For a copy of our catalogue, contact:

POLESTAR BOOK PUBLISHERS
P.O. Box 5238, Station B
Victoria, British Columbia
Canada   V8R 6N4
http://mypage.direct.ca/p/polestar